MW00770132

Also by Matt Strickland
Cask Management for Distillers

Batch Distillation
Science and Practice

Matt Strickland

White Mule Press, a division of
American Distilling Institute
PO Box 577
Hayward, CA 94541
distilling.com/publications/books

ISBN 978-1-7369802-5-5

To Lorelei and Sadie,
Thank you for being the most honest, interesting,
and patient teachers I've ever had.

Contents

Foreword

Matt is a prolific writer who is regularly published in industry publications. Even knowing this, I read the draft copy of this, his second textbook book in wonder and fascination; in wonder of how Matt was able to churn out two high-caliber distillery textbooks in under 12 months, and in fascination of his ability to present the subject matter of the science and practice of batch distillation with such clarity and approachability.

I have been active in the technical and R&D side of the distilling business since 1980 and today I operate my own distillery consulting and beverage development company in Canada. I have met many aspiring young (and old) distillers in my years in the business and have had the pleasure of knowing Matt for about 3 years. Matt and I first met in Edinburgh Scotland as new recruits to the Examiners Board of the Institute of Brewing & Distilling. Since then, I have been able to engage Matt for speaking at various distilling seminars and he and I have co-authored a chapter in a soon-to-be-released whisky textbook.

In early conversations with Matt, it was evident that his intricate knowledge of distillery science and distillery operations belied the fact that he had 'only' been working in the industry since 2012 (which it turns out is really an eternity in the craft distilling field). Matt stepped into craft distilling after grad school, at a time when American craft distillers were beginning to truly earn respect from consumers and the giant mainstream producers and were doggedly pushing the boundaries of distilled spirits innovation. Matt fit the mold of the new craft distiller. Following positions with two notable craft distilleries in the US, Matt the intrepid adventurer, moved from urban DC to rural Quebec in 2018 to head up a family farm distillery and malt house, and to immerse himself and his family into the inviting and perhaps intimidating French Canadian culture. I look forward to someday sampling Matt's creations at the Distillerie Cote des Saints, and knowing what I know of Matt's capabilities, I am confident I will be impressed with his handiworks.

In this highly detailed book, Matt enlightens the reader on key distillation developments throughout history, and then effortlessly guides the reader through the weighty subject of distillation theory, bringing clarity to concepts that I have struggled to grasp myself, let alone be able to explain with any sort of confidence. He then exposes the reader to the pot still in all its elements and forms, playing on his insights and practical experiences to enlighten the reader on the sizing, purchasing, startup and operations, and maintenance and troubleshooting of various still types and different distilling scenarios.

Matt has this innate ability to explain complex distillery processes with confidence and ease and in a manner that makes you want to pay attention and understand. He puts a conversational spin on some seriously heavy science and engineering and finds a way to distill the subject into a conversational format that reads like a casual chat with a good friend. With his sociable appeal and self-deprecating manner in a very Canadian way (how quickly this transplanted American adapts to his new environment), Matt succeeds in instructing the reader on 'how to distill', so whether you are producing vodka or neutral spirits, rum, gin, brandy, any style of whisk(e)y, or even Mezcal or Pisco, you will find helpful insights and techniques of practical value. This book truly is a journey into the technology and practices of distillation, and I encourage all practical distillers, distillery enthusiast and curious fans of distilled beverage products, or those who, in Matt's words, figure that 'knowing this stuff might make you more interesting at parties', to read this book. It will enlighten you, and heck yeah, it will make you a better distiller.

Steve Wright
Founder, Spiritech Solutions Inc.,
and Canadian Whisky Blender/brand owner

Introduction

After completing my last book, *Cask Management for Distillers,* I felt like I was at a mental and emotional impasse. Completing your first book is always spelled out to you in such monumental and heroic terms. At least that's how it felt. You work at a tearing pace, mentally puking your knowledge and research onto the page, carefully playing and arranging the words so that they not only comprehensively convey your ideas but are also written in such a way so as to keep the reader from falling asleep. Afterall, textbooks and academic writing are sometimes the worst offenders when it comes to turning off the reader from learning. What's the point in spending all that time writing down your ideas if you've done it so dryly and dully that the reader dozes off every third sentence?

So, there I was in June 2020, book completed, dealing with COVID lockdown depression, and trying to figure out what to do next. Should I go back to writing monthly pieces for the venerable trade magazines in our industry? Maybe I should pick up a hobby like bread baking or become a Harry Potter fan-fiction writer.

Then a flash hit as these things are wont to do. I would write another book. Immediately. But on what? I had just finished a book on spirit maturation which felt like the end of a story to me. I couldn't possibly go back and fill in the earlier blanks, could I? And yet, that seemed to be the thing that made the most amount of sense.

And it's that kind of "fuck it" attitude that brings us here... to a book on batch distillation.

It makes more sense the longer I think about it. My last book spoke of how to produce quality spirits through proper maturation techniques with an understanding of the underlying chemistry. The curious reader might have left with loads of questions pertaining to the spirit going into the cask and how to shape and mold it to their wills, thereby setting themselves up for a better situation at the start of maturation.

Admittedly, another impetus for this book was my never-ending fascination with the world's different spirit traditions. I passionately believe that the more we understand how different spirits are made, that we in turn can take some of those lessons and put them into practice with our own spirit production practices. Trust me, if you're a traditional bourbon distiller, there is loads of interesting information surrounding French brandy or mezcal or even gin production that can help you become better at your craft.

We all want to put something out there that consumers will want to drink. But for some of us, that isn't enough. We want to put something out that illustrates a bit of ourselves and our philosophy. We're trying to convey something of "us" to the royal "them," the consumer. You're trying to create a liquid masterpiece and you'd like the world to experience the fruits of your artistic toils. Hey, there's nothing wrong with that. Consider me an appreciator of the fine liquid arts and if you've got something to say, then I want to experience it in a glass. If it's great and novel, then believe me, I'll be one of your biggest champions.

Make no mistake: spirits have a way of telling stories. They can serve as liquid time capsules that convey a distiller's work philosophy and ethics. If the spirit is distilled with care and appreciation, then trust me, the drinker will know. They'll understand it. They'll trust it. And they'll come back for more. How you reach that level of honesty and authenticity and how you express that to the consumer is really on you. In this day and age when everyone is walking around with Internet access in their pocket, there is no point in trying to fake it. The modern spirits consumer is savvy, and they can spot a Caulfieldian phony from a mile away.

The reason for writing this book is that as I looked more and more into the written technical works for distillers, I found little in the way of *how to actually distill*. Certainly, there are books out there that dance around the act of distillation. Most of them seem to be related to amateur moonshine production and/or talk too much in generalities. The literary pantheon has been tragically short on specifics.

I've been fortunate to learn from a large number of incredibly talented and knowledgeable people in my career. But even I have had to struggle at times to find the information I needed to understand a certain method or technique. For all our techno wizardry and online info sharing social connectedness, the world of distillation is often a lonely glacier pocked with informational crevasses that can feel nigh impossible to navigate for the neophyte. I desperately wanted to change that. In my talks, classes, articles and now this book, one of my primary professional missions has been to make information on the production of fine spirits more readily accessible. I don't know if I've succeeded and honestly, I may never feel like I've done enough, but damn it, I've tried.

This book serves as largely a technical work though not in the strictest traditional sense. I don't believe in telling people that there is only one singular royal way of doing something. In distillation such mono-decisional situations are rare. There are almost always multiple paths to take. And these paths may themselves be layered with countless other factors and decision trees, making for a bewildering array of choices that have to be made. For the new distiller it can be borderline paralyzing and even for seasoned veterans, some decisions and techniques are fraught with immobilizing confusion. Hopefully, this book will help to break down some of the confounding mysteries and production factors to make the art and science of beverage alcohol distillation seem less labyrinthian. I don't want you to be afraid of all the production choices at your disposal. I want you to be inspired and energized by them.

Every book has to start somewhere for us the natural beginning is a brief discussion on the history of distillation. Chapter 1 looks at distillation's humble beginnings thousands of years ago, moving through the millennia steadily gaining technological traction until we reach a point around 500 years ago when beverage alcohol distillation really started to come into its own. Through it all we will discuss the philosophies and equipment used to distill all kinds of concoctions over the course of centuries as our humble industry steadily evolved into the economic powerhouse it is today.

Chapter 2 discusses distillation theory. This can be a heady topic, but I have tried to present here in easy-to-understand terms. We talk about what the process of boiling really means, how ethanol and water can be separated in the still and much more. We also look at the separation efficiency of using columns and trays during distillation. This will include a discussion on basic column and tray design for hybrid batch systems. These systems are incredibly popular for many distillers across the globe, so this section should be of interest to some folks. Chapter 2 ends with a brief discussion on the merits of copper, that glorious metal nestled in the middle of the periodic table. As we'll soon see, copper is used for a lot more than just its looks.

Chapter 3 discusses the chemistry and considerations for making distillation cuts. When I speak with new distillers this is a subject that often comes up. They are confused and often afraid of making mistakes with their distillation fractions. For many, the concept of distillation cuts feels mysterious and even arcane. This chapter hopes to break down some of the mysteries and give you a set of techniques and parameters for you to use when making decisions on your distillation fractions. Upon reading this chapter you'll hopefully see that it really isn't too complicated or difficult and you'll be off the races with your distillations in no time.

Chapter 4 takes an in-depth look at the basic pot still. We'll cover the major components of pot stills as well as several important add-ons that modern stills often have. The second half of the chapter briefly discusses several specific still designs and types that are commonly used in specific spirit categories such as mezcal's Filipino clay stills and cognac's alembic Charentais still.

Chapter 5 is for anyone looking at purchasing a still. I've gone through the purchasing process a number of times in my career and when that much money is on the line, the sheer breadth of decisions that must be made can be daunting. This chapter attempts to give advice on choosing the best still for the spirit you're trying to make as well as things to consider when looking for a manufacturer to work with.

Chapter 6, though brief, is an important topic. Here, we discuss the various quality parameters of your alcoholic wash and how they affect the outcome of your distillation. I've tried not to retread well-trodden ground with this chapter. There are multitudes upon multitudes of books out there detailing how to properly process and ferment grains, fruits, sugar, and agave. Instead, this chapter looks at several points of important consideration for the distiller prior to turning the still on. Many of these factors can potentially be of concern to consumer safety such as ethyl carbamate and NDMA. Others such as the various issues that come with microbial contamination are more qualitative in nature but no less important to your business.

Chapter 7 outlines the basic double distillation process. This is the basic distillation technique used by distillers all over the world to produce everything from brandy to rum, though it is arguably most strongly associated with single malt whisky production. The chapter concludes with brief discussions on specific double distillation techniques related to cognac and cachaca production.

Chapter 8 is where we dive into the often-confusing world of neutral spirit distillation on a hybrid still using multiple columns. A growing number of distillers all over the world have begun to distill their own neutral spirit instead of purchasing it from larger producers. Their aim is to produce a vodka or neutral base spirit with improved character and mouthfeel. These distillations are usually very hands on and can be frustrating for the novice distiller. The hope is that this chapter gives some clarification on the basic principles. I also offer a brief troubleshooting guide to aid in making operational decisions throughout the process.

Chapter 9 offers a brief discussion on triple and single distillation techniques. Triple distillation is often closely associated with Ireland and its whisky, however many of the more complicated triple distillation methods come from Scotland. We even look at one curious case of triple distilling in the bourbon industry. The final section of this chapter briefly looks at single distillation practices and why this may be one of the most challenging distillation processes of them all.

Chapter 10 is a patchwork of thoughts on gin distillation. I start out by giving a rough operating procedure for a basic gin distillation. This discussion is then followed up by a series of quick bites on some of the many factors and decisions that can affect the final quality of your gin. This *amuse-bouche* of ideas includes things such as overall botanical loads, maceration strength and timing, as well as performing multi- and single shot distillations.

I hope that no matter where you are on your distillation journey, that you can find something of use in these pages. Perhaps more than any other alcoholic beverage category, distilled spirits suffer too much from clandestine inner circles of knowledge. Whether you are just starting out or if you're simply trying to learn and apply new techniques, it can be immensely frustrating to try and find reliable information to help you get on your way.

I've no illusions that this book will answer all your questions. How could I do that when I myself am asking new questions on the art and science of distilling every day? What I hope though is that this book helps to grease the wheels a bit and provides you with inspiration mixed with a little bit of myth dispelling. If I've done that then I've done my job and I'll be able to sleep easy. Now without further ado, let's start walking through the wonderful world of distillation. I hope you enjoy the trip.

Cheers.

Chapter 1

A Brief History of Distillation

I find the beginning to usually be a good place to start most journeys. Of course, this being the science and art of distillation, the beginning is obscured by a cloud of oral tradition, alchemical beliefs, wizardry and perfume production. It's complicated, but that doesn't mean it's impossible to understand.

First things first: Let's define distillation.

Distillation is the act of separating substances and/or components from a liquid mixture using differences in boiling point and condensation.

The word distillation derives from the Latin *destillare* which roughly translates "to trickle down" (Kockmann, 2014).

So, you take a liquid mixture that contains some component you're interested in. You apply heat to the mixture and eventually one or more components begin to go into a vapor state. You can then condense those vapors through cooling and hopefully you've obtained the component you want from the distilled vapors or left behind in the original heated vessel. If that isn't simple, then I don't know what is...

In essence the practice of distillation can be, and commonly is, used to separate all kinds of substances outside the spectrum of alcoholic beverages. You can desalinate seawater through distillation. The oil industry uses distillation to convert crude oil into all sorts of things such as fuel and chemical feedstocks. The perfume industry uses distillation to make expensive scents designed to hide our scuzzy human smells. Distillation as a separation technique has an immense amount of uses. And as we're about to see most distillation throughout history was *not* used to produce beverages for casual consumption.

The Beginnings...

It's important to realize that prior to distillation and certainly the distillation of alcohol for hedonistic enjoyment, mankind stumbled onto fermentation. And stumble we did. We may never be sure exactly how humans figured out the art and practice of fermented beverages; their inception came before the written word.

The most likely form of events was possibly a pot of unattended grapes or grape juice was forgotten about for too long. The person responsible for said pot comes back for a belated inspection and notices that the resulting liquid smells different. Perhaps he or she gets a little curious and finds the courage to taste the new liquid; it did come from grapes after all, what could be the harm? A few sips later and the person begins to feel the inebrious effects of the liquid... nay, nectar! They go tell others about their serendipitous discovery and eventually they begin the process of trying to repeat the results so that a constant supply of alcohol-laden ambrosia is always readily available.

Maybe that's how it happened. Maybe not. There are certainly other substrates out there available for fermentation into beverage alcohol. In fact, one of the current theories is that grains were likely fermented regularly before wine grapes. As human civilization become increasingly and more formally civilized in the area of the Fertile Crescent (located mostly in modern day Iraq, Syria and Kuwait), they learned to work with grains for early bread production. Speculation abounds as to what grain was primarily used. It could have been an early form of barley or and early form of wheat. Regardless, some semblance of the hypothetical scenario mentioned above probably played out, though with a few more steps and input from luck. Maybe some grain was left out in a pot after a light rain. Upon picking up some moisture the grains begin to sprout, but then a few days later a heat spell kicks in. The hot weather dries the grains back out and one lucky SOB happens upon the forgotten grain and tastes it. It has now taken on a unique sweetness. A few more accidental steps and it's foreseeable that they could wind up with an early version of beer.

We know that the early forms of beverage alcohol were not much like what we consider refined refreshment today. Everything was fermented by native yeasts as pure yeast cultures were millennia away. Surely there were natural co-cultures of bacteria that may have lent sourness to wines and beers alike. The beers were not filtered in any form, leaving the grain solids themselves to be consumed along with the liquid. Quite literally "liquid bread" in this instance. There are famous pictures on Egyptian artifacts showing how people thousands of years ago consumed these beers with a straw. And forget about carbonation or refrigeration. These brews were consumed as fresh as possible, sometimes after only a day or two of fermentation.

The early alcoholic beverages were used for an assortment of cultural purposes including as currency, and religious ceremonies. Wine and beer were arguably safer to drink that many water supplies, a fact likely discovered by simply noticing the differential in deaths that occurred after people consumed water versus alcohol. Early civilizations didn't really know what they had, but they knew they had it good.

It wasn't long before the demand and *need* for fermented beverages became a powerful economic factor. Breweries and wineries big and small sprang up all over the place to provide the necessary volumes of liquid sustenance. It was something the population wanted and that provided a lot of avenues for power and influence accumulation for a lot of folks.

But, what about distillation you ask? Well, we know that distillation came after our buddies of wine and beer, but perhaps not as long after as you might suspect.

Some have posited that the first possible distillation took place around 2000 BCE in Babylonia (present day Iraq and Syria) (Hudson & Buglass, 2011). However, others contend that the Sumerians were using evaporation and condensation techniques to extract essential oils around 3500 BCE (Kockmann, 2014). While this was not an "active" distillation, it loosely fits the definition of the process and so allowed for a nice platform of knowledge for future distillers to build from.

The Sumerian method of distillation involved a clay pot with a diameter of about 50 cm and a height of 25–50 cm. Liquid inside would heat up from rising temperatures outside the pot and evaporation of lighter components would occur. Note the heat was not "applied." This was passive heat supplied from the environment. No vigorous boiling here, just gentle vaporization of lighter elements rising off the surface of the mixture.

The vapors would rise and condense on the roof of a lid placed on top the pot. Some of the condensation would trickle down into a curved ring formed above the liquid level inside the pot. This ring would be packed with special herbs for oil extraction.

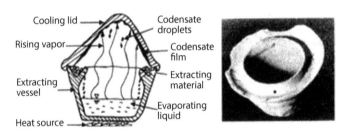

Figure 1-1. Early Sumerian Essential Oil Still (Kockmann, 2014)

From the Sumerians, the knowledge of distillation seemed to spread in all directions. Around 2000 BCE we find evidence of the Chinese using similar practices to the Sumerians. Egyptians were distilling essential oils by at least 500 years after that.

Who can say if these techniques were ever applied to beverage alcohol? If it was, the historical evidence has yet to be found. Likely, drinks such as beer and wine were deemed too precious, too valuable to be put through the arcane paces of primitive distillation. And in any case, given the distillation practices and technology of the day, it's unlikely that the distillation yield would have been particularly good, making the whole process an unworthy slog.

Essential oils on the other hand were incredibly important to early medical practices. People got sick. Medical treatments were crude and sometimes painful. Synthesized antibiotics didn't exist. Essential oils from indigenous plants provided the most efficient means of dosing a patient with a potentially life-saving compound. Not that the early doctors understood how or why any of these oils worked, if some of them even worked at all. But progress has to start somewhere and distillation, however primitive in practice, was certainly an important technique to move society up a few yards on the cultural playing field.

Early distilling practices effectively required the collection of internal reflux as product. So, the distillation would proceed and at a certain point the distiller would need to remove the lid of the pot and collect the liquid now residing in the internal rim. Obviously, this is not the most efficient way to collect a distillate. So, what is one to do?

The next technological leap in distillation was to design an external receiver. This would allow the distiller to continuously collect distillate without having to interrupt the process by taking the lid off of the distillation pot.

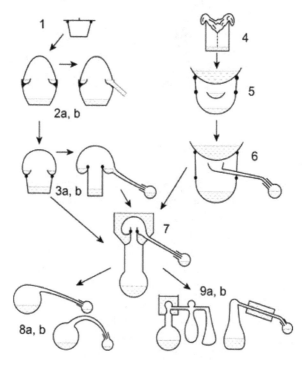

Figure 1-2. Early Still Development (need to have this readapted) (Kockmann, 2014)

The original receivers were simply attachments to tubes that extended from the pot internal ring structure. Condensed distillate would collect in the ring and then trickle down the tube to the external collection point. Meet the world's first still safe!

Of course, this wasn't the only improvement that needed to be made. A proper collection point made things easier, sure, but we still needed better heating and cooling methods.

No one at the time really understood this. After all, the internal ring structure system coupled with an external receiver was probably deemed the Ferrari of stills at the time. For many practitioners and early alchemists, it was likely deemed sufficient and even if they suspected that improvements could be made, many may not have possessed the enterprising mind to pull of the technological hat trick.

As these things often do, the improvements came slowly via incremental pushes. Active heating was introduced through the use of hot water or a hot sand bath. Remember, this at a time when pottery skills were still comparatively primitive and a full-blown fire beneath the pot might damage or even break the distillation pot. These cultures used what they could, and hot water and/or sand were the best solutions at the time.

This also helps to explain why alcohol was not likely distilled during the first millennia of distillation. It would have required too much energy to properly pull off. Think about it. If you don't have a proper fire going then boiling water is going to be difficult. Without boiling water, you wouldn't have enough heat energy to see an alcohol distillation through to its completion. A double boiler system like what is found in many kitchens to melt chocolate or make delicate sauces would have been a perfect solution, but this was another technological jump that had yet to be made.

The issue of cooling had to be addressed as well. If you rely on long periods of time to allow for simple evaporation to take place, then you can get away with external air temperatures to properly reflux the distillate from the lid of the pot back down to the collection point. However, once you begin applying more heat in the form of hot water or sand, now you've got to remove that heat at a similar rate per unit time in order to effectively condense your distillate. This was often accomplished by ensuring that cooler air was available, but eventually someone stumbled onto the idea of wrapping the tube to the collection vessel in wet linen. Water is a great heat repository and if you can keep a steady supply of cool wet linens around, you could potentially remove a lot of heat rather quickly, albeit at the expense of a lot of physical effort.

And for all our technology and historical hindsight, as far as we know, this is how things stayed for quite some time in the realm of distillation. There are a lot of blanks in the distilling historical record. Who can say exactly why this is? Perhaps it was because distillation was viewed as some sort of mystical art and therefore approached by only an intrepid and clandestine few. We know that by the time of Pliny the Elder, distillation was an accepted practice for the production of turpentine from pine resin. Turpentine was used for all sorts of things ranging from ship building (it is a water repellent) and lamp fuel (highly flammable) to medicinal uses such as treating depression in ancient Rome (Ewbank, 2018). (Turpentine has numerous deleterious effects on the human body including severe lung and kidney problems and, oh... death. However, it was still being used as a medicine and "snake oil" for all sorts of ailments on into the 1800s.)

Beyond medicine, another important use for distillation during this period was for the desalination of seawater. As civilizations got more advanced and curious, sea faring become increasing more important. You need potable water aboard the ships and drinking salty ocean water (about 3.5% salinity) just wasn't going to cut it.

The Early Alchemists

I've often said that distillation is the modern alchemy. It's a bit silly to say that because if you look at the history of alchemy, distillation was often right there in the center. Sure, these early alchemists weren't distilling fine single malts or 96 pt. brandies, but they used similar tools of the trade to explore some unique theories and concepts.

There's a common misconception about the alchemists. Many folks liken their practices and goals to magic or witchcraft shrouded in secrecy like some kind of proto-Illuminati. While there are some grains of errant truth in this belief the reality is much more nuanced. Many of the most prominent early alchemists were essentially the forefathers of modern scientific thought and process. They performed experiments on various materials using prescribed methods and aimed to repeat the results in a rigorous fashion. This was the beginnings of what would eventually become the scientific method.

If you've heard the term "alchemist" before then you may have also heard about some of their aims. First was often the transmutation of various metals into "noble" metals. The most common version of this was transforming lead into gold. Other projects included searching for an elixir of immortality, and the creation of medicines that would cure any disease or disorder. Lofty goals indeed.

There were quite a few serious practitioners and philosophers involved with alchemy and their works often carried a powerfully spiritual bent. Part of the aims behind much of the work surrounding metal transmutation and immortality also involved the perfection of the human body and soul.

The exact time and origins of alchemy can be hard to pin down, but it is believed that the earliest so-called "alchemists" emerged in Egypt during the Hellenistic Period (323–330 BCE). One of the earliest alchemical writings was *The Papyri*, a series of Greek-written recipes found in Egypt and dated to somewhere in the third century CE. On the surface, the recipes dealt with producing valuable metals such as gold or silver and precious stones. A deeper dive and you discover that the recipe aims were often to make mere *reproductions* of these items, often by using methods to change the color of say, copper to silver (Principe, 2013).

If cheap knockoffs of the real artifact were all the alchemists accomplished, then we wouldn't need to discuss them. However, for all the hucksters honing their "craft" during this period, there were quite a few individuals working towards higher scientific ideals. Many of these projects eventually involved some form of rudimentary distillation techniques and equipment.

Of the many important alchemists to our story on distillation few factor in as heavily as Mary the Jewess. Mary the Jewess is believed to have lived sometime between 1–100 CE I say "believed" because the truth is we don't know when she lived or even if she lived at all. None of her writings have survived so, most of what we can say about her comes from one source, a third century alchemist named Zosimos of Panopolis. Zosimos was a Greek born in Egypt and his writings on alchemy are some of the oldest and most well-known on the subject. It is through his writings that we know about Mary and her accomplishments.

It is believed that Mary taught her alchemical beliefs and skills to several students leaving an indelible mark on the history of proto-chemistry and distillation in particular. She is said to have developed several inventions to aid in her processes of alchemical discovery including several distillation apparatuses. She is credited with inventing (or at least describing as Zosimos puts it) the tribikos which is a simple alembic with three out ports for collection. More importantly, she was purportedly the inventor of the bain-marie boiler system which was one of the world's first double boilers. The bain-marie allows for a gentler heating of a substance with less risk of scorching. The technique is used in many distilleries and kitchens to this day. (Figure 1-4)

The tribikos is admittedly a bit of an oddity and not of much use to the commercial beverage alcohol distiller. (However, versions of it are still used today in chemistry labs all over the world.) The bain-marie is certainly Mary's most important invention for the modern distiller. With the bain-marie boiler distillers had a reliable and efficient heating method that largely eliminated the risks of heat prematurely decomposing or otherwise ruining their starting material.

After Mary the Jewess and the teachings of Zosimos, it would be a few hundred years before much of any import would occur in the world of distillation. That's not to say that this period in the world was boring or that it bore no relevance to our story, far from it. During this period, we see the fall of the Roman Empire and the founding and rise of Islam as a major world religion and cultural force. It is with the Muslim scholars that the next part of our journey takes place.

Islamic scholars were often fascinated by the tenets and aims of the old-western alchemists. Enlivened by their curiosity and thirst for knowledge, many of these scholars embarked on research of their own. And fortunately for us, these Arabic practitioners were much better at taking notes.

In the eight century CE we meet Jābir ibn Hayyān (later Latinized to Geber). Geber took his research and work very seriously and developed his own methodology for working in the realm of alchemy based on rigorous scientific approach and controlled experiments. In this light, he is sometimes regarded as the father of modern chemistry. For our story, Geber was also the person that introduced and pushed hard on the idea of using glass stills for distillation.

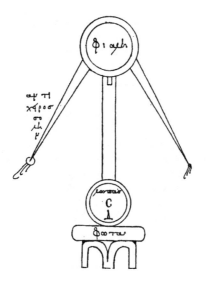

Figure 1-3. A Tribikos distillation apparatus

Figure 1-4. Bain-marie system

Figure 1-5. Jābir ibn Hayyān

The idea of using glass for distillation at the time was somewhat novel. Glass is non-porous and generally resistant to chemical attack i.e., non-reactive. This flows well from Geber's strict scientific stance. If your starting distillation substance reacts with your apparatus material, then how can you be truly sure of your distillate results?

The other important reason for our mention of Geber is that he was arguably one of the first to make mention of distilling alcohol from wine. It is a long-held belief that due to Islam's prohibition on alcohol, this kind of distillation did not take place or that Muslims never consumed alcohol. Interestingly that turns out to not be the case, especially in these early years of the religion (Al-Hassan, n.d.). Still, these early distillations of alcohol were likely used more for medicine and other scientific pursuits than recreational beverages.

This is where we'll leave our alchemist friends. Alchemy and its practitioners eventually transitioned themselves into actual science, studying the intricacies of the world around them and looking for answers to questions beyond the spiritual context of things like the Philosopher's Stone. The next major developments in distillation history took place among groups of people outside the alchemical realm.

800–1800 CE

The Western and Islamic alchemists laid bare an impressive body of work over centuries dealing with the practice of distillation. While no one was ever able to transform lead into gold or to find an elixir for immortality, these proto scientists were able to make major inventive inroads to the science of distilling.

During the roughly 1000-year period after 800 CE we find the sciences beginning to harden around the need to better understand the natural world while leaving the more esoteric fantasies of traditional alchemy behind. And with the advent of alcohol being distilled from wine in the Arabic world, there gradually grew an interest in other forms of distilled alcohol.

Sometime between 700–800 CE we know that the Chinese and Mongols distilled karakumyss which is a distillate produced from fermented mare's milk (Kockmann, 2014). Fermenting milk into alcohol is not the easiest of tasks and generally requires a completely different genus of yeast than *Saccharomyces* spp. The fact that these peoples were distilling the fermented milk suggests that the base fermentation had been around for much longer. And while we don't really hear about karakumyss in Mongolia today, they are still fermenting mare's milk into the regional specialty, kumis (also referred to as *airag*) which is most often made from cow's milk at 2% abv, though stronger and more traditional horse milk versions do exist (Rummel, n.d.).

Sometime during the 1200s, Albert Magnus of Cologne, was said to have distilled wine. Albert was a Dominican friar and bishop with a seemingly insatiable curiosity about science and the material world. He left behind numerous writings on a myriad of subjects and it is said that he held an interest in alchemical distillations. One recipe he supposedly gave was to "take thick, strong and old black wine, in one quart throw quicklime, powdered sulphur, good quality tartar, and white common salt, all well pulverized, then put them together in a

Figure 1-6. Depiction of Albert Magnus in his lab

well-luted cucurbit with alembic; you will distill from it aqua ardens which should be kept in a glass vessel." We don't actually know if this is really one of Albert's recipes or if it was simply a copied Arabic recipe recorded by one of his students (Forbes, 1948).

Not long after Albert's lifetime (and possibly even during or slightly before) we start to see the beginnings of some of the spirits that we know and love today. In 1310, the first reference to Armagnac is made by Prior Vital Dufour. He details "40 virtues" of the spirit which included the usual suspects of "render[ing] men joyous" and "enliven[ing] the spirit" but he then goes onto claim that it cures hepatitis and staves off senility (Davis, 2014).

The first pseudo-reference to gin occurred in 1269 with the publishing of *Der Naturen Bloeme* by Jacob van Maerlant te Damme. He lists the "recipe" for a sort of juniper-based elixir to fight off stomach pains.

> *"He who wants to be rid of stomach pain should use juniper cooked in rainwater. He who has cramps, Cook juniper in wine. It's good against the pain." (Duff, 2009)*

The Irish and the Scots often debate ad infinitum on who distilled the first "whisky." While the research and arguments have gone back and forth for decades, the evidence suggests that it was the Irish who distilled the first spirits from grain. In *The Annals of Clonmacnoise* published in 1405 states that "Richard Magrannell, Chieftain of Moyntyreolas, died at Christmas, by taking a surfeit of aqua vitae." (The Life and Times of Aqua Vitae, n.d.) Once again, this suggests that aqua vitae distillation was occurring well before the time of recorded mention. Some have even suggested that there is evidence of aqua vitae distillation in Ireland in pre-Christian history, which if true, would place beverage alcohol distillation occurring there prior to the fifth century CE (Irish Whiskey Museum, 2019). (Considering everything else in our story, I find this a bit suspect, but who knows? Maybe more direct evidence will come to light.)

In 1440, Johannes Gutenberg unveiled his printing press to the world. His invention heralded a revolution in the printed word and the availability of knowledge to the masses. Every aspect of learning and scientific discipline was impacted by these new machines that could more efficiently and accurately print page upon page of knowledge and theory for binding into books.

Along with the rapid dissemination of knowledge through more affordable printing and books came a slew of distillers and scientists willing to share their knowledge. This point cannot be understated. By putting their ideas to page in an affordable book format, more people had access to these new distilling theories and were then able to iterate and gradually improve upon them, thus pushing our nascent distilling industry further forward. These books also allowed for specific recipes to more easily and widely shared. As the recipes were shared, more producers and subsequently products were able to spring into the burgeoning spirits industries.

The first book of serious import was *Ain gûts nutzlichs Büchlin von den aussgeprenten Wassern* (roughly translated to "A good, useful little book about extracted waters") posthumously released in 1477 by Viennese physician, Michael Puff von Schrick (1400–1473). The book gives over 80 recipes for herbal distillates for medicinal use.

The next major distillation work to appear in print was that of Hieronymus Brunschwygk (sometimes seen as "Brunschwig") from

Figure 1-7. Title page from Hiermonyus Brunschwygk's seminal work on distillation (note the various still types depicted)

Strasbourg, Germany who wrote *Liber de arte destillandi (The Book of the Art of Distillation)* in 1500. This was arguably the first tome dedicated solely to the art and practice of distillation. Brunschwygk was a surgeon and so his book still focused heavily on the use of distillation for the obtainment of medicines. However, the book is still important to our story because he went into great detail regarding the techniques and equipment required to produce quality distillates.

Twenty-five years later saw the publishing of *Coelum philosophorum seu de secretis naturae liber* by Philip Ulstad, another German doctor (see a pattern, here?) who elaborated on the distillation theories of many who came before him, including Albert Magnus. By the time we get to the 17th century we get the first published work on distillation in England by John French. His work, *The Art of Distillation*, was published in 1651 and has been widely influential in the anglophone distilling traditions. However, this work has not escaped controversy as much of it is seen as simply translations and wholesale lifting of Brunschwyk's work.

The 16th and 17th centuries were also when we began to see the emergence of spirits being produced in the New World colonies, particularly rum on the Caribbean sugar plantations and agave spirits in Mexico.

Prior to colonization the "New World" of North and South America had little in the way of distilled alcohol production. In fact, it is theorized that distillation really didn't take place until the Spanish arrived in the 1500s. They brought with them a thirst for liquors and the equipment and knowledge to produce them. When the colonists' initial supply of liquor ran out, they would often look around them to find a suitable substitute. In Mexico, they knew the natives often consumed a low alcohol fermented beverage produced from the agave plant. Imaginations spurred, the Spanish soon realized that they could make a distilled spirit from agave as well and the tradition of mezcal (and subsequently tequila) was born.

Edward Curtis was a photographer and researcher of all things pertaining to the American west. He spent a lot of time studying the various groups of Native Americans in the American Southwest during the early 1900s. In his 20-year researched opus, *The North American* Indian, he says of mezcal:

> "*Another intoxicant, more effective than túlapai, is made from the mescal—not from the sap, according to the Mexican method, but from the cooked plant, which is placed in a heated pit and left until fermentation begins. It is then ground, mixed with water, roots added, and the whole boiled and set aside to complete fermentation. The Indians say its taste is sharp, like whiskey. A small quantity readily produces intoxication.*" (Curtis, 1907)

The origins of rum are arguably a bit more tragic. While there are mentions of distillation from sugar cane in ancient Sanskrit texts dating back to the 7th century, the rum as we know it today arguably originated in the New World. Colony building began in earnest in the 1500s upon the realization that sugar cane could be grown efficiently in various parts of the Caribbean and South America. Unfortunately, sugar cane is an incredibly labor-intensive crop, and the colonists needed a large workforce to ensure enough sugar was produced to satisfy the monarchies and controlling interests back home an ocean or two away. So, they forcefully enlisted (read: enslaved) local native populations to do the work for them.

The work was hot, miserable, and sometimes dangerous. Physical, mental, and emotional reprieves were few and far between. The one bit of solace a plantation slave might find would be in the occasional drink. Fortunately, with the sugar cane refineries operating at full tilt there was a lot of readily available fermentable substrate in the form of molasses to ferment into alcohol.

There are a lot of byproducts of the sugar making process and early refineries were considerably less efficient in their sugar extraction than they are now. At the end of the refining process, the refinery would be left with large amounts of seemingly useless molasses. Considering it to simply be organic trash with no real value, many refineries simply dumped it into the surrounding ocean. Nowadays, we realize that molasses still retains a lot of sugar and flavor and has all sorts of culinary uses. The plantation slave labor realized the same thing and eventually began fermenting some of the leftover molasses to produce alcoholic beverages. Couple that with colonially introduced distillation technologies and the slaves were able to begin producing rum by the early to mid-1600s. The resulting liquor was referred to by various names such as "rumbullion," "kill devil," or "rumbustion."

The 1800 – Present

It was during the 1700s that we really began to see the various distilled spirits industries take off commercially. As technologies improved and colonization continued across the globe, we see the first glimpses of modern globalism. People gradually began to travel to farther flung places and experienced different cultures, foods, traditions, and of course beverages. They would come back from their travels with tales of fantastical flavors and powerful liquors, seeding the curiosities and imaginations of others. It wasn't long before many spirits such as cognac, gin, absinthe, rum and whisky were being traded between countries. As demand rose for various spirits both at home and abroad, further advances needed to be made to increase production efficiencies and product quality.

At this point one of the primary issues facing many distillers was the type and amount of heat available for the distillation apparatus. In small laboratories this wasn't much of an issue. A simple gas flame or small double boiler would suffice. However, in commercial spirits production many distillers wanted something gentler and more consistent than open flame (never mind the potential safety hazards of mixing ethanol and fire). Direct fire stills are harder to control and there's always the risk of scorching the fermented wash and potentially producing some unwanted flavors and aromas in the process. Conveniently, much of the Western distilling world was teetering on the edge of the impending industrial revolution.

Steam engines had already been shown capable of powering trains. Surely it would be possible to utilize steam to heat a still.

In some ways, this technology had existed for centuries. Many distillers understood the concept of the double boiler and how it gently applied heat to the still. The Chinese had been experimenting with an early form of direct steam heating since the 7th century. Unfortunately, none of these techniques were easily scalable for large-scale industrial distillations.

Along came the steam boiler. In the late 1700s onward, there was increasing interest in pushing the limits of using steam as a source of power. Experiments and applications started small but by the mid-1800s the steam generation industry had begun. Distillers eventually took notice and began to implement steam power in their distilleries. While some spirit traditions such as French brandies, remained steadfast in their use of direct fire for heating, other spirits such as whisky gradually transitioned over to steam to a great extent throughout the last quarter of the 1800s and into the new century. The famous Glenmorangie Distillery in Scotland was the first Scotch Malt Whisky distillery to switch to steam in 1887 (The Whisky Professor, 2019).

Columns Rising

Perhaps no single innovation in the distillation space has had more of an impact than the invention of the continuous still. I know. I know. This is supposed to be a book on BATCH distillation, but I can assure you that having an understanding of how a continuous column still works will benefit your understanding of some of the batch techniques we discuss later in the book.

Many folks know the name Aeneas Coffey and his invention of the famed Coffey still. To hear some tell it, you would be forgiven for having the impression that Coffey birthed his still from absolutely nowhere into the modern world. Everyone has reference points and while Coffey's invention is important (and we will discuss him in a moment), he was not the first person to work with continuous distillation.

First, we need some cultural context. You'll soon no doubt notice that many of the names to follow are French, and that is no mere coincidence. In the early 1800s during his final rises to European domination and eventual defeat, Napoleon Bonaparte became increasingly fascinated by the commerce potential of the sugar beet. His main concern was weening his empire off the more difficult to get colonially produced sugar overseas. (Napoleon's navy had been decimated by England in 1805, leaving him with little in the way of Caribbean commercial opportunities as a result.) The sugar beet seemed like a possible alternative and so he poured a lot of government money into projects that might utilize the sugar beet. Some inventors realized there may be an opportunity for sugar beet usage in the production of industrial alcohol and so research began in earnest.

One of the first people to bring forth an idea was Jean Edouard Adam. Adam was a French chemist and inventor who lived in the second half of the 18th century. He made several improvements on the standard batch distillation systems of the day. Most notably, in 1805 he developed a *dis*continuous fractional distillation system. This system provided a convenient springboard for further developments.

Adam's still was an interesting contraption for batch distillation that allowed for better separation of multiple components in a distillation system. It wasn't really the most efficient method of component separation and there was definitely room for improvement. Fortunately, improvements were not long behind. (Figure 1-8)

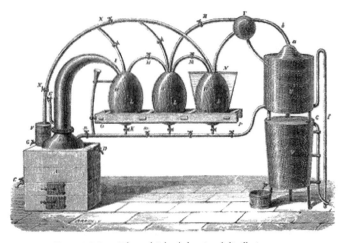

Figure 1-8. Jean Edouard Adam's fractional distillation system

Figure 1-9. Bérard working next to his still.

In 1806, Isaac Bérard, a French brandy maker, released the first still with a partial condenser. The partial condenser increased the amount of reflux inside the still and increased the amount of alcohol in the distillate while reducing the amount of flavor congeners. (Figure 1-9)

So, now we had two major breakthroughs in distillation technology. First, we had the added enrichment of the distillate through scaled-up fractional distillation. Second, we had added enrichment from increased reflux due to a partial condenser. All we needed now was a way to somehow combine these ideas into a single apparatus.

This brings us to the next Frenchman in our story, Jean-Baptiste Cellier-Blumenthal. Cellier-Blumenthal created what was arguably the first truly continuous distillation system in 1813.

The Cellier-Blumenthal still was a dramatic leap forward in distillation technology and allowed for further developments to come about more easily. The column was composed of a lower stripping section and an upper rectifying section with bubble cap trays. Above the column is a partial condenser. (Figure 1-10)

The next several decades saw a number of iterations on the concepts that Cellier-Blumenthal introduced. In 1822, Anthony Perrier patented his "baffles" tray design for a whisky distillery. These were effectively altered versions of bubble cap trays, but his work showed the growing interest of the whisky community in continuous distillation technology.

The Coffey Still

A continuous series of improvements and iterations on the continuous distillation concept were made in the first half of the 1800s. Robert Stein of Scotland made his own contribution in 1828. The still consisted of a series of three vessels and a large horizontal cylinder. The cylinder is divided into eight compartments separated by cloth. Wash was fed into the three vessels and vapors eventually make their way through the compartments (Underwood & Underwood, 1830). Truthfully, it was all a bit complicated, but it did make more efficient use of fuel which was certainly a benefit to some. A few distilleries including the famed Cameron Bridge did install one of these beasts, though their use was short lived as a new still was about to come to the fore.

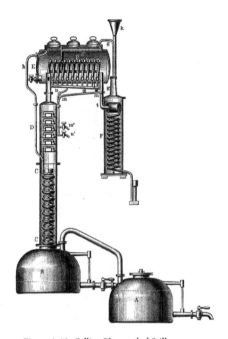

Figure 1-10. Cellier-Blumenthal Still

Figure 1-11. Aeneas Coffey (1780-1839

Aeneas Coffey (figure 1-11) was an excise officer working in Ireland for 25-years. This experience gave him an intimate knowledge of the distillation process and the problems distillers faced at the time concerning the government and production efficiencies. Apparently, he was also quite the clever tinkerer and by paying attention to the continuous still designs that came before, he was able to design and patent his Coffey still in 1830.

Coffey produced a two column still with an "analyzer" section for stripping the incoming wash and a "rectifying" section for increasing alcoholic strength and removing unwanted congeners. The still cleverly had his incoming wash piping pass by some of the hot distilling vapors. This allowed for cooling of the vapors and a preheating of the incoming wash creating a valuable energy savings. He also utilized sieve trays in the column which could handle washes with high amounts of grain solids without clogging.

In figure 1-12 you can study how Coffey's design works. The incoming wash (A) travels through piping in the rectifying column through pipe (B), picking up heat and providing some cooling to the rising vapors along the way. The wash is eventually dumped onto the

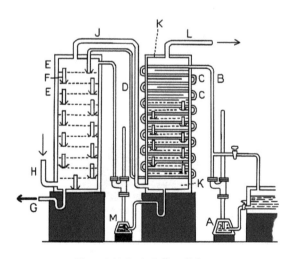

Figure 1-12. Basic Coffey still design

top of the analyzer column (column on left) where it travels downward and meets incoming steam from the bottom. The incoming steams pushes the more volatile substances in the wash into a vapor state and they begin traveling upwards through the analyzer and back into the rectifying column. Meanwhile the spent dealcoholized solids from the wash exit the bottom of the analyzer through gravity.

Coffey's design permanently changed the landscape of distilling. All of a sudden, companies had an efficient method to produce large amounts of alcohol at higher concentrations and purity, using less fuel. It opened the door to the numerous spirit styles from Scottish grain whiskies to light style rums to modern vodka and more.

Coffey's design has been changed and iterated upon a bit since its inception, but the core concepts of his invention have largely stayed the same. There are even a few older wooden Coffey stills from the 1800s still in use today such as the one used by Demerara Distillers Ltd in Guyana who make the highly respected El Dorado line of rums.

Distillation Today

Up till now we've only given the briefest of glimpses into the fascinating history of distillation and distillation technology. The necessity for brevity has forced us to fly over more than a few things. Hopefully, you've still gained a sense of the fantastic strides we've made as distillers over the course of the past few thousand years.

If we jump forward to today (which is not unreasonable given that the focus of this book is "modern" distillation techniques), we see a fascinating array of distillation techniques and equipment employed to produce everything from beverages and medicines to fuels and so much more. Imagine if Aristotle or Geber were able to gander upon our progress in distillation. I'm sure they would have a difficult time believing what their eyes were showing them.

However, imagine that someone like Elijah Craig or Jack Daniel were alive today to see our whiskey making practices. I'm sure they'd be impressed, but I suspect they would also grasp the technology fairly quickly. The truth is that for all our "smart" technology, boson hunting and polio eradicating progress, at least in the realm of beverage making we've largely stuck to the basics. This is not to say that there haven't been advances, of course there have. However, from a big picture perspective, I would argue that these advances have largely been iterative rather than revolutionary especially when it comes to the batch distillation space. The continuous still distillers have all sorts of automated programming, fusel oil decanters, demethylizers and so on, but pot distillers operate very similarly to the way that distillers worked 150 years ago.

There are certainly some things of note worth mentioning. Shōchū distillers in Japan have access to vacuum distillation technology for some interesting results. The gin guys utilize ever more elegant still designs for the perfect fusion of botanical with spirit.

But, perhaps the most important design leap for the modern batch distiller has been the advent of the hybrid still design. This is the still type that combines both a basic pot with some combination of plated columns which you might normally find in a continuous system. Some argue that these systems offer the best of both worlds. And while, I wouldn't go *quite* that far, I will say that they have been a boon to small distillers looking to have large portfolios of different spirit types. Because these stills behave a bit differently, we'll look at specific techniques and operating protocols for them later in the book.

And there you have it, a brief history of distillation. Understanding where we came from can sometimes help us to see where we're going or at the very least where we *should* go. With that in mind, we can comfortably move on to something a bit more formalized and technique oriented: distillation chemistry.

Chapter 2

Distillation Theory

I came to the world of distillation through winemaking. I was leaving graduate school where I studied wine microbiology and did research for the Oregon wine industry but realized that I didn't want to work in wine. It was too seasonal and at times felt a bit elitist (my views have since softened, but I have still had no regrets about moving into distillation). As I looked around for a post-graduate job, I was clued into a distillery back in my hometown of Nashville and that they might be looking for someone. After a few emails I was hired to handle their research and development. Great... except I had no distilling experience (outside of some lab work in the chem lab at university). My new employer said it was no problem. They would teach me.

And teach me they did. I learned how to operate all their stills, from the tiny benchtop units all the way to the large production vessels for whiskey. It was a pretty loose and paint by the numbers like process. Turn this valve one-quarter turn. Turn this one three turns. Collect spirit to X-number of gallons then change the receiver to this vessel. Collect until abv reads X-percent. It was a recipe and usually a damn good one at that. It got results and problems were rare.

Something was missing, however. I'm a bit of a nuts-and-bolts kind of guy and I like to know what's going on under the hood, so to speak. It took a bit to realize that they weren't really showing me much of the underlying chemistry.

Maybe it wasn't important. Afterall, we had loyal customers, good sales numbers and we were winning awards. You don't need to know why a donut tastes good, just that it does and how to make it consistently.

Of course, that mentality only works if everything is going according to plan or if you aren't interested in being able to push the limits of your craft. If you're driving through the desert and get a flat tire, you should know how to change a tire. (Sure, you could call a tow truck or the auto club, but you might be stuck in the hot desert for a while... no fun.) In order to properly change a tire, you have to have a basic understanding of how a tire works and how it connects to your car. I'm not saying you need to know exactly how the Otto Cycle in your engine works, but a simple grasp of a few basic car concepts can really help you get where you're going.

The same can be said for distillation. If something goes wrong, like say your distillate strength is 10% lower than it normally is, you would do well to understand some of the underlying chemistry so that you can pinpoint where the problem is and hopefully correct it. Otherwise, you may find yourself perpetually stuck in the desert, and the desert gets HOT and miserable, my friend. (We'll end that strained metaphor, here.)

What if you want to develop a new product or distill one of your existing spirits in a new style? Say you're a brandy distiller who normally produces highly flavored distillates, but now you'd like to produce some lighter spirit for a fortified wine project. You could spend hundreds or even thousands of dollars on a consultant to show you how, or you could save your money, get an understanding of the distillation chemistry and process, and tackle the problem on your own. (Sorry, to all my consultant friends out there.)

Now, I'm not going to lie. This chapter gets a bit heady and there are some things in here that might be viewed as knowledge for knowledge's sake. You may not feel like you need or want to know much about distillation chemistry. While I would suggest you strongly reconsider, it's perfectly acceptable to skip this chapter and move on, though the later chapters that discuss specific techniques will reference a number of the concepts here so it might be worth your time to go through it. I promise that even if you hated chemistry in high school and/or college, I'll help you move through it. Trust me: it's not that bad.

Some Definitions

Just what is distillation, exactly? Well, if we go back to the beginning of the last chapter, we'll find a definition already laid out for us.

Distillation is the act of separating substances and/or components from a liquid mixture using differences in boiling point and condensation.

When we distill a substance, we are actively exploiting known (or sometimes suspected) differences in boiling point and volatilities between the substances contained in the mixture being distilled. This is a physical separation, not a chemical one. By that I mean, if we have a mixture of water and ethanol, we can separate the water and ethanol from each other using distillation. This is a physical process. However, if we were to separate hydrogen and oxygen from each other in our water to make hydrogen and oxygen gas, *that would be a chemical separation.*

Something else needs to be addressed in our definition of distillation: the term boiling point. Sure, we think we know what boiling point means. After all it's simply when a liquid gets really hot and goes into a vapor state, right? Well, yes and no. It's possible to boil water at temperatures below zero degrees Celsius. And just because ethanol reaches a temperature of 78.3°C does not mean that it will go into a vapor state. There's obviously more to the boiling point story here so let me explain.

Make no mistake: "boiling point" IS a temperature. However, *what temperature* a liquid boils at depends entirely on PRESSURE.

The boiling point of a liquid is the temperature where the vapor pressure of the liquid is equal to the surrounding atmospheric pressure.

Atmospheric pressure (also known as the barometric pressure) as we know is simply the pressure that air exerts onto us in our local environment. Atmospheric pressure differs depending on where you are in the world with elevation having a big impact on the total force. At sea level, atmospheric pressure is 1 atm or 760 mg Hg or 14.696 psi or 1.01 Bar (take your pick of units). However, at the summit of Mount Everest the atmospheric pressure is 0.333 atm, a full 67% lower than at sea level.

Now what exactly is "vapor pressure"? Many substances such as water and ethanol exist in multiple phase states at the same time. If you have a glass of water sitting on the kitchen counter, just above the liquid surface in the glass, there are also molecules of water *vapor* hanging about. Since they are in a gaseous state, they are moving to and fro and this movement exerts a pressure back on the liquid surface and the surrounding atmosphere. This the vapor pressure.

Vapor pressure is the pressure that a vapor/gas exerts on its surrounding while in thermodynamic equilibrium with its liquid state at a given temperature.

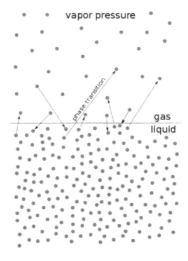

Figure 2-1. How Vapor Pressure Works (Used with permission and copyright of the Institute of Brewing & Distilling)

That gets us through the basic concept of boiling point, but there are a few other definitions that we'll need before moving forward.

Volatility: Volatility is simply a measure of how easily a liquid will move into a vapor state. Generally speaking, *higher volatility* compounds have *lower boiling points* and vice versa.

Mole: a mole is a numerical unit of measurement. Specifically, it is 6.02214076 x 10^{23} (also known as Avogadro's number) particles of a compound. One mole of ethanol would be 6.02214076 x 10^{23} molecules of ethanol. It seems a bit arbitrary until you understand that a mole of a substance has a mass of that substance's atomic weight in grams. So, one mole of ethanol has a mass of 46.07 grams (also known as the molar mass).

Mole Fraction: The mole fraction is the percent *in moles* of a substance in a mixture divided by the total amount of all substances in the mixture *in moles*. By definition, the total of all mole fractions must equal one.

Partial Pressure: We've dealt with vapor pressure, so the concept of partial pressures should be easy to understand. We know that liquids have their own vapor pressures, but what happens when you have a mixture of liquids such as a mixture of ethanol and water? Well, each component, in this case ethanol and water, would continue to exert their own vapor pressures on the system, almost working independently of each other. Thus, the *total pressure* of the system would be the sum of the partial pressures of the individual components. This is also known as **Dalton's Law of Partial Pressures**. Dalton's equation looks like this:

$$PT = Pa + Pb + Pc + ...$$

Where PT is the total vapor pressure of the system.
Px is the partial pressure of each individual component in the mixture.

Raoult's Law: Law in thermodynamics originally studied and stated by Frenchman François-Marie Raoult. Raoult's Law says that in an ideal mixture of liquids, the partial pressure of each mixture component is equal to its partial pressure in an unmixed state multiplied by its mole fraction in the mixture.

Pi = Pi* (xi)
where Pi is the partial pressure of component i in the mixture, Pi* is the equilibrium vapor pressure of component i in its unmixed state and xi is the mole fraction of component i in the liquid mixture.

Basic Distillation Design

I don't have a lot of spare time. I've got two adorable and precocious daughters, a distillery to run, articles to write and clients I consult with. When I get a moment, I enjoy the wind down that cooking a nice meal provides. There is something inherently Zen-like about processing ingredients on my stove, oven or grill into something (hopefully) edible. Many of these processes require heating water or some other liquid until it boils.

Imagine a pot of water on the stove, say for eventually boiling pasta. You turn the heat on and before long you've got steam coming off the top of the liquid surface. Not long after that you see bubbles emerging from the bottom pot, rising through the liquid and breaking at the liquid surface producing even more steam. Now we're at a full boil. Leave the pot long enough and the liquid will eventually boil away to nothing. It will have all escaped as steam. This is nothing more than the act of boiling water. Not too complicated and most of us have done it countless times for all sorts of reasons throughout our lives.

If we look at things a little more closely, the simple act of boiling water becomes a tad more exciting. As we apply heat energy from our stove, it passes onto the metal of our pot which in turn travels into our water. The water molecules steadily gain increasing amounts of energy from our stove and as this happens, their kinetic energy goes up and they begin moving around more frantically. While this is happening the vapor pressure continues to increase.

$$\textit{Molecules } H_2O \textit{ liquid} \leftrightarrow \textit{Molecules } H_2O \textit{ vapor}$$

Above we can see the basic relationship between liquid water and its vapor state. At a given temperature, these things are in dynamic equilibrium with each other. In other words, at the surface of the water you have some molecules gaining enough energy to enter a vapor state while there are also vapor water molecules that lose just a bit of energy and revert back to a liquid state. By increasing the heat energy in our liquid system, we shift the equilibrium more towards the right, i.e., the vapor side.

Eventually we reach a point where the water molecules have enough energy to begin exerting a vapor pressure equal to that of the surrounding atmospheric pressure. The temperature at which this occurs is the boiling point. If we are at sea level, this temperature is 100°C for water. But if we were atop Mount Everest that temperature would be 71°C because the higher elevation gives us a lower atmospheric pressure. The bubbles that you see rising to the surface of the water are water molecules that have transferred from liquid to vapor inside our pot. They rise to escape the liquid surface and move into the atmosphere.

Now back to our pot of water. What if you put a lid on the pot as you might if you were braising some meat or working with some vegetables. Apply heat, steam is formed and begins to rise only this time the steam can't escape the confines of the pot. It rises up until it hits the slightly cooler surface of the pot lid where it cools just enough to condense back into its liquid form. If you lift the lid off for a second and mop the condensed water clinging to the pot lid with a towel, you can wring it out into a glass. Congratulations. You've just distilled water. Not very well or very efficiently, mind you, but it was a distillation, nonetheless.

How could we make our little water distillation experiment more efficient? How about if we put a fan next to the pot and blew cool air onto the lid? We could even go so far as to place a small bucket of ice just in front of the fan so that we were blowing colder air onto the lid. This would certainly increase the temperature differential between the lid and the boiling liquid below thus increasing the rate of condensation on the lid.

Further improvements could be made. We obviously need a better way to collect the water than repeatedly lifting the lid and sopping up the liquid with a towel. A better method would be to lead a pipe from the top of the lid away from the pot into a collection vessel. We could then place our fan to blow cold air onto the pipe instead of the pipe lid, increasing our efficiency all the more.

If you've paid even glancing attention to the art of distilled beverages, you have likely realized that I have effectively described a very crude pot still. The stove is our heat source. The pot is... well, our pot. The pipe coming of the lid would be our "lyne arm"/condenser and the fan serves as our cooling medium for condensation.

That's essentially all you need for distillation. You need:

1. a heat source
2. a vessel for the liquid to be distilled
3. a way for the vapors to reach the receiving vessel

4. a cooling medium to condense the vapors back into liquid

As we continue to progress through the book, we'll see that there are all sorts of gadgets and equipment alterations that we can use to make our jobs easier, but the above list serves as our minimum equipment order.

Yes, we're only distilling water, which admittedly is not really that difficult to wrap our brains around. It's when we get to true mixtures of liquids where things get interesting.

Binary Mixtures and Their Distillations

If you're reading this book then I will assume that you are either currently distilling alcohol, thinking about distilling alcohol, or at the very least interested in distilling alcohol. So, I can also assume that distilling water is not that interesting to you in the long term.

Nope you want to know how to distill alcohol and for that we need to discuss the concepts and chemistry of simple mixtures. Specifically, we will primarily be dealing with a binary mixture of ethanol and water.

You've likely come to this book with at least the general understanding that alcohol boils at a lower temperature than water. In fact, when I go on distillery tours, that is the most common base explanation I hear.

"We take our fermentation, put it in the still and heat it up. *Since alcohol has a boiling point lower than water, we can distill it all off, condense it and get our spirit.*"

Yes, I understand that tours are not the time and place for a lesson on distillation chemistry and physics, but I feel like this explanation and its many (many) iterations leave quite a bit to be desired. Most notably if we distill all the alcohol off then we can easily imagine a situation where we wind up with 100% alcohol, which under normal beverage alcohol distillation conditions is impossible.

In order to parse out what's really happening when we distill alcohol in our distillery, we can set up another hypothetical. First, some basic chemical ground rules. Water boils at 100°C and alcohol (ethanol) boils at 78.4°C. We have a strictly binary mixture of alcohol and water; no other "congeners" are in the system. Finally, our mixture is sitting at sea level with an atmospheric pressure of one atmosphere.

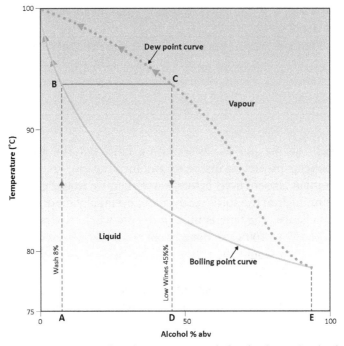

Figure 2-2. Vaporization and Condensation Diagram of Ethanol and Water (Used with permission and copyright of the Institute of Brewing & Distilling)

Figure 2-2 is a classic vaporization and condensation diagram for an ethanol and water mixture. This kind of diagram can be used to give an approximation of initial spirit strength from a wash with a known alcohol concentration. If you've never seen one of these diagrams before, fear not. Reading them is simple. Start on the horizontal x-axis to find the alcohol by volume concentration that corresponds the liquid you wish to distill (your "wash"). From that point draw a perfectly vertical line up to the first curve, the boiling point curve. The temperature corresponding to that point on the vertical y-axis is the boiling point of your liquid. Next, draw a horizontal line from the point where your vertical line intersected the boiling point curve out to the vapor curve on the right. Then draw a final vertical line directly back down to the x-axis. The alcohol concentration that you land on is the concentration of your distillate from the liquid you're distilling.

Looking specifically at the points on the above diagram, Point A on the x-axis indicates a wash with an alcohol concentration of 8% abv. (Remember, that for this scenario our "wash" is nothing more than alcohol and water.) This is pretty standard for a lot of distilling traditions such as whisky, rum and even some brandies, so it makes for a good place to start.

Let's say we put our wash into a basic pot still with all four components previously discussed and turn the heat on. If we adhere to idea that alcohol boils before water, then we would get pure ethanol running into the spirit receiver and eventually there would be an abrupt change. The temperature in the pot would rise rather quickly from 78.4°C to 100°C as the ethanol is rapidly depleted. Our distillate's strength would then drop to zero percent alcohol by volume within an instant.

Of course, we know that's not what really happens.

As the distillation process starts, we get a distillate that comes over at a starting concentration of roughly 45% abv. This occurs when the 8% wash boils at approximately 94°C. Not too bad. We've gone from our 8% abv wash to 45% so we've increased our ethanol concentration considerably. The other 55% of the distillate is composed of water.

But wait, a minute. If water boils at 100°C, how is water coming over in our distillate at such a low temperature? Similarly, why is the alcohol waiting to come over at 94°C?

The answer is that we're dealing with a mixture of substances. The water and alcohol both exert an influence on each other's volatility. For us this means that a mixture of alcohol and water will boil at some temperature between either compound's boiling points. And that relationship is heavily influenced by the amount of each component in the mixture. If we have more alcohol in the mixture, then our initial boiling point will be closer to 78.4°C and if we have more water, then the boiling point will be closer to 100°C.

Back to our diagram. So, the initial distillate that comes off the still has been enriched from 8% abv to 45% abv. What this means is that we have effectively vaporized some alcohol and water inside the pot and recondensed it in the form of our distillate. However, we were obviously more effective at removing alcohol from the pot than water. This means that the alcohol concentration in the pot is now lower than when we started. If we look back at our diagram, you can see that as more alcohol is removed from the pot, the lower the pot alcohol concentration will continually become. This means that there is subsequently less alcohol to remove and enrich as the distillation proceeds and therefore our emerging distillate has progressively less and less alcohol and more water in concentration. Indeed, in actual practice this is what we observe during a "standard" whiskey or brandy distillation, for instance. As the distillation progresses, the emerging distillate has a lower alcohol concentration. So, the end result of our distillation of an 8% abv wash does not give us a final distillate of 45% abv, but more typically something in the range of 20–25% abv.

Vapor–Liquid Equilibrium

So far, so easy. But things are a bit more complicated under the surface. Some of this stuff can get a little confusing and admittedly when I first learned it, I felt like I had stepped into a Lewis Carroll fantasy. Suddenly up was no longer up and symbols seemed to fly off the page at me with menacing abandon. However, it's important stuff to know, so I'll do my best not to lose you as we go down the rabbit hole. Let's take a closer look at what's going on here.

We are starting off with what we might call an "ideal mixture," which is simply a mixture of substances that are completely miscible in each other. Both alcohol and water are exerting their own vapor pressures in our system with alcohol exerting a greater pressure due to it having a higher volatility than water.

Raoult's Law, if you remember, tells us a bit about vapor pressures in mixed systems. Here's a quick refresher from a few pages earlier:

$$Pi = Pi^* \ (xi)$$

where Pi is the partial pressure of component i in the mixture, Pi* is the equilibrium vapor pressure of component i in its unmixed state and xi is the mole fraction of component i in the liquid mixture.

Easy, right? One of the main inferential takeaways from Raoult's

Law is that the higher the concentration of a substance in a mixture, the higher its partial pressure will be.

Think about that for a moment. Remember when we said that the more alcohol you have in your binary mixture, the closer the mixture's boiling point would be to 78.4°C? That's because having a large amount (i.e., mole fraction) of alcohol in the mixture increases alcohol's partial pressure and its overall influence on how the mixture behaves.

Also, if we know the partial pressures of our ethanol and water, we can find the total vapor pressure of the mixture using Dalton's Law. If you'll remember from our definitions Dalton's Law says that the total vapor pressure of the system is simply the sum of the individual vapor pressures.

$$PT = Pa + Pb + Pc + ...$$

Where PT is the total vapor pressure of the system.

Px is the partial pressure of each individual component in the mixture.

We can also approach this from the opposite direction by looking at the composition of our mixture components sitting in the vapor phase.

$$Pi = PT\ (yi)$$

Where Pi is the partial pressure of component i, PT is the total pressure of the mixture, and yi is the mole fraction of component i in our vapor.

Quickly going back to Raoult's equation, if we do a little rearranging, we can make the equation look like:

$$Pi^* = Pi\ /\ (xi)$$

Now rearranged, the above equation states that vapor pressure is equal to a component's partial pressure divided by its mole fraction in the liquid mixture. So, as the mole fraction in the liquid goes up then the total pressure goes down and vice versa. This might sound obvious, but what's important about this equation is that it is essentially the definition for volatility.

Here's the thing with volatility: the bigger the difference between the volatilities of mixture components, the easier they are to separate through distillation. That's the good news.

The bad news is that on a relative scale, the volatilities of ethanol and water are actually fairly close to one another. Fortunately, they aren't so close that they become inseparable, but they are still close enough that we have to be careful with our distillation procedures in order to get the best results.

This idea of differing volatilities brings us to the concept of "relative volatility." As you might expect, relative volatility is simply a way to quantify the difference between mixture component volatilities *relative* to each other. The equation for relative volatility (α) looks like this:

$$\alpha = Pa \, / \, Pb$$

Or as would be the case for our ethanol and water mixture:

$$\alpha = PE \, / \, PW$$

Through a slew of algebraic substitution, we can arrive at the following relationship:

$$\alpha \, (xE \, / \, xW) = (yE \, / \, yW)$$

This relationship is important and illustrates a few key points. First, if our volatilities are equal to each other, then relative volatility becomes equal to one and therefore no separation can occur between the mixture substances. Secondly, relative volatility is not a constant number. As distillation proceeds, we are changing the mole fractions of each substance in both the liquid and vapor states, and therefore our relative volatility will also change.

If the relative volatility of a substance is greater than one, then the compound is more volatile than ethanol. If the value is less than one, then the substance is less volatile than ethanol.

But for all this talk about volatilities, mole fractions and the like, what does it all really mean when we get to our ethanol and water mixture? Fortunately for us, some industrious researchers a long time ago plotted out the values of mole fractions for ethanol in both the liquid and vapor states when mixed with water at atmospheric pressure.

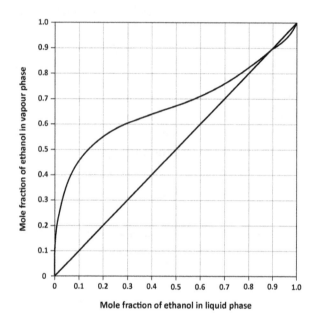

Figure 2-3. Vapor–Liquid Equilibrium Diagram for Ethanol and Water at 1 bar

Figure 2-3 is what we call a Vapor Liquid Equilibrium plot, or VLE diagram. It plots out the mole fraction of ethanol in liquid and vapor phases for a binary ethanol/water solution. There are a few things worth noting about this particular plot. First, notice the straight diagonal that splits the graph in two. These are all the points where the mole fraction of ethanol in the vapor phase is equal to the mole fraction of ethanol in the liquid phase. If our VLE curve touches this line, then no separation can occur. Second, notice how quickly the curve moves upward, giving us a graphical depiction of how much more volatile ethanol is compared to water. Finally, remember that mole fractions in a system should add up to one. If we see a mole fraction of 0.4 for ethanol, then the water in the mixture at that point has a mole fraction of 0.6.

Azeotropes

You may have heard at one point or another that beverage alcohol producers are not physically able to distill ethanol to 100% abv level of purity. You may have even heard the term azeotrope. Few people really seem to understand what these two related concepts actually mean, however. Before proceeding into the thicker weeds of distillation chemistry, we need to have a good understanding of what an azeotrope is and why it is important to beverage alcohol distillation.

An azeotrope is a constant boiling mixture where the composition of the vapor is the same as the liquid being distilled. Once we've reached the azeotrope, we cannot separate the individual components of a mixture through normal distillation practices.

If we look back at the VLE diagram from before for our ethanol and water mixture, we can see that our curve crosses the horizontal line when ethanol has a mole percent of 0.89 in both the liquid and the vapor phases. Remember: we said that when the curve touches that line, there is no more separation possible. That means 0.89 mole percent of ethanol is our azeotrope. That works out to 97.17% abv in more recognizable terms.

Under these conditions, we could throw all our distillery's energy at the mixture, but we will never be able to distill past 97.17%. (Honestly, most distilleries don't get much beyond 96.4%, but that is more an issue of equipment practicality that will become clearer soon.) There are ways to "break" the azeotrope, but most methods on an industrial scale require the addition of things such as benzene or dehydration techniques to produce nearly pure ethanol. These techniques are typically done on large continuous systems which is beyond the scope of our little tome here on batch distillation.

Reflux

Reflux is another term you've likely heard. It's an important concept in batch distillation circles, particularly in the ever-expanding world of mercurial craft distillers looking to make a wide array of spirits on a single still. On the surface the idea of reflux is quite simple.

Reflux is the condensation of vapors inside the still, where they will be re-vaporized and enriched with a greater amount of high volatility components.

In our world of batch distillation, reflux serves the oh-so important purpose of increasing the amount alcohol in our spirit, while also reducing the amounts of heavier congeners such as fusel oils. All stills are able to produce some amount of reflux, though some are considerably better designed for this purpose than others. Controlling the amount of reflux that occurs during distillation is important to the final quality of the spirit.

An important concept to understand with regards to reflux is the reflux ratio. The reflux ratio is the ratio of liquid returned to the pot from internal reflux to the amount of liquid leaving the still as distillate. The higher the reflux ratio, the more reflux you have, and the less distillate comes off at any given time. The design of the still as well as the heating and cooling settings all have a significant impact on the reflux ratio. Running a rudimentary pot still with a lot of heat and little cooling produces an incredibly low reflux ratio inside the still. These conditions will also tend to produce a lower quality spirit. "Standard" reflux ratios used in the industry will vary from below 1 to around 1.3–1.5.

Some spirit types and styles require extraordinarily little reflux such as heavy-type rums, many American whiskeys, mezcal and brandies meant for long maturation. On the other hand, some spirit types wouldn't exist without copious amounts of reflux, particularly vodka.

As we will discover in later chapters, there are a number of factors that can increase the amount of reflux inside the still. These include:

- distillation speed
- cleanliness of surfaces inside and outside the still

- the charge volume inside the still
- the addition of rectification equipment such as columns, trays and purifiers
- still geometry
- the temperature of the air surrounding the still

Increasing Distillate Strength

Let's take a look back at our Vaporization and Condensation plot again.

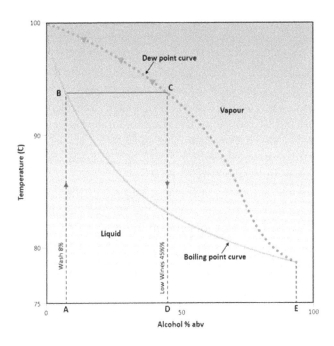

Figure 2-4. Vaporization and Condensation Diagram
(Used with permission and copyright of the Institute of Brewing & Distilling)

At Point A we are starting with a fermented wash of 8% alcohol by volume. We turn the still on, heat things up and the first distillate that comes over in condensed form is going to be approximately 45% abv. As the distillation continues, we are constantly removing alcohol from the wash, concentrating it and collecting it in our distillate receiving tank. Except that as we remove alcohol from the wash, the concentration of alcohol in the condensed distillate coming over in the still gets progressively lower so that by the end of our distillation we have an average alcohol concentration in our total distillate of around 20–25% abv. For virtually every major spirit category in the world today, that would be considered too low. And we have not even considered how to fraction the distillate to avoid unwanted flavors coming over into our distillate. So clearly, we need to boost the alcohol concentration somehow. We could start by simply redistilling our first distillate. Let's take a moment and see how this plays out.

Let's say we start with a liquid containing 25% abv. We can now use our Vaporization and Condensation diagram to estimate what the initial distillate concentration will look like. Starting on the x-axis and finding the point that roughly corresponds to 25% abv, we draw a line upwards to the boiling point curve, move horizontally to the right towards the vapor curve and then vertically back down again to the x-axis. The alcohol concentration that we land on should be approximately 75% abv. That's not too bad. In fact, that's fairly common for initial distillate strength of double pot still distillations such as single malt whiskies and cognac-style brandies.

As before, we know that the emerging distillate will steadily decrease in alcohol concentration as the distillation progresses. Let's assume that the final alcohol concentration of our total distillate for this session winds up around 50% abv. OK. Now we're getting somewhere, but what if we want to go above 50% abv? Let's distill our liquid a third time.

Same as before, trace a line up from 50% abv on the x-axis to the boiling point curve, move over to the vapor curve and back down to the x-axis. The initial distillate should be somewhere around 80% abv. After the distillation is done, we might find ourselves with an average of 65% abv in the spirit receiver. What if we want to get an even higher alcohol concentration? Maybe we're trying to make some neutral spirit at 95–96% abv. Can we do it with the procedures we've outlined here? Let's do one more distillation to see what happens.

Starting around 65% abv and moving through our plot shows us that we get an initial distillate concentration of around 85–90% abv. After the distillation is finished you can bet that we'll be lower than that and still far off from our goal of 95% abv.

Notice a few things happening here. First, we're taking everything that comes off the still, which in the real world doesn't happen that often for potable spirits. If we made a few "cuts" (which will get further explained later in the book), then there are ways for us to increase the alcohol concentration of our finished spirit, but only by so much.

Secondly, notice that we're already up to four distillations and seemingly nowhere near our goal. That is compounded by the third thing I want you to notice which is that with each distillation there are diminishing returns on the amount of alcohol we can concentrate in the final distillate. Essentially, we're putting a lot of time, work and literal energy into a distillation system with little reward for our efforts. I suppose, in theory we could just keep on keepin' on and distill our distillate several more times to steadily inch our way to our goal, but it's not the most efficient use of our time or equipment. (There are also some practical safety issues with redistilling increasingly higher amounts of ethanol inside a pot still. If you distill something at 94% abv to hopefully reach 95% abv, that means you would have very little liquid left inside the boiler which creates some dangerous pressure issues. Don't try it.) There has to be a better way, right?

You bet there is.

Columns

This is the point in the chapter where we begin to pull all the preceding and seemingly disparate ideas together. We want to increase the alcohol concentration of our distillate, and we'd like to do it efficiently. The answer lies in creating reflux within our still.

There are many ways to create reflux within a distillation system, but they all work by creating a temperature gradient that the vapors must come into contact with, thus causing some condensation and re-vaporization with further enrichment of alcohol.

The "easiest" way to create some reflux in our still might be to increase the distance the vapors have to travel. Thought experiment time!

Imagine a basic pot still with a neck protruding from the top of the pot. By increasing the height of that neck, we can create a temperature differential between the top of the neck with the bottom of the neck connected to the pot. In other words, the section of neck piping closest to the pot will be a higher temperature than the section of the neck piping higher and further away from the pot. As the distilled vapor travels up and away from the pot, it enters the neck piping where it encounters increasingly cooler temperatures. Some of those vapors with lower volatilities (high boiling point) will condense and fall back down into the pot while some of the higher volatility compounds (low boiling point) will proceed to the condenser and emerge as distillate.

This system is heavily dependent on environmental conditions and the neck length. If you've got a room with a cool breeze blowing through, then you'll set up a better temperature gradient than if you were distilling in a room that's hot and stagnant. Likewise, you'll get more reflux down the neck if the piping is taller rather than shorter from simply setting up a larger and longer gradient. If you think this at all sounds silly note that popular single malt maker Glenmorangie makes excellent use of stills designed in this fashion to produce a lighter take on single malt whisky and that is in part due to the increased reflux they get from inside their very tall pot stills.

Another example of this from my own experience comes from when I used to work for Corsair Distillery in Tennessee. One of the primary stills that Corsair has traditionally used to produce their whiskies is an old pre-Prohibition era pot still. Stories about the still's actual provenance and original use abound, but one of the most interesting things about this 250-gallon beauty, was that it came with an incredibly tall neck. So tall, in fact, that the total height of this relatively small pot still was around 18–20 feet (about 6 meters). When the company decided to move the still from their Kentucky-based distillery into their warehouse space in Nashville Tennessee, they realized that the ceiling height was too low to fit their prized piece of equipment. Unfortunately, their Nashville distillery was located in a long defunct 100-year-old auto factory and was a registered historical landmark, which meant no alterations to the building could be made. Their only option was to cut about six feet (2 meters) out of the neck piping. This had the interesting effect of lowering the overall distillate strength down to roughly 67% abv from well above 70% abv. Fortunately, it worked out well for them and with the lower levels of reflux inside the still, they were able to get a heavier, higher congener distillate that was well suited to barrel maturation.

However, Glenmorangie doesn't produce distillates with the kind of strength we're talking about. We're looking to push our distillate to 95% abv or higher, so what can we do? Well, I suppose we could just make the neck piping even higher. That might work.

How high would we have to go? Well, without providing a long mathematical explanation that would put you to sleep long before you reached the conclusion, let's just cut to the chase and say, "VERY HIGH." In fact, to base our ethanol enrichment needs solely on still height would be cost prohibitive for any distillery based on the amount of piping required and the amount of height needed, let alone the issue of being structurally unsound from the column's sheer enormity. Remember that by only increasing the height of the neck piping to increase reflux, we would be relying only on the microclimate surrounding the still to provide the proper temperature gradient for reflux. Not ideal.

We could install a small counterflow chiller at the roof of the neck piping and that would certainly increase our reflux for us. However, this "pre-condenser" will only take us so far. In order to reach the level of purity that we're after, we would still need a really tall column and an immense amount of cooling going through the chiller to make things happen. So, we're still not in a satisfactory situation just yet.

What we need is a way to shorten the column while providing the proper amount of reflux and subsequent alcohol enrichment. For that to happen we need a something that allows the hot rising vapors to mix and exchange heat with the descending condensed liquid. Once proper mixing and heat exchange happens, the vapors should be more enriched with high volatility compounds such as our precious ethanol, while the liquid should contain more of the lower volatility compounds such as fusel oil and water.

What we're describing here is effectively a distillation tray or "plate." Distillation trays are more often associated with continuous distillation techniques, but in the past few decades they've made serious inroads into the world of batch distillation, especially with smaller craft distillers. This isn't a new technology. Remember that during the latter half of the 18th century and into the beginning of the 19th, we saw a number of industrious inventors iterate on column design with pre-condensers and yes, trays.

Tray Design

It might help if we take a few moments to discuss distillation tray design, specifically. These are generally simple structures but the impacts that they can have on the distillation process when properly used are profound.

A distillation tray has four primary functions.

1. Provide a surface for the mixing of vapor and liquid for proper heat exchange between the two.
2. Provide a space for the liquid and vapor to separate after heat transfer has occurred.
3. Provide a route for high volatility vapors to rise above the plate and continue through the still.
4. Provide a route for liquid and low volatility compounds to fall below the plate and lower back into the still.

There are multiple tray designs in use throughout the distilling industry. Indeed, many still manufacturers seem to have their preferred types. The simplest type commonly found in beverage alcohol distilling is the sieve tray.

Sieve trays are composed of a basic metal plate, most often made of copper (but sometimes steel), that has numerous perforations drilled throughout. There is a weir on one side of the plate which is simply a slightly raised piece of pipe that allows liquid to flow into it after liquid levels on the tray have risen to a certain level. The weir descends in the form of a downcomer pipe to the tray below where it will deposit condensed liquid. Downcomer pipes are typically placed as far apart from the opposing weir as possible to force the liquid to sit on the tray for longer periods of time and cover more surface area.

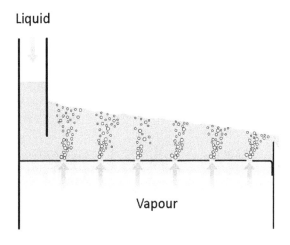

Liquid

Vapour

Figure 2-5. Sieve tray
(Used with permission and copyright of the Institute of Brewing & Distilling)

Notice that in figure 2-5 we have structures and design that satisfies all our requirements. From the left of the diagram and moving right we have a downcomer pipe leading depositing liquid onto the tray from the tray above. We have a series of perforations in the tray that allow vapor to rise and mix with liquid. On the far right we have a raised piece of pipe, our weir, that only allows liquid to overflow into the downcomer pipe once the liquid has reached a certain level. That downcomer pipe will then allow the liquid to flow to the tray beneath, while the newly enriched vapors will rise above the tray and push up through the perforations on the tray above.

You might be wondering why the liquid on the tray doesn't just fall through the perforations. This is because the upcoming vapors from the tray below keep the liquid from falling through the holes. Also, vapor can't easily travel up the downcomer pipes because their openings are placed beneath the desired liquid level on the tray.

When liquid falls through the tray perforations, this is called "weeping" and is due to there not being enough energy being applied to push ample amounts of vapor upwards through the perforations. The opposite situation can also occur where the tray becomes completely flooded well above the weir piping and can't properly drain to the tray below. This is called entrainment and usually occurs from too much energy being applied to the distillation system. (We'll look at techniques and troubleshooting advice to avoid both of these situations later in the book.)

Sieve trays are not the best at providing high amounts of separation between different volatilities. They just don't give the same level of mixing as other tray designs. However, they stand out for some important reasons. First, they are inexpensive to manufacture. Some of the other tray designs cost a pretty penny to produce and set a small distillery back a small fortune for only a few trays in a column. Sieve trays, due to their inherent design simplicity, are also one of the best tray types for handling large amounts of solid materials in the wash. In batch distillation systems this is usually not as much of an issue as there shouldn't be any solids from the pot still pushing into the column trays. However, in the world of continuous distillation this can be incredibly important. For instance, in bourbon production, the high grain solid liquid feed enters near the top of the column onto a sieve tray. In fact, on bourbon columns, the bottom 16 or so trays are usually sieve trays in order to deal with the solid materials, while the top 3 or 4 trays are more complex in design for increased rectification without the need of handling grain solids.

The other commonly seen tray type in the world of batch distillation is the bubble cap tray (Figure 2-6).

Bubble caps are formed from a short rise pipe that rises through the tray to sit just above it. Covering the end of the pipe is a small cap. The cap sits so that there is a small gap between it and the pipe end. This allows vapors to rise up from the tray below, through the pipe and pour over onto the current tray from redirection by the domed cap. As liquid fills the tray it covers the perforations in the cap where the vapors push out which causes the appearance of bubbling in the liquid, hence the name.

Bubble caps are considerably more efficient at rectification and

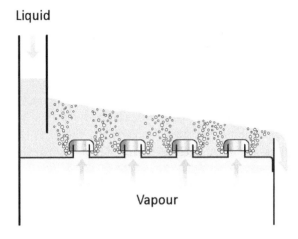

Figure 2-6. Bubble cap tray
(Used with permission and copyright of the Institute of Brewing & Distilling)

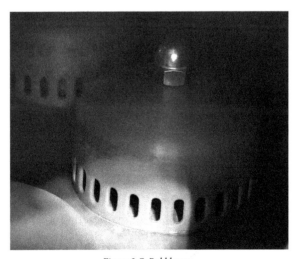

Figure 2-7. Bubble cap

producing higher concentrations of high volatility compounds in the distillate. Unfortunately, they are much more expensive to produce and easily clog with wash solids. As a result, they tend to be found in the upper regions of columns where solids won't likely reach. However, they hold their liquid levels well and are less prone to weeping.

There are other tray designs that occasionally pop up. Disc and donut trays are another choice if high solids are a concern and valve trays have great mixing capabilities akin to bubble caps. However, sieve and bubble cap trays are certainly the trays beverage alcohol distillers are most likely to encounter in hybrid discontinuous column systems.

Calculating Theoretical Plates

Of course, the next legitimate question one would likely want to ask is, "How many plates do you need to reach 96% abv?" It's a complicated question.

If we were dealing with the design of a continuous distillation system, we could make use of several calculation methods including the famous McCabe-Thiele method, pioneered by two graduate students in the 1920s.

The problem is that we're not dealing with a continuous system. Continuous distillation columns typically have feeds entering onto a feed tray and the trays beneath it serve as the "stripping section" (also called the "analyzer") while the trays above it work as the rectifying section. Each section has its own associated calculation that when plotted onto our VLE diagram would allow us to find the necessary number of plates to reach a desired spirit strength.

Take a moment and look at figure 2-8. Parsing out the various calculations in the McCabe-Thiele Method that allow us to arrive at the above plot is well beyond the scope of this book. (If you are curious about the subject, the internet is your friend but be warned that it can be a bit of a mental rabbit hole...) What you're seeing is our VLE diagram overlaid with some extra data. Through a behind-the-scenes set of calculations we've established an operating line for the rectifying section and the stripping section and then "stepped off" the two lines to establish the required number of trays to reach 95% abv. We see that 14 trays are needed to meet our goals. (In most beverage alco-

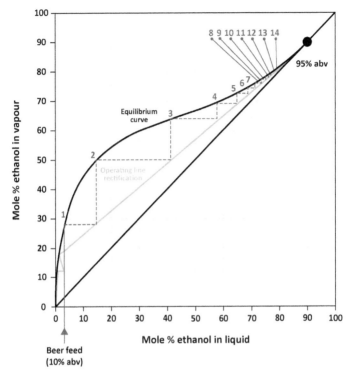

Figure 2-8. McCabe-Thiele Plot for continuous alcohol distillation with a 10% abv feed and 95% abv spirit (Used with permission and copyright of the Institute of Brewing & Distilling)

hol systems, the number would be somewhat higher.)

This all gets rather more complicated when we factor in other congeners such as iso-amyl alcohol into our system. The congeners shown in figure 2-9 (page 60) are fairly common during beverage alcohol distillation and behave differently depending on alcoholic strength and distillation technique. This is to say that real life distillations are a bit more complicated than our "ideal" binary system.

In a batch distillation system, we don't have a continuous feed of wash with a constant alcohol percentage. Instead, we have a "pot" that continuously loses alcohol (and usually other congeners) in the form of vapor. Assuming we have a column with trays fixed atop the pot, then we can indeed get enough reflux with enough plates to reach

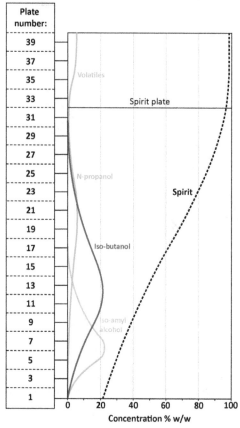

Figure 2-9. *Typical concentrations of congeners in the rectifying section of a continuous distillation column (Used with permission and copyright of the Institute of Brewing & Distilling)*

95–96% abv but calculating the required number of trays seems to be more a matter of tray design, manufacturer experience and distillation technique rather than calculating out mass balances and operating lines onto a VLE plot.

> *I spoke with my friend Mike Jackman at Specific Mechanical in British Columbia, a well-regarded still and brewing equipment manufacturer. I asked him about how they decide on the number of necessary trays in a neutral spirit batch system and if they use*

the traditional McCabe-Thiele Method in any form to make this decision. He said, "Our starting point of 20 trays for a neutral spirit is largely based on experience but it really depends on how the still is run and where the cuts are made."

"...since there's no feed point in the columns, it's all rectifying and the stripping section would essentially be the pot still... Therefore, the operating line ends up being the 45-degree line representing full reflux which isn't the case. So again, it's good for illustration purposes but the data needs to be taken with a grain of salt." (Jackman, 2020)

So, what's the answer to our query? For a batch distillation system with column(s) the answer depends on quite a few factors, all of which you should discuss with your chosen still manufacturer. How big do you want the system to be? What kind of tray are you wanting/willing to use? How much cooling power do you have? There's a lot you could discuss, but *in general,* you can expect to need around 20 trays with bubble caps (or something similar) to reach 95% abv. If you want to push up to 96% abv without much trouble, you may find that you'll need to double that number. Discuss your needs with your manufacturer.

Packed Columns

Increasingly we're seeing more and more so-called "packed column" designs entering the distillation marketplace. It has become so common that I felt it warranted a brief discussion on the subject. The manufacturers of these stills promise unparalleled performance in separation and rectification capabilities. Many come with moderate to high levels of automation to boot.

A packed column forgoes traditional tray design in favor of a hollow column filled with packing material. This packing material may be copper scrubbing "wool," ceramic rings or beads, stainless steel "springs" and many other designs.

The packing acts as a series of innumerable plates, in theory

Figure 2-10. Stainless steel packing for distillation column

giving you incredible rectification in the column. With so much reflux happening in the column, these systems effectively form a liquid column, held afloat by rising vapors from the pot. Subsequently, the operation of packed column systems requires some counterintuitive thinking on the part of the distiller. Generally, we're taught that running a distillation low and slow on power will give us maximum separation ability. However, because a packed column requires a completely filled liquid column to be maintained, they typically require you to push the distillation a bit harder which also means you need a fair amount of cooling coming from the other direction to compensate.

Without getting into too much of the nitty gritty of these systems, I'll say that I'm personally not much of a fan. I know they're popular with some folks, but I've spent some time working with packed columns and have never been happy with the results. This has a lot to do with the caliber of the companies that offer these stills to the trade and quite frankly, the level of build quality is just not up to snuff. And despite promises of being able to produce 96% abv spirit off these stills, the designs that I've played with require a LOT more time and effort to pull that feat off and so total distillery operational efficiency suffers as a result.

If you are considering the purchase of a packed column still, I would strongly urge you to rethink things. Yes, many of the companies that tout them offer competitive pricing, but let's just say that you get what you pay for. I've spoken with quite a few distillers over the years about these systems and have not once met someone who uses them that doesn't have serious complaints or issues. And with that we will leave the subject of packed columns alone.

Copper Chemistry

The last bit of chemistry that we need to discuss pertains to the use of copper during distillation. Take a tour of any modern batch distillery and you'll likely be confronted with stills that serve as towering gleaming monuments to the miraculous metal that is copper. The copper still in all its shining glory leaves a visual impression on the beholder, a mental mark that indicates craftsmanship and traditional methods are somehow nebulously at play in the distillery.

Of course, we don't use copper for distillation simply because it looks good. That's just a side perk. There are countless distilleries across the globe that are not open to the public, but still make heavy use of copper in their stills.

What many folks think of when they think of a "still" are the copper behemoth pot stills dotting the whisky-scape of Ireland and Scotland. These glorious distillation pieces are often characterized by a large and wide copper pot with a simple and narrower neck rising above. The next piping extends at roughly a right angle to a vertically situated condenser. The whole apparatus is burnished bright shiny copper.

But why copper? There are less expensive metals that could be used for sure. Or how about making the whole thing out of stainless steel? It's a tougher metal and requires less cleaning and maintenance. Why do we, as distillers, put ourselves through the physical and financial paces of purchasing and using stills so heavily clad in such seemingly soft and precocious metal?

There are four primary reasons for the use of copper in distillation.

1. Copper is more malleable and easier to work with than many other metals, including stainless steel.
2. Copper is a good conductor of heat.
3. Copper catalyzes many positive flavor reactions during distillation.
4. Copper reacts with several sulfur-containing compounds and removes them during distillation.

The first two reasons were arguably more important a century ago than they are today. Certainly, copper is considered one of the softer metals and is relatively easy to bend and shape, but technological progress over the last 100 years has made it easier to perform similar processes with other harder metals including stainless steel. And with regards to copper's conductivity of heat, we have so many clever heating options available to us these days along with more efficient forms of heat insulation that this too, is not as much of a modern concern. However, the last two reasons for using copper still hold their weight in the current era (and at the risk of being proven wrong in the next several decades, will likely always prove to be important for quality spirits production).

First, we have the fact that copper catalyzes reactions that result in positive flavor contributors to the final spirit. Copper has been shown to aid in ester formation during distillation. Some folks suspect that the heat from the distillation process might be what is really driving these reactions, but the evidence does seem to suggest that copper plays at least some part in the process. One theory suggests that copper aids in the reduction of aldehydes to their respective alcohols. These alcohols can then go on to combine with organic acids to produce new esters (Miller, 2019).

Secondly, copper reacts with several important sulfur containing compounds and subsequently removes them from the final spirit. Sulfur is a fairly reactive element and plays an important role in the formation of many intensely aromatic compounds found in spirits. Some of these compounds are quite nice smelling, but many are things we would like to avoid having in our spirit. Compounds such as hydrogen sulfide (H_2S) and the aforementioned DMS/DMTS are all capable of coming over into the distillate from the fermented wash and all of them are generally deemed to be negative aromas with low sensory thresholds. Fortunately, in addition to being highly volatile compounds, they all readily react with copper inside the still to form copper salts that precipitate out and won't affect the final distillate.

This is all well and good, but copper is expensive stuff and so, do we really need to have our entire still made out of copper? I would argue that if you can afford it, a little more copper is never a bad idea in the distillery. That being said, there has been some interesting research on this subject, and it turns out that there are ideal points for copper placement based on what you are distilling. Don't get too hung up on some of the terminology here as it will all be explained in more detail in upcoming chapters.

If we are distilling a fermented wash it has been shown that copper is most effective at removing sulfur compounds when it is primarily placed inside the condenser. But when we are distilling the subsequent low wines (that we obtained from the previously distilled wash) the ideal copper placement is inside the pot, itself (Harrison, Fagnen, Jack, & Brosnan, 2012). Thus, if you should be so inclined to purchase a still that will only be for distilling either low wines or wash, you can, in theory at least, preferentially place copper in areas and parts of the still that will have more of an effect on the sulfur content of the spirit.

This is not the last time we will discuss copper placement in the still. When we get to Chapter 4 on the physical still components, we will need to talk about copper even more, particularly when we come to the discussion on the different varieties of condensers.

Chapter 3

Chemistry and Cuts

Even if you've never distilled before, you have likely heard the term "cuts" before in relation to spirit production. Hell, even if you're just a fan of spirits and have no intention of starting your own distillery, you've probably come across the term. It gets bandied about in marketing materials for distilleries all over the world often describing the action of "taking the perfect cut." You may have even heard the terms "heads," "hearts" and "tails."

"Making cuts" is often spelled out in eerily arcane terms as if only a distiller with 50 years' experience could possibly perform the action correctly. When I attend conferences, this is actually one of the most common areas of questioning I get from folks. "How do I take my cuts on the still?" My initial response is to tell them just to practice, but I'm here to tell you, it really isn't that complicated. For this somewhat brief chapter let's take a closer look at what it means to take cut fractions during a batch distillation.

First, let's describe what a "cut" or "fraction" is when it comes to batch distillation.

> *A "cut" or "fraction" is simply a choice of what part(s) of the distillate a distiller chooses to keep in the product and which part(s) he or she chooses to recycle, repurpose, or destroy. These decisions are typically based on efforts surrounding consumer safety, product sensory quality, and/or maturation potential.*

As spirit comes off the still during a batch distillation, the character is constantly evolving. In other words, the first liquid to come off the still will not smell or taste like the stuff that comes off an hour later and even more different than the stuff that comes off at the end of the distillation.

If you've been following along in the previous chapter, then you have possibly put together some basic lessons regarding how various congeners in a batch distillation system behave when they have different volatilities. Quite simply, compounds with lower boiling points and higher volatilities will come off the still earlier in the distillation process than those with high boiling points and lower volatilities.

Examples of high volatility congeners include methanol, acetaldehyde and ethyl acetate plus many more.

Examples of low volatility congeners include phenols, fusel oils/higher alcohols, fatty acids, water and many more.

You might be wondering how we decide what it means to be "low" or "high" volatility. Afterall, aren't these relative terms? Absolutely. For the purposes of beverage alcohol, we define ethanol as having the "standard" volatility and the rest of the volatilities are defined in relation to ethanol.

Unfortunately, it gets a bit more complicated than that. It turns out that in a mixed system, the volatilities of several important congeners will vary depending on the concentration of alcohol. This isn't too hard to understand, though. If you think about it, there is a certain amount of elegant sense to it. Some compounds are more soluble in water than ethanol and hence will have higher volatilities in systems where there is a lot more alcohol. Other compounds are more alcohol soluble and will therefore have their volatilities go up as the alcohol concentration goes down in the still. (This is a gross oversimplification of the chemistry, but I fear offering a full explanation would put most readers to sleep.)

In figure 3-1 we can see how some of this plays out. The relative volatilities of several common congeners found in batch distilled spirits are plotted in relation to ethanolic strength. Some are fairly predictable and seem to act independently of ethanol concentration such as acetaldehyde and diacetyl. Others are very much influenced by how much ethanol is in our system. Methanol has a higher rela-

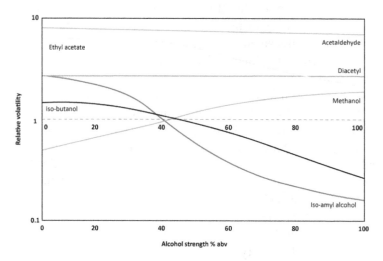

Figure 3-1. Relative volatilities of common congeners in relation to ethanol (Used with permission and copyright of the Institute of Brewing & Distilling)

tive volatility to ethanol when the ABV is above 40%, but it rapidly decreases below ethanol when the ABV is below that point. Conversely, iso-amyl alcohol and iso-butanol have higher relative volatilities beneath 40% abv, but dramatically lower values above 40% abv.

In figure 3-2 we can see this information presented in relation to distillation progress and time. Here we have simply grouped the various congeners into volatility groups with alcohol as the reference compound. Group A has higher volatilities than ethanol which includes methanol, simple aldehydes, many higher alcohols and esters. Group B has approximately the same volatility as ethanol and includes "lighter" higher alcohols. Group C1 has lower volatilities than ethanol with Group C2 having even lower volatilities than C1. These groups include some heavier higher alcohols and fatty acids. It's an interesting plot because it brings to the forefront the idea that many congeners actually bleed into our hearts fraction.

This flies a bit in the face of the blindly accepted orthodoxy I often hear in the distilling community with regards to removing things such as methanol from the product spirit coming off the still. It is fairly common to hear such statements as, "We take a big heads cut so

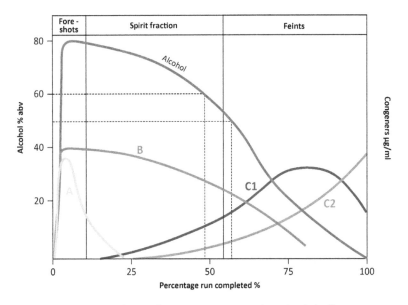

Figure 3-2. Behavior of various congener groups during batch distillation
(Used with permission and copyright of the Institute of Brewing & Distilling)

that we can remove ALL the methanol." Understandably, we want to remove methanol from our final distillate. High amounts of methanol can damage our optic nerves (hence the apocryphal stories of people going blind from drinking poorly distilled "moonshine"), however it also just doesn't smell or taste particularly good in high amounts.

As we'll see in upcoming sections, there is no way to simply remove *all* the methanol (or any other compound for that matter) from our distillate during batch distillation. Even during neutral spirit distillation, there will always be at least trace amounts of congeners remaining in the final spirit. At that point it is certainly no longer a health issue, but rather an issue of flavor. Even minute amounts of certain congeners of both high and low volatility types can contribute either positive or negative sensory impacts to your spirit depending on their relative concentrations.

I had a bartender friend in D.C. who used to vacation
every year in Oaxaca, Mexico. One year he brought back

several bottles of "small batch" mezcal. And by bottles, I mean he brought back a few plastic water bottles of illicit mezcal he had purchased from a clandestine distiller with a supposed legendary local reputation for his skills with a still. My friend was excited to see what I, as a distiller, thought of his find. I carefully unscrewed the cap, sniffed the inside of the bottle, and carefully screwed the cap back on. I politely told my buddy that he had been sold a bottle of incredibly "heady" spirit and that I didn't feel comfortable drinking it. My friend was undeterred in his pride for his "find." Oh well.

And that is perhaps the crux of our discussion here. Cuts are important from not only a consumer health point of view, but also from the perspective of consumer acceptance. You should certainly be careful with regards to providing something wholly potable to your customer, but that's not enough. You want to make something delicious and paying proper attention to where your cut point is can have a profound impact on how the final spirit tastes. For spirits destined to sit in cask, the congeners that emerge from these cut points can play important roles in chemical reactions that occur during maturation, adding to the final spirit's complexity in extremely nuanced ways.

Foreshots and Heads

The first bit of distillate that comes off the still during distillation is commonly called the heads and/or foreshots. This fraction is composed of aldehydes, esters, higher alcohols and more high volatility congeners. In other words, this fraction is intensely aromatic.

Now, depending on who you talk to and what distilling traditions you follow, these terms may be equated to each other or may be considered different things entirely. In the UK, you'll often hear the term "fores" which encompasses everything that comes before the "hearts" (which we will discuss in a moment). In France, this fraction is often referred to as *tetes* (simply French for "heads"). In Mexico, this cut is called *cabezas* (Spanish for 'heads').

I personally have always considered the foreshots and heads to be two separate entities, even if I don't always treat them as such in my own distillery.

The foreshots are the very first distillate to emerge from the still. They are full of high volatility compounds but also fatty acids and esters that have clung to the walls and piping of the condenser from the previous run.

The heads are the fraction that comes after the foreshots. This fraction is composed primarily of high volatility congeners such as acetaldehyde, methanol, and ethyl acetate but also contains some ethanol as well as smaller amounts of other congeners with differing volatilities.

We'll get into specific techniques for deciding when to take these fractions in later chapters. For now, we can simply say that different distilling traditions approach the heads fraction from different perspectives. Some base the cut point on the amount of time the distillate has been coming off the still. Others use alcohol percentage or volume as their preferred metrics. Still others opt for an old school approach and use sensory analysis of the spirit to decide when to cut.

Regardless of the method to make the cut or even the source fermentable material it is distilled from, there are a few commonalities that bridge all batch spirit styles together on heads. First, is that the heads cut is typically small compared to the rest of the distillation fractions. Numbers vary based on distilling technique, spirit style, still design and more, but in general the heads volume is between 1–3% of the total still charge. In other words, if we put 1,000 liters of liquid into our still and we begin to distill it, we should expect about 10–30 liters of heads to emerge before we can feel comfortable cutting into our hearts stage. (This is a gross over generalization, but I merely offer it to give you a basic guide. We'll get into more specific techniques and numbers later.)

Second, heads have some tell-tale aromas and sensory qualities associated with them. The smell of heavily concentrated heads from a neutral spirit distillation is intensely solvent heavy, akin to nail polish remover and sometimes paint thinner with a slight hint of fruitiness. In spirits distilled without massive amounts of rectification such as many whiskies and rums, the aromas are more subdued, but still very obvious. In both instances, the aromas start out incredibly strong and gradually lower in intensity as the initial cut point to hearts gets closer.

Hearts

Hearts are where the bulk of our precious alcohol resides. The hearts cut is the fraction we want to immediately keep. Once we have collected it, we can redistill it into something else, place it in a cask, or send it to further processing for added flavor additions or packaging.

While the hearts contain the bulk of our alcohol, they also contain smaller amounts of other flavor important congeners. This is incredibly important for spirits meant for maturation, but also for "neutral" spirits. As I mention above, we can't remove every congener from our distillate leaving only ethanol and water. Even under the most diligent distillation techniques with the fanciest of fancy equipment, the best we can hope to do is to remove most of the congeners. There will always be other things that remain. But don't fret. If you've done your job right, the minute amounts of residual congeners will give your spirit added character and texture, even if it's destined to be vodka.

Batch distillation cut point location

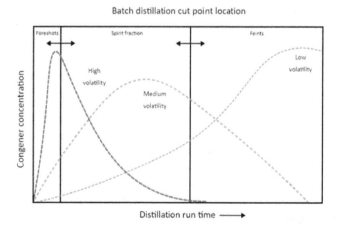

Figure 3-3. Congener behavior during distillation (Used with permission and copyright of the Institute of Brewing & Distilling)

Figure 3-3 is a simplified version of one of our previous diagrams. It shows how some of our heads congeners continue to bleed into our hearts cut and sometimes even a bit into the tails/feints fraction. Likewise, it shows how low volatility congeners that make up the tails/feints will actually start coming over early in the distillation, even near the beginning of our heads fraction.

Giving hard cut points for where hearts begin and end is something that new distillers always want to know. I can empathize. When I started my distilling career that was something that I desperately wanted to understand. Unfortunately, there's no simple answer outside of "It all depends." Don't worry. This is not to say it's hard or difficult to determine, just that every spirit and still is different. I hesitate to even give an expected volume percentage because this too will be different depending on what type of spirit you are distilling. The amount of hearts collected during a distillation of single malt whisky may be vastly different to the amount collected off a similar charge for a gin distillation. Further along in this chapter I'll give some pointers for deciding general cut points if you're just starting out.

The aromas and flavors of the hearts are going to vary with the type of base fermentable. In other words, rum hearts are sensorially different from whiskey hearts which are different from grape brandy hearts and so on. Fortunately, there are some commonalities we can cling to.

When I started distilling the general advice I received regarding the sensory perception of hearts was that compared to the heads and foreshot fractions, they smelled almost neutral. I'd argue that's only partly true. The initial distillate aromas of heads are…well, pretty heady and kind of intense. So, when you compare those aromas to the aroma of the incoming hearts, by comparison the hearts do indeed smell somewhat neutral. However, the problem with this advice is that you can really only benefit from it if you truly understand what the heads smell like. On top of that, in most batch distillations, the point from heads to hearts doesn't simply change magically from smelling intensely solvent-like to "neutral" in a matter of seconds. Instead, it's a gradual change over time. Therefore, the elucidation of the difference between the two is more subtle in real time as opposed to being abrupt and obvious.

What I prefer to tell people regarding hearts is that the aromas are going to be more closely related to the starting fermentable material. If, for instance, you are distilling bourbon, then the hearts should take on more grain-based aromas, particularly those related to corn. Rum hearts should have an aroma related to either molasses or sugar cane (depending on what the starting material was). Brandy hearts should come off with aromas related to the source fruit.

I don't believe that sensory analysis for cut point decisions is the wisest way to go, reasons for which will become clear nearer the end of this chapter. I do think that sensory analysis is an important part of the overall quality equation and can help you assess how your distillation is proceeding. Obviously, based on the advice I just laid out, you need to have a good understanding of what your base materials and fermentations smell and taste like in order to understand how that translates through distillation. This kind of knowledge and understanding takes time to acquire. Therefore, towards the end of this chapter we will tackle some other methods for deciding cut points that will make this puzzle feel less puzzling.

Tails

After hearts comes the tails, the other volumetrically large fraction in our distillation. Tails are largely composed of ethanol, water and decreasing amounts of low volatility fusel oils/higher alcohols.

The tails fraction can be a little tricky for some folks to determine. This has a lot to do with not only what makes a "good" distillate, but particularly what makes a good distillate for its intended purpose. If your intention is to release an unaged eau de vie, then very narrow cuts preventing much in the way of heavy fusel oils to creep into the hearts fraction would be the order of the day. On the other hand, if you want to lay your spirit down in cask for 10 to 15 years then those more complex higher alcohols can be potentially beneficial to the final mature character of the spirit.

Much of this thought process can and should begin with the raw material selection, processing and fermentation practices as these forerunner activities have enormous impact on the overall composition of the low volatility congeners found in the tails fraction. All the same, we need to know what tails smell and taste like to understand what's happening with our distillate.

When I talk with other distillers regarding the tails cut, more than any other part of the distillation process, I hear an incredible array of seemingly disparate sensory descriptors. I've gotten everything from "minty" to "spoiled milk" to "smokey" and much more. This makes choosing a tails cut point quite tricky for the beginning distiller. And because the tails portion of the distillate contains mostly low volatility congeners, a poor tails cut has the potential to be disastrous for the overall final spirit quality. This is because, unlike the high volatility congeners in the heads, these compounds will not dissipate or evaporate over time very easily. A slightly sloppy heads cut can be somewhat ameliorated (although not completely) by letting the spirit rest for some time exposed to air, which in turn will allow some of the high volatility congeners to evolve out and away from the liquid spirit. This doesn't really work with tails. So, what do you do?

Well, first we need to understand when to look for the tails. As the hearts fraction proceeds, the emerging distillate will continue to pick up an increasing intensity of new aromas and flavors. These aromas and flavors will heavily depend on raw materials and fermentation conditions, but generally, the aromas will steadily move away from the core source material. Even more tellingly, the flavor will pick up an ever-increasing bitterness that is well perceived on the back of the palate. Beyond that I hesitate to give much in the way of sensory descriptors because it can be so variable between people. So, let's take a look at how cuts can be better approached for the distiller.

Fraction Chemistry

In case it isn't obvious by now, the reason we are concerning ourselves with these three primary distillate fractions is because their innate chemistry gives them certain sensory characteristics that we can use to alter the final flavor of our spirit. To pull all this together let's take a closer look at how these fractions can chemically affect the product distillate.

Some interesting studies have been done on the chemical composition of the various distillate fractions, but let's take a look at just one of them from 2011. Researchers in Brazil decided to investigate the effects of various distillation cut points on the chemistry and sensory aspects of their local sugarcane distillate. During the study, they compared traditional whisky distillation techniques to those of cognac and others. We'll get to the specifics behind these techniques in later chapters. For now, all we need to know is that the distillates in their study were all distilled twice. The first distillation concentrated and collected the alcohol and congeners from the fermented sugar-cane wash. These low wines were then distilled using one of several prescribed distillation methodologies such as what might be common in Scotch whisky single malt production. Fractions were taken during this distillation and analyzed for their overall composition.

In the data set from the study (figure 3-4) you can see the chemical composition across the three cuts made during the distillation. We can see across the data that the general trends of what we've discussed hold up. Esters, aldehydes, methanol and higher alcohols are in greater concentrations within the heads fraction. Higher alcohols gradually decrease throughout the run while volatile acidity reaches its peak in the tails.

Chemical composition of distillate fractions from the first and the second distillations, according to double distillation methodology used in the whisky production

	Low Wines	Second Distillation		
		Head	Heart (Spirit)	Tail
Alcoholic concentration[1]	39.84	84.19	78.55	35.09
Copper[2]	0.09	0.13	0.08	0.13
Volatile acidity[3]	39.82	7.06	7.56	42.32
Furfural[3]	0.10	0.00	0.00	0.00
Aldehydes[3]	21.11	76.25	9.60	0.00
Esters[3]	20.84	75.24	10.39	0.00
Methanol[3]	14.60	92.32	9.45	6.06
High alcohols[3]	548.19	455.87	401.90	180.79
Congeners[3]	630.06	614.42	429.45	223.11

[1] in %v/v 20°C, [2] in ppm, [3] mg.100mL-1 anhydrous alcohol

Figure 3-4. Chemical composition results of cognac distillation (Alcarde, Araujo de Souza, & Eduardo de Souza Belluco, Chemical profile of sugarcane spirits produced by double distillation methodologies in rectifying still, 2011)

In figure 3-5 we see the same composition variables measured for a cognac distillation. Remember that these distillations used the exact same fermented wash. The only variable at play here is the distillation technique and here, we can see that it does indeed play a huge role on the levels of many congeners in the final spirit. Overall, the cognac distillation gave a higher level of congeners for the hearts fraction than the whisky technique.

Finally, we can take a look at how much these techniques reduce some of these compounds from the low wines to the final distillate. In the table from the same study (figure 3-6), we see that the whisky distillation reduces the total congeners by nearly one third from the low wines to the spirit. The cognac distillation saw a reduction of 16% from the low wine.

Chemical composition of the distillate fractions obtained in the first and second distillations, according to double distillation methodology used in the congnac production

	First Distillation			Second Distillation			
	Head	Brouillis	Tail	Head	Heart1 (Spirit)	Heart 2	Tail
Alcoholic concentration[1]	81.10	41.39	1.85	84.15	80.32	31.86	3.25
Copper[2]	0.18	0.10	0.15	0.14	0.06	0.38	0.15
Volatile acidity[3]	11.41	29.42	642.16	7.41	11.09	55.93	639.69
Furfural[3]	0.00	0.00	0.00	0.00	0.00	0.00	0.00
Aldehydes[3]	101.17	19.25	0.00	88.01	9.42	0.00	0.00
Esters[3]	179.11	19.23	0.00	71.38	8.68	0.00	0.00
Methanol[3]	67.99	12.57	0.00	29.41	9.40	7.47	0.00
High alcohols[3]	987.19	497.91	12.33	460.67	448.51	81.95	0.00
Congeners[3]	1278.88	565.81	654.49	627.47	477.7	137.88	639.69

[1]in %v/v 20°C; [2]in ppm; [3]mg.100 mL^{-1} anhydrous alcohol

Figure 3-5. Percent reduction in compounds through different double distillation techniques (Alcarde, Araujo de Souza, & Eduardo de Souza Belluco, Chemical profile of sugarcane spirits produced by double distillation methodologies in rectifying still, 2011)

Percentage of reduction in the concentration of secondary compounds of the spirits produced by double distillation, taking as reference the concentration of secondary compounds in the distillate of the first distillation

	Methodology of double distillation		
	10-80-10	Cognac	Whisky
Volatile acidity[1]	19[c]	62[b]	81[a]
Aldehydes[1]	41[b]	51[ab]	55[a]
Esters[1]	35[b]	55[a]	50[a]
Methano1[1]	35[a]	33[a]	35[a]
High alcohols[1]	-10[c]	10[b]	27[a]
Congeners[1]	-5[c]	16[b]	32[a]

[1]mg.100 ml-1 anhydrous alcohol. Different letters in same row indicate statistical difference by Tukey's test at 5% significance

Figure 3-6. Percent reduction in compounds through different double distillation techniques (Alcarde, Araujo de Souza, & Eduardo de Souza Belluco, Chemical profile of sugarcane spirits produced by double distillation methodologies in rectifying still, 2011)

We have to be careful about drawing too many conclusions surrounding the effects of different techniques here. This was only one study on one type of spirit from one type of wash on one type of still. There are so many other factors that can throw some inconvenient wrenches into our meta-analysis. Still, studies like this allow us to gain some general glimpses into how these different distillation techniques will affect our own distillates.

Sensory Implications of Chemical Composition

I've already alluded to some of the perceived sensory characters experienced by the various fractions. It might be beneficial for you to have a more detailed explanation of some of the sensory characters these compounds contribute to spirit quality. This list is by no means exhaustive, but it does cover several of the most important sensory compounds commonly found in batch-produced distillates.

Methanol – On its own methanol is actually somewhat similar in aroma to ethanol. The aroma is a bit sharper and more pungent, however though it is still a little sweet smelling similar to ethanol.

Fortunately, there's not really going to be a situation in a batch distillation program where you have methanol simply by itself; it is always going to be accompanied by other compounds many of which are more aromatically intense than methanol. Mostly found in the early stages of distillation.

Ethanol – Contrary to what some folks believe, ethanol is not actually odorless. Even 100% lab grade anhydrous ethanol has an aroma to it. It is generally characterized as being slightly sweet and lightly fruity. It is altogether a more subdued aroma than that of methanol.

Ethyl acetate – This is the most common ester found in distilled spirits. There are numerous origins for its formation. In low amounts it can lend a subtle fruitiness to the spirit, but in high amounts it is incredibly pungent and solvent-like and highly unpleasant. During distillation, it is generally found in the early stages, though in poorly produced washes with high levels of ethyl acetate it can persist longer throughout the distillation run.

Isoamyl Alcohol – This is a fairly pungent higher alcohol that can create problems for inattentive distillers using continuous columns. It can also go on to combine with acetic acid to form isoamyl acetate which in low levels produces a pleasant banana-like aroma in the distillate. Along with iso-amyl alcohol, 2-methyl-1-butanol (active amyl alcohol), 2-methyl-1-propanol (iso-butyl) and 1-propanol often make up the bulk of the higher alcohols in the distillate (Spaho, Dürr, Grba, Velagić-Habul, & Blesić, 2013).

Acetaldehyde – This compound is highly volatile and is generally not much of an issue for properly produced spirits. In low concentrations it has a green apple aroma. Though much of it comes over the still during the first parts of distillation, it readily reacts with other components to form a variety of other flavor-active congeners.

Diacetyl – Also known as 2,3 butanedione, diacetyl is well known for its aromas of butter and sometimes butterscotch. It is fairly volatile and will come over in the still early but may persist into the spirit if there is enough of it. Odor threshold in whisky has been shown to be as low as 0.2 ppm (Spedding, 2015).

Phenethyl Alcohol – Another important higher alcohol, though this one has the aroma of roses. It is a positive aroma found in some whiskies with levels ranging from 5–131 ppm (Spedding, 2015). It is also found at similar levels in brandy (Ferrari, et al., 2004).

Ethyl hexanoate – This is an ester that produces a kind of red apple aroma and is sometimes simply described as "fruity." It and along with a host of other so-called "fruity" esters are important contributors to a swath of batch distilled spirits. It is formed through a combination of ethanol and caproic acid, a fatty medium length chain acid. Many fatty acids found in later parts of the distillation have unpleasant sensory characters (caproic acid = cheesy, butyric acid = baby vomit) but when esterified produce an array of pleasant fruity notes.

DMS and DMTS – Acronyms for dimethyl sulfide and dimethyl trisulfide, respectively. These compounds are highly volatile and come over early in the distillation of many grain-based spirits. They can easily wind up in the hearts fractions. Both compounds have varying degrees of cooked corn/cooked vegetable aromas which in high amounts would be considered a flaw in the spirit. Making matters worse, the aroma thresholds are low. DMS has a sensory threshold of only 35 ppb. The good news is that if given enough time, like say sitting in a cask for a year or more, these compounds easily evaporate and start to go away. (They are also adsorbed onto the char layer of charred casks.)

Making the Cut

So, how do you successfully decide on the right point and time to make a cut during distillation? Is it based on some kind of internal alchemical secrets only passed down through the family if your last name is Beam, Russell or Noe? Absolutely not. And I'm here to tell you that the subject is not really that complicated.

First, let's dispel the romantic notion of cuts being done using only sensory analysis. We've all seen and heard the story of the master distiller or moonshiner deciding on just the perfect point to make a cut on a distillate because he or she took a quick sip or sniff of the spirit off the pipe. These kinds of images and stories give the impression that distilling is much more art than science and therefore may require some innate ability that a few folks may never possess. This couldn't be further away from the truth.

Of course, you should get to know the sensory qualities of your new make spirits at all points during the distillation. You should smell it. You should taste it. You should rub a few drops between your palms to see how it feels. These are all important data points, but that's all they are: data points. In other words, they offer only fragments of the whole picture.

Basing your cuts on sensory analysis alone is a risky move in my opinion. Sure, it's romantic. Sure, it gives you that feeling of being a true craftsperson, enabled by the pure power of your highly tuned senses. But it also totally human and humans are incredibly fallible. Sensory analysis for cut points is therefore not the most consistent way to approach the process.

All kinds of things can change how attuned your senses of taste and smell are on any given day. Maybe you had a spicy meal the night before (or even worse the morning of) the distillation. Maybe it's allergy season or you're coming down with a mild cold and your sense of smell is taking a hit. Even your morning cup of coffee can throw things off enough to ruin your accuracy. If you smoke tobacco, then things are even more difficult.

On top of everything, this all assumes that you're the only person making the sensory-based decisions. What if you want or need other employees to also make the cuts based on sensory analysis? People perceive aromas and tastes quite differently from each other and adding another person to the mix throws another unpredictable cog into the machine.

When I was getting started in the distilling industry, the distillery that I worked for did all their cuts based on sensory analysis. It was incredibly difficult for me to learn how my boss "tasted" and "smelled" for different things. (It didn't help that I was a smoker at the time...) We could never seem to get to a point where my cut points were consistent with hers. Somedays I was being too "conservative" and others not conservative enough. Certainly, there may have been errors on my part (I was pretty new to the game after all), but I suspect there were also issues with general fluctua-

tions in sensory sensitivity for both of us. She never felt that my cuts were so far off as to make the spirit "bad," just that they were slightly different than hers. In other words, not consistent. We were still able to distill together and accomplished quite a bit, but that lack of perfect consistency really nagged at both of us.

What I am NOT saying is that sensory analysis for cuts is bad. You should absolutely sensorially assess your spirit during the distillation process. *It just shouldn't be the ONLY thing you do.*

There are several other parameters that distillers use to make a decision on cut points. Some of the more spirit specific techniques such as the demisting test in single malt whisky or the three pearls method for brandy will be discussed in their own sections. Here, we want to tackle bigger concepts and eschew some of the more colorful minutiae for now.

Parameters that are commonly used to determine cut points during batch distillation include:

- Time
- Volume
- Alcohol Concentration
- Temperature

Many of these are used in concert with each other and some such as alcohol concentration and specific temperature readings are closely related.

I met a brandy distiller from Austria a few years ago. He and I were discussing the differences between distilling in his home country and that of the United States. One of the interesting things I learned from him was that in Austria, he was not allowed to access the distillate as it was being distilled as per government regulations. Therefore, he had no way to perform sensory analysis on his new make spirit. All his decisions on fractions and cut points had to be based on things such as volume, alcohol concentration, and so on. Despite not being able to taste his new make spirit, he was able to make excep-

*tional Austrian-style eau de vie and he did it consist-
ently every year. And I'd like to point out that even
though he wasn't tasting through every cut, I would in
no way consider him any less of an artisan distiller. He
knew his spirit better than many of his American peers
and could tease out impossibly pure varietal flavor and
character from his source material without having ever
sipped a drop off the still.*

Time

Let's start with the concept of using time as a distillation variable. Many distillers, myself included, use time as a check variable for
deciding when to cut from heads/foreshots to the hearts fraction. For
myself, from the moment the first few drops of distillate emerge from
the still, I set the time for 30 minutes. Why 30 minutes? It's not an
arbitrary number. I arrived at 30 minutes based on experience with
my low wines composition, and yes, sensory analysis. I know that
somewhere between 30–35 minutes at my standard power setting on
my still, I will get the correct flavor and aromas I'm looking for in a
hearts fraction beginning to emerge.

Why does this work? Look back at the earlier diagram from this
chapter that shows congener behavior over time during a batch distillation. You'll quickly notice that high volatility compounds making
up the majority of the heads fraction dwindle quickly down to reasonable levels early on in the distillation.

Now, exactly *how long* that time is, is really affected by how much
power and cooling you are using during distillation, subjects we'll
delve deeper into in another chapter. And no, it isn't as simple as
running things faster to decrease the amount of time you collect heads.

If you are pushing your still pretty hard with a ton of heat energy
and possibly less cooling, then you will push more vapors from the
pot towards the condenser and therefore more distillate per unit time
will emerge. Makes sense. If you add more power then you're going to
go faster, not unlike driving a car. Hit the gas and go. Push the pedal
to the floor and you'll zoom, zoom, zoom. However, if you only lightly touch the accelerator, you'll probably just creep along as if you were

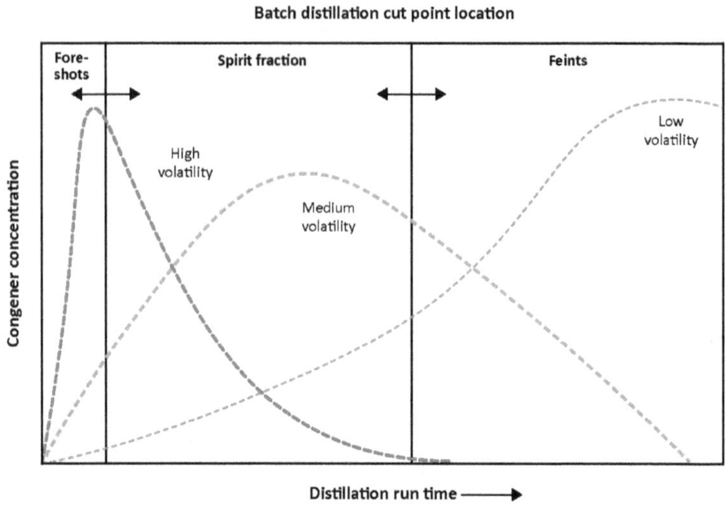

Batch distillation cut point location

Figure 3-7. Congener Progression Over Distillation Time
(Used with permission and copyright of the Institute of Brewing & Distilling)

following a shopper from a packed holiday season mall out to their parked car so you can have their coveted spot.

What also happens when you apply tons of heat to your distillation is that you get what I call "smearing." If you look at the previous diagram, you'll note that the various fractions bleed into each other a little bit. These overlaps are exacerbated by applying loads of heat to the contents of the still, stretching out the tails of those curves in both directions. You'll extend the length of time that your heads extend into your hearts fraction and you'll allow the tails fraction to start earlier. The curves essentially "smear" into each other. In effect, by trying to speed up the distillation, you make your distillate fractions a bit sloppy.

The other side to the time coin is to run everything as slow as possible. The problem with this route is that you get diminishing returns for your efforts in a simple batch distillation. If you don't have in place much in the way of rectification systems such as trays, then there's only so much fraction separation you can realistically do. "Low and slow" does help with some separation, but after a certain point you will just be wasting valuable production time.

The amount of time, heat and cooling needed to obtain a desired fractionation of the heads is going to vary quite a bit depending on what your end-goal is for the spirit and the type of still and heating you have. I'll give some real-world examples for guidance near the end of this chapter.

Volume

I won't say too much about volume, because, quite frankly, there isn't much to say. Some distillers use volume as a guide for deciding when to cut from heads to hearts and even more rarely from hearts to tails.

The idea is simple. Distillate starts to come over, collect to a certain volume, and then cut to the next fraction. It works for some people and some distilling traditions. I use volume as an ancillary guide along with time, alcohol concentration and sensory.

The problem with volume is that it is affected by temperature. If you are cooling your condensers with some form of ground water or municipal supply, then your water supply temperature will likely vary throughout the year with warmer temperatures during the summer months and cooler temperatures during the winter months. This in turn can affect the temperature that your distillate comes out at which will also affect your volume readings. If you are relying on precise volumes for you cut decisions, then using volume as your sole guide won't work. I suggest using it as an additional piece of information to aid in your decision-making process.

But, if this is something that seriously interests you, then it would probably be helpful if I provided some sample volumes for you.

For heads/foreshots on many distilled spirit types, you can expect about 1–3% volume of the total spirit charge. So, if you charge the still with 1000 liters of low wine, you can expect about 10–30 liters of heads. How much you choose to cut out depends on factors such as your intended spirit style, fermentation and more.

The amount of hearts volume you obtain from a typical distillation once again varies based on quite a few parameters. However, I typically say that you can expect somewhere between 15–50%

volume of the initial still charge. I know, I know. That's a pretty big range, but it's based on a quite a few variables and that will become clearer as we proceed throughout the book, and we begin to look at style specific techniques. (If it helps to have a reference point, most of my single malt hearts cuts are usually around 18–20% of the initial charge volume inside the still. But keep in mind, that's for MY distillations and yours may and probably will be completely different.)

The volume that you might collect for a tails fraction is even more variable. This is because not everyone has the same ideas surrounding the keeping and possible recycling of tails (more on recycling later). Also depending on the type of distillation you are doing the volume of tails can be heavily impacted. In a hybrid batch column system where you're producing neutral spirit, you will likely have a far lower volume of tails than if you are distilling whiskey on a simple pot still. This is because the level of rectification and concentration of unwanted or otherwise unusable congeners is different between the systems.

One of the more famous examples of the use of volume is the 10-80-10 distillation technique sometimes used in cachaça production. I'll describe it in more detail in a later chapter, but for now all you need to know is that 10-80-10 refers to the volume percentages of the heads, hearts and tails. As we will see, it's simple…often to a fault.

Alcohol Concentration

This is probably the metric that gets used the most by distillers the world over for deciding cut points. It is easy to check, easy to understand and assuming the production team has been consistent with their processing techniques up to that point, it is the most reliable.

To understand how we can use the metric of distillate alcohol concentration to our advantage, it helps to understand what is going on inside the still. We know that as the distillation progresses, the alcohol concentration of our outcoming distillate also steadily goes down. We also know that the remaining liquid inside the still is also steadily having its alcohol concentration lowered. The two are closely correlated with each other.

The other important thing to remember here is the volatilities of various compounds are at least in part affected by the alcohol concen-

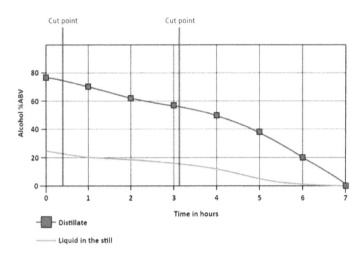

Figure 3-8. Alcohol concentration of the spirit vs liquid remaining in the still over time (Used with permission and copyright of the Institute of Brewing & Distilling)

tration. This is certainly relevant for many of the tails-based fusel oils that we may generally want to keep out of our hearts fraction. Through trial and error, we can establish ethanol levels that indicate the appropriate cut points.

What commonly happens during a standard batch distillation is that the very first distillate coming out of the still starts out at a slightly lower alcohol concentration and then rapidly rises. This is in part due to low ethanol levels in the distillate within the first few minutes of distillation but also the composition of fatty acids and residual esters being rinsed from the spirit piping early on. Eventually the alcohol concentration hits a peak and begins its slow descent for the rest of the distillation. At some point after the alcohol peaks, we generally take our heads cut. The distillation is then allowed to proceed as we collect our hearts fraction. Eventually, we reach a point where we want to cut the hearts and begin collecting tails.

This is where the trial-and-error methodology comes into play. We need some understanding of the sensory characteristics of our distillate to understand what is happening and when.

Just as importantly, we need to ensure that the liquid we are distilling is consistent from batch to batch as much as possible. Otherwise, the use of alcohol concentration as a viable metric is not going to work. (Of course, none of the other metrics will work that well if batch consistency is not maintained, so this really speaks to a broader point of being diligent in your processes and record keeping throughout the manufacturing process.)

What alcohol concentrations should you use? Well, once again, the answer is that it really depends. Quite a few factors come into play here, including (but certainly not limited to), still type and rectification level, cooling and power applied, starting alcohol concentration inside the still, and so much more.

For a simple single malt distillation, you might expect the following number ranges. (Once again, do not take these as gospel. Experiment with your own equipment and distillations.)

Heads to Hearts — cut between 75% and 72% abv.

Hearts to Tails — cut between 65% and 55% abv.

Notice that I have given ranges and not absolutes because every situation is a bit different. For instance, if I were distilling a peated whiskey with lots of phenolics and smokey notes, I might cut to tails closer to 55% abv or even lower in some cases. This is because I know that those phenolic smoke compounds from the peat tend to come a little deeper into the tails and so I would need to cut a little later in order to properly capture those. There are dozens of other examples we could look at, but you get the point. Experiment with the alcohol concentrations that give you the new make spirit with the congener profile you want.

Temperature

As a metric for cut-making decisions, temperature is a bit more fraught and not quite as useful as our other metrics. Even still, we can gleam valuable information from temperature measurements at certain points during our distillation to help us in the decision-making process.

We know that different mixtures of ethanol and water have different boiling points. Therefore, if we place an accurate thermometer probe in the line of vapors, we can approximate their alcohol content fairly well.

This means that we are using temperature as a way to indirectly measure our alcohol concentration, which is admittedly only valuable when we want to know the alcohol concentration of a vapor in some part of the still. The most common scenario where you will come across vapor temperature as a valuable metric is during distillation on hybrid pots using columns and trays, in particular with regards to neutral spirit distillations.

We'll dive into the specific techniques for neutral spirit distillation on batch columns later in the book, but for now we can simply say that these distillations generally require a deft hand and fine control over multiple vapor points in the still. It helps to know what the temperature and subsequent vapor alcohol level is at various points in the process in order to make decisions in a timely manner. On many batch column systems, the difference between a successful neutral spirit distillation cranking out 95% abv or higher spirit and pumping out something beneath that level is often only a few tenths of a degree in temperature. Here, using temperature of the column(s) and vapor streams in conjunction with the outcoming alcohol concentration is invaluable when producing a quality neutral spirit.

What Have We Learned?

Look, if you've reached this point and are still confused, I completely understand. Making good cuts on the still and producing a high-quality distillate is priority number one for everyone and if you are new to distilling, this can be a very intimidating part of the process. What I can tell you is that you just have to practice.

But the word "practice" comes with some caveats. After all, it can be difficult to practice if you are not sure what your end goal is supposed to be. So below are some tips and a potential road map for learning the process of making successful and consistent distillation cuts.

1. Be consistent.

I cannot stress this enough. *Every decision you make in your distillery affects every downstream process after the fact.* If you decide to use some moldy grain then it will affect your mashing, fermentation, distillation and maturation processes. If you decide to change your yeast from a whiskey yeast to a more neutral yeast then your fermentation, distillation and maturation will all be affected.

Basically, anything you do prior to distillation can have an effect on your cut points, so it pays to find a set of operating procedures that you are happy with and stick with them. Be as consistent as you possibly can with each recipe so that when you get to the distillation process, you can remove as much human error from cut fractioning as possible.

2. Know your spirit.

Like the back of your hand. And I'm not talking about just the spirit coming off the still, but the spirit you've envisioned in your mind that you would like to eventually put into a bottle for the thirsty consumer. If you are wanting to mature something in a cask for a long time, then you can (and probably should) be a bit less conservative with your cuts than if you are wanted to release something unaged. Conversely, if your goal is to release an unaged spirit then you would likely want to be a bit more conservative with your fractioning.

It can help to go out and purchase bottles of spirits that are produced in a similar style to what you are shooting for. Taste and smell them. Get to know their quirks both good and bad as well as you possibly can. You want to understand what makes them tick. Take lots of notes and then use those thoughts and couple them with the lessons in you pick up in this book. Do certain aromas from a spirit smell head-like? Is there a slight bitter note on the palate that shouldn't be there? Maybe the spirit is really estery. All of these things may be influenced by cut points and you can use your sensory impressions along with what you learn from your reading to put the pieces of the puzzle better together. Then you will be better prepared to make distillation cuts in a way that drives the spirit in the direction you want. When you begin distilling your own spirit, taste the liquid as it comes off the still. Take notes after every sample. Write down the heat and cooling settings on the still. Write down at what time in the distillation you took the sample along with the alcohol concentration and any other concrete metrics you want. Take note of how the spirit smells. Make note of how these sensory and physical metrics evolve as the distillation proceeds. Do this a few times to make sure you understand the patterns that emerge.

3. Start small.

The easiest thing to do when you are ready to start taking cuts on the spirit is to simply take a lot of them. When the initial heads begin to come over on the still, take several smaller fractions, as many as you like and feel comfortable with until you are absolutely certain you are into the hearts fraction. Make note of the distillation time and the alcohol concentration of when you took the cut. When the distillation gets to a point that you think you might be looking for the next cut, begin taking another set of smaller fractions until you are absolutely confident you are into the tails of the distillation. After everything is done you can then go back and smell through all the fractions and blend back the ones that you feel good about.

4. Don't stress.

Seriously, don't over think it. Cuts management is not that difficult and with a little experience everyone can come up with an operating procedure for taking distillation fractions that not only produces a quality spirit but is also easy to teach to their employees.

5. Use multiple parameters to make the best decisions.

I don't rely on any one parameter above too heavily. Instead, I will generally look at several of them in order to decide on when to cut the spirit. For instance, for whisky production, I use time for my foreshots with an eye towards the total volume I'm getting. Once I reach a certain length of time, I'll begin checking the alcohol concentration to ensure everything is looking good. And for good measure, I will be smelling the distillate the whole time to make sure that I'm getting the sensory character that I'm after.

I interviewed for a distiller position a few years ago and the owner/head distiller of the distillery I was interviewing with told me that he was the only person allowed to do cuts on the spirit in his distillery. Despite the fact that I had more experience than him, he said that in no uncertain terms would he let me or anyone else on his team make the decisions on cut fractions. I understood and respected his reasoning, but I also felt that his philosophy just wasn't sustainable in the long term. By his line of thinking, he would have to be there for every distillation run. If he decided to go on vacation or if he got sick, the distillery would not be able to function to its best ability or capacity. He should have designed a protocol based on repeatable metrics so that the rest of his employees could also manage the distillations. I decided to not take the job.

Let's close this section out with a comparison of the cut points between some real-life distilleries. Specifically, we'll look at distillation data from several of the Islay malt whisky distilleries. These distilleries are all famous in their own rights. Many of them are known for producing a heavily peated type of whisky. Much of their equipment and distilling techniques share quite a few commonalities. Most of them are using similar if not the same grains and yeast. However, if you taste through the various expressions from these distillers you

	Ardbeg	Bowmore	Bruichladdich	Bunnahabhain	Caol Ila	Lagavulin	Laphroaig
Wash ABV	8%	7%	6% – 7%	6.5% – 8.5%	8%	8.9%	8.5%
Low Wines Collection Points	46% – 1%	46% – 1%	22.5% (avg)	46% – 0.5%	42% – 1%	50% – 0.1%	45% – 1%
Heads Length	10 min	15 min	40 min	10 min	25 – 30 min	30 min	45 min
Spirit Cuts	73% – 62.5%	74% – 61.5%	Varies (76%-71%) – 64%	72% – (64%-61.5%)	75% – 65%	72% – 59%	72% – 60.5%
High Wines ABV	70%	68.8%	Varies 69%-72%	68.5%	70.5%	68.5% (avg)	67.5%

Table 1. Distillation information from several Islay malt distilleries
(Adapted from data presented in Andrew Jefford's Peat Smoke and Spirit (Jefford, 2004))

would not easily mistake one for another. There are a lot of reasons for this, but some of these differences are in part due to subtle differences in distillation technique.

The table (previous page) has a ton of interesting information and if you know these whiskies well enough, you can easily see how some of the data presented here plays out in the final distillate. If we take a look at Ardbeg, Lagavulin and Laphroaig which are arguably the true peat beasts nestled next to each other on the Southeastern side of the island, you can see quite a few similarities, but some important differences as well.

First, you'll note that while Lagavulin and Laphroaig have similar alcohol concentrations in their wash, Ardbeg's is somewhat lower at 8% abv. The collection range for low wines is predictably similar though with the higher wash alcohol concentration, Lagavulin has a higher starting point than the other two.

Second, you'll note that the heads collection times are all incredibly different from each other. With Ardbeg collecting heads for a mere 10 minutes while Laphroaig collects theirs for a full 45 minutes. Lagavulin sits comfortably in the middle. Certainly, there are a number of reasons why these times are what they are. Everything from mash preparation and fermentation conditions to the amount of heat applied to the still and still geometry can affect how long you might want to collect the heads. So, it is not a simple question of one distillery being more conservative in their heads cut than another.

If we were to assume that all conditions were equal between the three distilleries, which having visited all three, I can most assuredly state that they are NOT, then we could possibly tease out some important information about the final spirit. A brief heads collection would mean that a greater portion of high volatility congeners are in the final spirit. Some of these compounds will be lost through evaporation during maturation, however some of them will play important roles in several maturation reactions such as the formation of ethyl acetate and other simple esters. Conversely, a longer heads cut would produce a "cleaner" new make spirit, but the subsequent maturation chemistry would be altered considerably.

Moving on with data in our table, we see that the cut points between our three distilleries are subtly but importantly different from each other. Ardbeg's cuts are arguably a bit narrower with the tails cut coming at 62.5% abv while Lagavulin goes all the way down to 59% abv and Laphroaig at 60.5% abv. The same caveats I mentioned above apply here. It can be a bit slippery to infer too much from such limited information, but these cuts are not chosen at random. Remember that these distilleries all produce fairly peaty and smokey spirits. The compounds responsible for those aromas and flavors are somewhat more low volatility in nature and tend to come over more in the early tails section. By Lagavulin and Laphroaig cutting a bit later, they are going to capture more of those phenolic peat compounds. Of course, there are other methods to eke out a few more ppm of peat. Ardbeg is generally considered the peatiest of the bunch at roughly 55 ppm of peat compounds in the spirit, while Laphroaig and Lagavulin are a little lower at 45 ppm. All this means is that despite the earlier cut point, Ardbeg has other techniques in the processes that accentuate the high peat levels in their whiskies. (The measurement of "PPM's" is fraught with all kinds of uncertainty and you shouldn't place too much emphasis on it in your assessments of these and similar whiskies.)

We could play this game with any number of distilleries, but I give you this table and the information it contains for a couple of reasons. One is to simply show you how some of the larger pot distilleries approach cuts. Second is to point out that while cuts are important, there are a lot of other factors that will come into play that will affect the actual cut point.

Let's look at just one example of how a cut point change can impact the distillate.

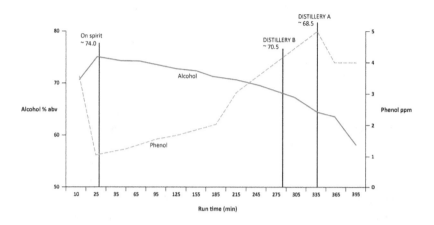

Figure 3-9. Effect of cut point on smoke character in malt whisky
(Used with permission and copyright of the Institute of Brewing & Distilling)

In the above plot we see a comparison between cut two distilleries making peated malt whisky. Distillery B chooses to cut their hearts earlier than Distillery A. This simple difference has an immense impact on the final distillate flavor. You can see that the phenols which are often responsible for the smoke aromas in peated whisky increase towards the end of the hearts fraction. Cutting a bit later can drastically increase the amount of phenol in the final spirit, thus increasing the overall smoke character for the whisky.

Other Cut Methods

There are two other cut methods worth pointing out. They both have their proponents and detractors, but I'll give each a brief discussion so that you can form your own opinion. The first is sometimes used in traditional French brandy production (and loosely in other spirit traditions) while the second is mostly discussed in the realm of single malt whisky.

The Three Pearls Method

The three pearls method is sometimes used in the production of traditional French brandies to make the cut from hearts to tails. Its adherents are a fast-dying breed, instead favoring more modern and consistent methods, but there are a few folks that still swear by it.

The way it works is pretty simple. As the distillation proceeds and you begin to feel like you are getting near the end of the hearts fraction, take a sample of distillate and put it into a standard sampling glass. Place your hand over the glass and give it a good shake, agitating the liquid inside. Make sure your hand is clean and doesn't have any heavy oils on it... this is *really important* for this technique to work. You'll notice that a bunch of bubbles form on the surface of the liquid and quickly dissipate. As the cut point draws near, these bubbles will linger for longer periods of time until you finally reach a point where there are two to three bubbles that cling to the side of the glass much longer than the others. These are the "pearls."

The underlying theory is that bubble formation occurs from air being agitated and surrounded by a certain amount of heavy tails compounds. When you get to a point where two to three bubbles can easily linger, then the levels of these compounds are too high and a cut needs to be made. This is loosely similar to how some moonshine and many mezcal producers gauge alcohol concentration in their final distillate, known as checking the "bead." Basically, anything below roughly 50% abv will not bead properly. Once again, it's a neat parlor trick but not that accurate for professional distilling purposes.

Proponents of the technique will quickly attest to its accuracy. It seems to work best with grape and fruit spirits, though I have used it somewhat successfully in whisky production as well. The problem is that I find the technique to not be quite as consistently accurate as I would like. It's just a little too flimsy in its methodology. Still, I find that it can be a nice way to double check your decisions from time to time.

The Demisting Test

The demisting test is most famously used in Scotch whisky production to identify the cut point between heads and hearts. This is another simple test that when done properly can be quite accurate.

As the distillate first starts to come through the spirit pipe at the beginning of a distillation run, it is heavily loaded with esters and fatty acids that have clung to the inside of the condenser piping from the end of the last run. They are often cloudy in appearance as a result.

The heads from the new run are essentially washing the pipework of the dregs from the last run. As the heads continue to evolve off the still, there is less and less to rinse out of the piping. The level of heady compounds also steadily decreases while the alcohol level slightly ticks upwards.

Take a sample of heads and mix an equal amount of distilled or RO treated water with it. If the spirit goes cloudy then you should continue collecting heads. If the sample stays clear, then you can cut to your hearts fraction.

Once again, there are some caveats worth mentioning. Mainly, this technique only works if your starting alcohol concentration inside the pot is less than 30% abv. Stronger than that and you run the risk of getting a "blank run" which may give you a false positive on when it's safe to cut. The same issue can arise if you are using enabled plates with your distillation. The initial alcohol level can be fairly high coming off the still, once again leading to the false positive of a blank run. Regardless, it can be a valuable tool when coupled with one or more of the other concepts discussed earlier in the chapter.

Figure 3-10. Demisting test results (From left to right: initial distillate; 20 minutes into heads fraction; 35 minutes into collection and cut point to hearts)

Chapter 4

Distillation Equipment

So far, we have talked about distillation history, distillation chemistry and how to approach the fractioning of distillate coming off the still. Before we move into the subject of style-specific distillation methodologies, we need to better understand our equipment. This chapter deals with the ever-humble pot still.

I say humble, but truthfully, the pot still has evolved into a modern technical marvel. Many manufacturers offer enough bells and whistles to make a car dealer's head spin.

However, the most fascinating thing to me about pot stills is that despite incremental refinements, the basic apparatus itself has not changed much over the past 200–300 years. If Elijah Craig or Jacob Beam were to come back from the dead and visit a small distillery, they would have a fairly good idea of how to operate the stills. In fact, I would go so far as to say that if they visited the modern sites of their namesake brands, they would be more confused by the methods and techniques employed to produce their own products than the processes used by most of the small craft distilleries currently dotting the world's evolving liquor landscape. This is because places like Jim Beam and Heaven Hill use technologically advanced continuous column stills to produce their distillates while the majority of small distillers use the less complicated pot still.

In fact, it's not just the small distillers that use pot still systems-many larger distillers use them as well. The Scotch single malt whisky industry, cognac and a lot of rum and agave spirits are all made with pot stills. Some of these plants are quite large in scale. The Glenlivet distillery in Scotland produces over 10,000,000 liters of alcohol per year with seven wash stills (15,000 liters each) and seven spirit stills (10,000 liters each). I would hardly call that a small distillery.

However, you can only maximize your distillation output if you thoroughly understand how your still functions. For that we need to do a deep dive into the fascinating world of pot stills.

> *To be successful in this industry you need to have a good understanding of your tools. A friend was recounting a story about this very thing to me a few years ago. A new distillery nearby was about to open their doors and begin production. But there was one problem. The "master distiller" couldn't get the still to heat up. He contacted the still manufacturer to complain that their still "wouldn't turn on." The manufacturer sent out a representative to see if they could assess the problem. The company had sold the distillery a steam heated still so perhaps it was just a boiler issue. The rep got to the distillery and began to look around. Within a few minutes, he had found the problem. The "master distiller" had not purchased a steam boiler to power the still, nor did he understand that he needed one.*

The Basic Pot Still

A still can be as simple or as complex as you want it to be. All you need for distillation are the following four things:
1. A heat source
2. A vessel for the liquid to be distilled
3. A space for vapors to travel without leaking to the atmosphere
4. A condenser to turn the vapors back into a liquid

That's it. It really doesn't have to be any more complicated than that. Forget all the doodads and whatchamacallits that you see on so many modern pot stills. We will definitely get to those, but without all four of the items listed above, your beautiful still isn't really a still at all. It quite simply will not do the job it is supposed to do, which is to distill alcohol.

If we look at figure 4-1 and sweep away some of the more extra-

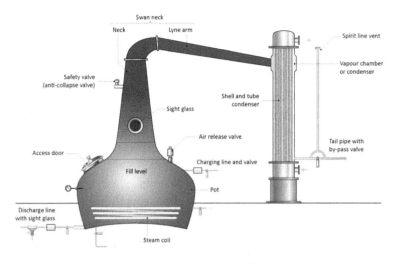

Figure 4-1. A basic modern pot still design
(Used with permission and copyright of the Institute of Brewing & Distilling)

neous (though still nice to have) features, we see that all four of our primary still design elements are in place. We have our heat source in the form of the steam coil which is placed inside the pot where we have our liquid to be distilled. Above the pot and moving to the right in the diagram we have piping that serves as directional space for our vapors to flow to the condenser where they will be condensed back into liquid.

Now, think back to the first chapter on the history of distillation and some of the early distillation apparatuses we discussed. It isn't too hard to see how despite the additions of a few modern conveniences, the diagram of our modern pot still is really not too different from those early stills. Because at the end of the day all we want to do is vaporize some liquid in one space and concentrate it back into liquid in another space. That's it. There's no magic or divine intervention here. The rabbit has been hiding up our sleeve the whole time. It really is that simple.

Of course, those modern conveniences are pretty nice to have, and we have indeed come a LONG way from allowing vapors to simply evaporate in a clay pot and hopefully collect on the upper rim.

It would serve us well to take a look at many of these modern components to understand how they affect a modern distillation.

The Heat Source

Let's start with the source of heat for our still. You might think that what type of heat you apply to your still doesn't matter. Heat is heat, right? Well, yes and no. The truth is that there are a lot of heating options out there and they all have their pros and cons.

Direct vs Indirect Heat

First thing's first. Are we using indirect heat or direct heat for our still? These are two very different options so let's break them down a bit.

> *Direct heat systems rely on the heat being directly applied to the liquid that is being distilled or directly to the metal of the still. Indirect heat systems involve heat that is conducted to the liquid through another material such as a pipe or jacket.*

The most obvious form of direct heat systems are the traditional open flame burners that sit underneath the still. I realize that the concept of having an open flame involved in distillation is probably frightening to many people but remember that folks have been using open fire to heat distillation equipment for centuries to great effect. Yes, there are definitely inherent dangers involved and every few years there seems to be some kind of tragic accident involving a still catching fire from an open flame source nearby. Honestly, this is not something that I would be overly concerned about so long as the still comes from a reputable manufacturer with a proven track record.

Direct flames are most notably used in the cognac industry to fire their alembic Charentais stills. The burners beneath the stills are usually fueled by propane or natural gas, but some old stills utilize wood fires or coal. The burners for this style of still are encased in brick so that the flames are not open to the atmosphere and well separated from the outcoming alcohol.

So, why would someone want to use direct flames on their still?

Well, the amount of heat generated is enormous and so the theory goes that the extra heat applied to the liquid inside the still can cause positive chemical reactions to occur such as the caramelization of various sugars. Opponents argue that these reactions may not really occur and even if they do, their effect on the final spirit would be minimal. For my part, I've yet to see an actual study that proves either side's points. I personally think there is room for well-designed direct heat systems in the distilling world and that the stills they are employed on often produce really fantastic spirits. Whether that has anything to do with the influence of direct heat or not, I'm not sure.

Indirect heat is far more common in the modern distilling industry. This is where heat is conducted to the liquid medium inside the still via a conductor material such as a metal pipe inside the pot or a metal jacket surrounding the pot. The heat is produced somewhere else in the distillery and is pushed into the distillation system through the use of pressure or pumps.

Proponents of indirect steam like its inherent safety (though accidents can still occur so never become complacent) and for how "gentle" it is on the liquid inside the still. Direct heat advocates argue that this type of heating system misses out on some of the aforementioned flavor reactions because the heat is not as intense.

In my opinion, either system works just fine as long as you have a soundly built still. I hold no adherence or preference to either one, except that I just happen to use indirect heat for both my own stills. This has more to do with the utilities at my disposal rather than some perceived increase in quality due to the heat source. Had I been saddled with a situation that required me to use direct heat on my stills I would have happily gone that route so long as the stills were built well.

This brings up another subtle but important point on the differences between direct and indirect heated stills. If you have an open flame heating the base of your still, you need to make sure that the copper is thick enough to withstand the continual heat stress that is being applied day in and day out over many years. Generally, direct flame heated stills need thicker gauged copper to withstand these stresses. The suggested thickness for stills in the Scotch whisky industry is 16 mm (5/8") while indirect heated stills can use a thinner gauge of copper of around 10 mm (13/32") (Nicol, 2014). Aside from the build quality issues, as you can imagine, a thicker copper gauge is more expensive to produce.

This all brings up the question of what fuel you will use to heat your still. We've already mentioned that direct heat stills using open flames are often fueled with propane or natural gas and even more occasionally hardwoods and sometimes coal. Your choice between these fuels is often dictated on availability which in most cases means you don't have a choice over one or the other at all. You just use whichever you have access to. If you are in the fortunate position of being able to choose, then there are a few things you should understand.

First, is that propane is a more efficient fuel. Propane provides more than twice the amount of heat per unit volume than natural gas. On the flip side, natural gas is usually cheaper than propane, but this really depends on where you are (occasionally propane is cheaper). Natural gas is generally piped to your building directly from the local gas authority, so as long as you pay the bill, supply should never be interrupted. Propane on the other hand usually requires the installation of a large tank outside the building. Tanks can go empty if you aren't paying attention, though many propane services these days offer wireless monitoring, so this is not as much of an issue as it once was.

When using a direct fired still that produces combustion products you will need to also consider how those products will be removed and vented from the distillery. You don't want these combustion gases to build up inside your manufacturing plant, so these systems generally require some kind of flue system to vent these gases to the outside atmosphere.

Another power source in the world of direct heated stills is plain old grid supplied electricity. This is not common per se, but there has been a slight uptick in distilleries using these types of systems in recent years. In my experience, most of what you find in this sphere are electrically supplied heating elements that are positioned on the inside of the pot. The switch gets flipped to turn the elements on and the liquid inside the still heats up.

I take a few issues with electric heating elements that I feel are worth mentioning here. First, is that they generally are not the fastest way to heat a still. This has more to do with sizing requirements than anything. It is possible to convince some manufacturers of these systems to put larger or a greater number of elements in the still to reduce heat up times, but most systems I've seen are somewhat to severely undersized. Also, there is a potential issue of scorching (this can occur with gas fueled flames beneath the pot as well). Direct heated electrical elements can easily burn liquids with high amounts of solids such as many traditional American whiskey mashes. They can also burn bags of botanicals if you are using the still to make gin or other botanical spirits. This scorching can cause awful smelling burnt notes to appear in your distillate. If you are considering going the route of electric heating elements, then speak with your manufacturer about potential scorching issues and any remediation efforts they can offer such as non-scorch coatings on the elements.

As we move into indirect heating systems, our fuel and heating options get a bit more varied. You'll certainly see plenty of uses for propane and natural gas, and sometimes even electric elements in this realm, though they are all used to heat something else that then goes on to heat the inside of the still.

Electricity is occasionally used to power heating elements that are inserted into a water or oil jacket that surrounds the pot. The elements in turn heat the water inside the jacket with then heats the contents of the pot itself. These systems tend to require more time to heat the still, but it also means that this is a gentle heating method with little to no chance of adverse scorching or overheating. In cases where oil is the heated liquid inside the jacket, these stills can be dialed into incredibly precise and stable temperatures with little in the way of the rise and fall temperature cycles associated with other indirect heating methods.

Finally, we need to discuss the use of steam for heating the still. Steam is arguably the most common and important heating method for the modern distillery. For the majority of batch distilleries, steam is generated by a separate boiler which is fueled by propane, natural gas, or oil. Smaller operations typically use a low-pressure boiler which is usually defined as operating at 15 psi (1.034 bar) or below.

The generated steam is then directed to the still via a variety of structures. Some stills, particularly smaller ones under 5,000 liters will often make use of jackets that surround the pot. The steam can be pumped through these jackets which in turn heats the contents of the still. Depending on the manufacturer the jacket configuration may be a simple single jacket that surrounds the bulk of the pot or something more complicated. One of my stills is a 2,000-liter system with both an upper and lower jacket that can be operated independently from each other.

Larger pot stills may make use of internal copper coils. These coils extend into and sit in the bottom of the pot. Steam is continuously pumped in and through the coils providing a large amount of heating surface to efficiently heat the still contents.

In all cases it is generally recommended to make sure you have enough liquid inside the still to completely cover the heating coils or jackets. If this isn't done, then you run the risk of possibly damaging

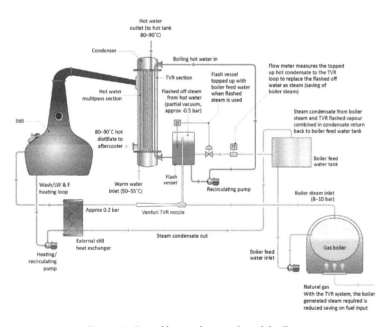

Figure 4-2. General layout of a steam-heated distillery
(Used with permission and copyright of the Institute of Brewing & Distilling)

your equipment. One of the nice things about my 2,000 liter still with an upper and lower jacket is that if I want to do a half-sized batch of something, I can just turn on the lower jacket and leave off the upper jacket without concern for potential equipment damage.

How Much Heat Do You Need?

I'm not going to go down the painful rabbit hole of distillery process engineering principles… too much. But we should address the question of how much heat you need to supply your still. (Note: many distilleries have heating needs beyond that of their still including things such as hot liquor tanks or cookers, so you would need to account for that in your heating calculations.)

Let's say we have a 1,000-liter still. Now, what we put in that still will have a determination on the amount of heat required to heat those contents to boiling. The **specific heat** (the amount of energy required to raise the temperature of one kilogram of substance by one degree Celsius, noted as CP and measured in kilo Joules per kilogram degrees Kelvin) will vary depending on the liquid being distilled and its alcohol content. For my purposes, I like to just assume that everything I distill is 100% water (CP = 4.184 at 20°C, atmospheric pressure). For the engineers out there, that might sound a bit extreme. Alcohol solutions have lower specific heat values and therefore require lower levels of heat energy to reach a certain temperature. However, I prefer to be conservative with these kinds of calculations. If I'm distilling a wash with only 8% alcohol by volume, certainly the specific heat will be lower and the initial boiling point will be below the boiling point of water (about six degrees Celsius lower, in fact). But remember that as the distillation proceeds, we're removing more alcohol and leaving a lot more water in the pot. This steadily increases our pot liquid's specific heat and therefore our energy requirements.

There is also the issue of heating efficiency. In the case of steam boilers, the amount of provided heat that they are rated for is not usually what you get in practice. Typically, depending on the type of boiler you use and the associated piping and insulation you can expect anywhere from a 10–20% drop in heat from the supplier rating to what you are actually pulling from the machine. The technology is getting better all the time, but in my experience no boiler has ever provided exactly the amount of thermal energy it is rated for.

All this means is that I would rather be more conservative in my required heating estimates and find myself with more power than I need instead of not having enough power. I've been in that situation and trust me, it makes the job of distilling a real chore.

The equation using specific heat, essentially how much heat energy we need to take 1,000-liters of water from 20°C to 100°C is simple:

$$Q = M \times CP \times \Delta T$$

Where Q is the heat required in Joules (J)

M is the mass of the substance in kilograms (kg)

CP is the specific heat of the substance in kJ/(kg°C)

ΔT is the change in temperature (°C)

So, the solution to our problem here would be:

$$Q = 1,000\ kg \times 4.184\ kJ/(kg°C) \times 80°C$$

$$Q = 334,720\ kJ$$

This is all well and good but if we are going to size our heating system appropriately then we need to know how much heat per unit time it needs to supply. This is an important question. How long are you willing to wait for your still to reach a boil? The industry standard (if there is such a thing) is somewhere between 30 and 60 minutes. However, I've seen stills that can heat up faster than that and others where it takes close to three hours. Too much heat might be harder to control, but not enough heat means your distillery is not operating at peak efficiency. There's quite a bit of wiggle room there, but you still need to come up with a number. For our problem, let's just make it simple and say that we want to boil our water in 60 minutes.

What we're looking for is the total wattage required where a watt is simply the number of Joules per second that are being used to perform an operation.

So, if we need to go from 20°C to boiling in 60 minutes (3,600 seconds) with our 1,000 liters of water, how many kilowatts do we need?

Since many regions use British Thermal Units (BTU's) instead of kilo Joules, we can offer a simple conversion factor:

$$1 \ kJ = 0.948 \ BTU$$

This means for our 1,000 liter still to reach a boil in one hour we would need a heating source that could produce 317,315 BTUs per hour.

For the process engineers out there, you may be wondering why I'm not calculating the amount of heat required to reach a full boil of our water using numbers for latent heat. (For those that need an engineering review, latent heat is the amount of heat required to make a substance undergo a phase change. When water nears it boiling point, it keeps absorbing heat even though the temperature doesn't change until it goes into a vapor. The heat that is absorbed is the latent heat.)

The answer to this is that we're not trying to boil water. Yes, there is some boiling action happening inside the still, but it is an alcohol mixture and alcohol has a much lower latent heat figure than water. By using the more conservative values I obtain with water as my liquid in the still, I am essentially covering my bases with the heat requirements.

The Pot

The pot or "boiler" is simply where we put the alcoholic liquid that we want to distill. There are innumerous varieties and iterations on shape and size. You'll find everything from the 80,000-liter giants situated at Ireland's Middleton Distillery to comically miniscule one-liter models used for small prototypes. (The Middleton Distillery has historically had a penchant for large pot stills, with one of their former stills from the 19th century reaching over 140,000 liters.)

The shapes are generally round but show a surprising variety in the level and placement of curvatures. Occasionally you may find square stills on the market but from what I've seen and discussed with other distillers, their quality is fairly suspect, so we won't consider them here.

Modern pot stills often have a variety of features that make the practice of distillation both easier and safer. In addition to the standard locking manway placed on the upper third of the still, there is usually a dedicated filling valve near the top of the pot and a larger diameter discharge valve for emptying the still on the bottom of the pot. There is also usually some form of air valve and/or anti-collapse valve placed on the top of the pot and sometimes on the neck. These valves help to ensure that in the event of an abnormal pressure increase or decrease inside the still, there won't be a catastrophic explosion or negative pressure collapse.

> *On April 24, 2015 at Silver Trail Distillery in Marshall County Kentucky a fire broke out. The cause was an over pressurization in their still. The safety valves installed on the still were rated incorrectly for the potential pressures in the still. Compounded with some subpar welding on the inside of the still, once the vessel had built up too much pressure it blew up causing the two distillers working that day, brothers Jay and Kyle Rogers, to suffer severe burns. Kyle Rogers ended up dying from the incident on May 11, 2015.*

The Neck

The neck (sometimes referred to as the swan or goose neck) is the narrowed piping that vertically rises above the pot. Its primary job is to allow vapors to rise up and away from the pot. While seeming simple, this is where we begin to see a lot of variation and innovation in still manufacture.

The neck can be a simple straight pipe with no frills that leads to a lyne arm or condenser (discussed below). Or it can have a series of trays, varying geometries and features, cooling coils and other assorted added doodads.

The neck can be short or incredibly tall and this will certainly have an impact on the amount of reflux happening in the still. You can see a picture of Corsair's pre-Prohibition era pot still below that has had the tall neck shortened so it could fit inside their warehouse.

When they shortened the neck, the resulting alcohol concentration was lowered, and the congener profile was altered due to lesser levels of internal reflux. Contrast that with Willett Distillery's pot still, also pictured below and you can see a tall and narrow neck which is not that common in the Kentucky bourbon industry. Given the correct running parameters, this still neck will produce a decent amount of reflux on the distillate. Glenmorangie in Ross-shire famously claims to have the tallest pot stills in Scotland. The necks of their stills are a crick-inducing 16 ft (4.9 m). The height of their necks allows them to produce their well-known light Highland style of whisky.

The necks of many pot stills have bulbous expansions at a point usually in the lower third of the total height. This bulge goes by many names, but the traditional term is "ogee." You can see examples of ogees on many of stills pictured below. There are a wide variety of sizes and shapes.

The how and why an ogee works is actually quite clever. Imagine a pipe with water running through it at a comfortable clip. That water

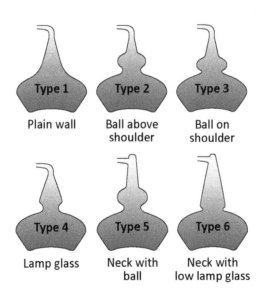

Figure 4-3. Various neck shapes commonly found on pot stills
(Used with permission and copyright of the Institute of Brewing & Distilling)

has a specific pressure associated with it. Now imagine that about halfway through the pipe, the diameter of the pipe suddenly doubles in size. When the water hits this point, its pressure and velocity drop significantly. This is effectively what happens to vapors rising from the pot when they hit the ogee in a still. Their velocity and pressure drop. How much they drop depends on a lot of factors not the least of which is the specific geometry of the ogee. Regardless, when the pressure drops this causes some of the vapors to condense and fall back into the pot. This is a small but important amount of reflux that can have an immense impact on the quality of the final distillate. Some have suggested that differences in still geometry can effect a 3.5% abv increase in low wines ethanol concentration (Whitby, 1992). Similarly, it has been shown that total acids in the distillate can increase by a factor of three using stills with a geometry that favors poor reflux (Hastie, 1925).

Of course, if we really want to increase reflux, we can add some tray components into our neck piping. Couple the trays with a well-designed pre-condenser at the top of the neck and we can force a large amount of reflux to occur inside our still. The number and design of trays varies considerably, though a common configuration within the craft spirits community is four bubble cap trays above the pot. These often have optional toggles so that the trays can be enabled and functional for full reflux or disabled and non-functional for less reflux.

There is also the famous case of the Lomond Stills. Invented by Alistair Cunningham of Hiram Walker in 1955, these stills have three sieve trays that can be individually and independently cooled. The idea was that by having multiple possible cooling and reflux configurations, multiple types of whisky could be made on the same still. They were primarily used in Scotland but never really took off. Today only a handful of distilleries use them including Loch Lomond, Bruichladdich and InchDairnie. Scapa on Orkney uses one as well but only as a wash still.

The Lyne Arm

The lyne arm is the pipe that curves somewhat horizontally away from the neck and connects to the condenser. It often (but certainly not always) tapers down in diameter from the neck piping to the condenser.

Perhaps the most important thing to consider with the lyne arm is its angle of placement. An arm that ascends to the condenser at an upward angle will cause some reflux to drain back into the pot. A lyne arm that descends in a downward angle to the condenser will not allow the reflux to fall back into the pot, thus nullifying the potential of any reflux that does occur. And there are certainly lyne arms that operate at a perfectly horizontal 90° angle.

Many distilleries will have a still for their wash distillations with a downward sloping lyne arm because for them, reflux during the wash distillation is not that important. They may take the resulting low wines and distill them in a separate still with an upward sloping lyne arm so that they can benefit from reflux on the second distillation.

Of course, everyone has their opinions on what works best for their own distilleries. In one of the pictures below you can see a picture of one of the stills in operation at Copper and Kings Distillery in Louisville, Kentucky. Their stills have a notoriously short neck with a large ogee attached to a steeply downward sloping lyne arm. This produces a full-flavored distillate rich in congeners, perfect for cask maturation.

Every year I travel to Scotland for an IBD Examiners meeting. A few years ago, I had the fortune to be able to get there a few days early and tour Speyside for a bit. Of course, I took this opportunity to visit some distilleries. Certainly, high on my list was a trip to the new(ish) home of The Macallan. I purchased my tour ticket and listened intently to the story of "The Six Pillars of the Macallan." These are the production components that the company feel make The Macallan what it is. One of the pillars is their "curiously small stills" of only 3900 liters each. They've got 36 of them each with fairly steep downward lyne arms. Another pillar is that they claim to take one of the smallest spirit cuts in all of Scotland. Being a distiller, I couldn't help but sit there and attempt to put the pieces together in my mind. Looking at their stills I suspected that the small hearts cut is somewhat necessary to produce a clean spirit without an over-abundance of fusel oil or feinty notes. My suspicions

Figure 4-4. Corsair Distillery, Nashville Tennessee 2012

Figure 4-5. Corsair Distillery, Bowling Green Kentucky 2012

Figure 4-6. Copper and Kings Distillery, Louisville Kentucky

Figure 4-7. Willett Distillery, Bardstown Kentucky

Figure 4-8. Distillerie Cote des Saints, 2000-liter hybrid still, Mirabel Quebec

Figure 4-9. Koval Distillery, Chicago Illinois

were more or less confirmed after the tour when they sat us down for the standard tasting. The last sample we got to try was some of the new make spirit (diluted to 40% abv). It was indeed slightly feinty with some fusel notes, but overall delicate and grainy – perfect for longer maturation periods in the well-selected sherry casks that The Macallan is known for.

Condensers

Ah the condenser! Without it our jobs as distillers would be virtually impossible. The condenser is fed vapors by the lyne arm and, through counterflow cooling, condenses those vapors back into liquid. This is another one of those seemingly simple processes that actually has quite a few variables to consider.

First, is what type of condenser you purchase. There are two primary condenser types at use in the batch distilling industry today.

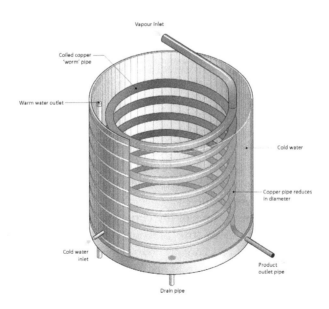

Figure 4-10. Worm tub condenser
(Used with permission and copyright of the Institute of Brewing & Distilling)

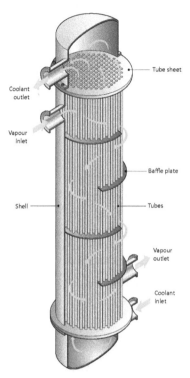

Coolant
outlet

Vapour
inlet

Shell

Tube sheet

Baffle plate

Tubes

Vapour
outlet

Coolant
inlet

Figure 4-11. Shell and tube condenser
(Used with permission and copyright of the Institute of Brewing & Distilling)

One is the shell and tube condenser, a more modern invention. The second is the worm tub or serpentine coil condensers, a living vestige of distilling times long past. Even though they do the same job, these two condensers behave fairly differently from each other so let's take a closer look at both of them.

You can view illustrations of the two condenser types in figures 4-10 and 4-11. Both make use of counterflow heat exchange to condense vapors. That is, a coolant flows in opposite direction to the vapor flow, maximizing heat exchange and removal in the process.

The worm tub condensers are the older of the two condenser types and have steadily lost favor over the past century in many spirit traditions. Invented in 1771 by a German chemist named Christian

Ehrenfried Weigel, they are still important to several distilleries and spirit types. Notably, cognac make practically exclusive use of these condensers in their distillations and a not insignificant handful of malt whisky distillers insist on their use.

The vapors leave the lyne arm section of piping and continue through a single pipe that gradually decreases in diameter as it downwardly spirals to the bottom of a large tank with cool flowing water. These condensers can be quite large at some distilleries with the coil piping often being around 100 m long and tapering from 40 cm in diameter down to 8 cm. The coiled piping is almost universally made from copper offering some reactive contact for the incoming vapors and condensed distillate. However, as we'll see in a moment the amount of exposed copper surface area is considerably less than many shell and tube heat exchangers, so worm tub condensers have earned a reputation for producing a slightly sulfured distillate. This is by no means a bad thing, however. Some sulfur compounds are considered desirable by a few distillers.

Of particular interest to some malt whisky distillers is a certain allowance for "meaty" aromas to persist into the distillate. The meaty aroma in question comes from 2-methyl-3-furyl disulphide (MMFDS). This heavier sulfur-based aroma and related compounds are important to some prominent whisky distilleries including Dalwhinnie, Mortlach and Oban. (Interestingly, these distilleries are all owned by Diageo who purportedly has more worm tub distilleries under their belt than any other whisky company.)

Mortlach is a famously quirky distillery based in Speyside. One of the many odd things that they do is to spray cold water on their lyne arm before the vapors hit the worm tub. This has the effect of speeding up vapor condensation and reducing copper induced sulfur reduction reactions. The net result is an overall increase in meaty character, more so than simply using their worm tubs alone.

These are fascinating and impressive condensers with a historical bent that always seem to intrigue the distillery visitor. However, there are some considerations that must be accounted for. First, these condensers tend to be expensive. In smaller stills, that may not be the case or much of an issue, but certainly in larger stills where a suitably large worm tub would be required, the price can be hefty. Secondly, there are some potential maintenance concerns. The coil is exposed to wide temperature differentials from being surrounded by a massive column of water that is cold at the bottom of the tank and quite warm (or even hot) near the top where the vapors enter the coil. This temperature difference puts a lot of strain on the metal and can potentially damage it over the long run. And should a leak develop in the coil, it can be hard to detect. Many distilleries with worm tubs regularly check the cooling water for traces of alcohol. Finally, if something does happen to the worm tub, they can be hard to replace due to their enormity.

The other condenser type commonly used in association with batch distilling today is the shell and tube condenser. These condensers are composed of a large metal shell encasing 100–200 tubes each with a diameter of about 3 cm. (This will vary depending on the size of the still and the requirements of the condenser.) Intermittently placed throughout the shell are horizontal baffle plates which the tubes pass through. These plates force condensed liquid to linger longer in the shell for greater contact time with the tubes. The lyne arm deposits vapors into the top of the shell while coolant flows through the small tubes upwards in the opposite direction.

Immediately, you can see that these condensers offer considerably more surface area for vapor contact than the worm tub design. This has two effects. First, is that these condensers are more efficient at cooling and thus require less coolant to work properly. Second, assuming the tubing is made from copper, these condensers offer more copper contact to the incoming vapors and therefore a better removal of sulfur compounds. However, not all shell and tube condensers use copper for the tubing, so it is still possible to produce a sulfured spirit with these condensers if the tubing is composed of another less or non-reactive metal such as stainless steel.

The difference in effects between shell and tube condensers should not be underestimated. Famously, Dalwhinnie at one point tried to change over to shell and tube condensers away from their worm tubs. They immediately noticed a significant change in their spirit, notably a loss of their prized meaty aromas in the new make. They subsequently went through the time and expense to change back to the old worm tubs.

Many shell and tube condensers will also have an additional external pipe that rises from the base of the condenser to the top terminating in a small vent. This is so that if too much liquid or vapor/liquid mixture floods the condenser column, the stream can be vented out. This situation happens if there is not sufficient cooling in the condenser and/or if too much heat is being applied to the still.

> *For my preferences, I choose copper as the tubing metal without hesitation every time on these condensers. It is less expensive to go with stainless steel, but the conductivity of copper is more efficient at heat removal plus I like the sulfur removal that the copper provides. To compensate for the drop in cooling efficiency, some manufacturers will simply add more stainless-steel tubes. It is an important decision and one that you should spend time discussing with your manufacturer.*

Two distilleries, Ailsa Bay and Roseisle, have done something rather clever and have installed two shell and tube condensers per still. One condenser is made of copper while the other is made of stainless steel. This allows them to switch between the two condensers when they want to produce a different character of spirit, say using the stainless condensers when a more meaty and sulphured spirit is called for.

Pre-condensers

Pre-condensers (or partial condenser) are used to provide a bit of reflux in the neck of the still. They are usually a shell and tube design that sits atop the neck, often with some trays immediately below. Older pre-condensers would be smaller copper coils inserted somewhere in the neck though this isn't as common anymore. Look back at some of the still photos. The older still in Corsair's Nashville location has an ogee with a coiled pre-condenser placed inside. Their former Bowling

Green Kentucky location used a small 55-gallon gin still with a shell and tube pre-condenser at the top of the neck, certainly the more modern of the two styles.

An increasingly common still configuration found in smaller distilleries throughout North America is to have a neck with four bubble cap trays, crowned with a suitably sized shell and tube condenser to push the appropriate amount of reflux on the trays. These condensers are even more prominent on modern hybrid stills where they sit atop one or more columns in the system. If a distillery is trying to make neutral spirit on a batch system, they absolutely need a pre-condenser in place to reach the proper level of separation on the trays.

Another name that you have or will hear for the pre-condenser is "dephlegmator." It's kind of a funny looking word and I've never gotten much of a consensus on how it is supposed to be pronounced. There are two main schools of thought. Some think it should be pronounced "de-fleg-mator" (with a hard 'g' sound). Others think the 'g' is silent and say, "de-fle-mator" assuming the middle of the word is kind of like the word "phlegm."

I sit comfortably on the side of the latter pronunciation because there are some historical references to "phlegm" in the still which is usually taken to mean the heavier components that drop back down into the pot... and this is exactly the job of the "de-fle-mator."

There is also some debate about whether a dephlegmator is different than a partial condenser. Some argue that a dephlegmator works with less cooling and is not designed be as efficient as a partial/pre-condenser. To this I say tomato and they say tomahto. I would argue they are effectively the same thing and there is little point in dividing them up based on perceived minutiae such as slight cooling differences. This is one of those areas where it just isn't worth the effort to split hairs.

Where do you get your cooling from?

This is an unbelievably important question that you have to answer for yourself and ultimately your bottom line. Distilleries are incredibly utility intensive, both on the heating and the cooling fronts. And it's the cooling needs that often hurt many distilleries the most when it comes to variable costs. The amount of water that distilleries use is high. By some estimates many distilleries use around 12 liters of water to produce one liter of spirit and much of that has to do with cooling needs (Mikuka & Zielinska, 2020).All that heat you are pumping into your still contents? That has to be removed in order to get your vapors to condense back into liquid form. The amount of cooling required to do that is immense and you should plan on cooling requirements that match the number of BTU's you intend to put into the system.

How you supply that cooling is going to be heavily affected by the size of your distillery, number of distillation cycles per unit time, distillery location, local climate conditions, utility pricing and much more.

For instance, smaller distilleries may be able to get away with using water from the local municipal water supply. It's expensive but it may cost you less than installing more complicated equipment. This all depends on what your municipal supplier thinks of having a distillery using that much water. There is also the issue of running the hot water return back through the municipal lines and the amount of heat you're putting back into their system. For most places, this is not likely much of an issue if the distillery is small enough. But larger distilleries are a different beast entirely.

Large distilleries have to get a bit more creative with their water usage. There is a reason why many distilleries are located near large moving bodies of water such as the River Spey in Scotland. The distilleries have been able to traditionally take advantage of the massive water flow to cool all manner of distillery equipment, including the still condensers. Modern conservation and environmental concerns have made this method a bit more complicated. In many regions, a new distillery much obtain proper permitting and water usage rights. They also have to control the amount of heat being returned to any effluent system. You can well imagine that if you have a bunch of distilleries pumping hot water back into a flowing river at the same time, it might have an impact on local fish and wildlife among other things.

In some regions, water may not be readily available for cooling for some or even most of the year. In the American Southwest, there are serious concerns with industrial water usage and distillers there have to either severely limit their production or come up with other suitable cooling methods. Other areas in the world may experience seasonal droughts which will impact water availability for the distillery. This doesn't just affect the distillery's ability to cool their condensers but could be a problem for other water intensive procedures as well such as mashing for whisky.

Another issue that arises is the seasonal change in ground water temperature. This can occur not just in rural regions, but in municipal water sources as well. During the winter the incoming ground water may be nice and chilly at 5°C (41°F) only for it to rise to 20°C (68°F) during the warmer months of the year. Those temperatures can go even higher if your distillery is located in a hotter climate. I've seen summer ground water temps reach above 30°C (86°F) in some areas. As you can imagine this scenario of seasonal fluctuations can make your distillations rather difficult to manage. The warmer the incoming coolant is (in this case ground water), the more you'll have to use in order to remove the necessary amount of heat. And in many instances, if the incoming temperature is too warm, you may not be able to properly cool your spirit well enough without risking things like evaporative alcohol losses.

So, what are distillers to do? Seasonal temperature variations are painful. The conservation of water for the sake of the environment is important to a lot of people. There may be supply issues in some areas and the costs of water can be frighteningly costly.

Well, many distillers have opted for cooling loop systems and/or the use of cooling towers. A cooling loop is exactly what it sounds like. Your condenser fluid is passed through your condenser where it picks up heat from your distillate vapors. It is then looped through a cooling system where it passes off that heat to a different medium such as glycol or air and then returns freshly cooled back to the condenser.

There is an issue of bacterial buildup in systems that are completely closed loop. Bacteria such as legionella can grow in these systems if not properly controlled or monitored for. Legionella easily disperses in the air and can cause pneumonia-like symptoms in vulnerable employees. Not fun. However, if properly maintained and kept clean, even legionella is of little concern.

This isn't really the place to dive into the specifics of how these systems work. For one, they are incredibly varied in design so a complete explanation would be nigh impossible with the space I'm permitting myself here. Besides, your engineering consultant would be much better suited than I to give you all the available options for your area.

If such a system sounds expensive, you'd be correct for assuming so. Even the simpler systems can be quite costly. But you should look at such a system as an investment. The upfront cost is higher, sure, but the long-term costs tend to be lower. Certainly, you are using more electricity to run and cool these looped systems, but in many areas, those costs still wind up being cheaper than the water costs they are replacing.

For some perspective, let's break this down a bit. I'm proposing a fairly small distillery with a single 500 gallon (1,900 liter) pot still with a 500 gallon mash cooker and a couple of 500 gallon fermenters. The distillery does only three mashes per week. Let's see how that adds up in water usage.

Mash Water: 6,000 gal (22,700 liter)/ mo
Cooker Cooling: 59,040 gal (223,490 liter)/ mo
Tank/Cooker cleaning: 2,880 gal (10,900 liter)/ mo
Condenser cooling (single pass): 144,000 gal (545,100 liter)/ mo
Total: 211,920 gallons (802,200 liter) per month

This does not include dilution water, general cleaning, boiler feed, etc.

First off, let me say that these numbers are *conservative*, meaning they are probably quite a bit higher in reality for many distilleries of this size. Granted, I've avoided information on incoming water temperature, utility costs and water sourcing. This stuff is different for everyone.

Finally, and most importantly, you'll note that condenser cooling is by far and away the biggest issue we have when it comes to cooling. I've seen distillers about this size pay around $4000–$5000 per month sometimes in water utilities. So, can a looped system benefit your bottom line? Quite possibly.

Additional Equipment

With the advent of so many new distilleries opening their doors, there has been no shortage of functional improvements and technological doodads added onto the traditional pot still. In this section I'll briefly cover a few of the most common items that you're likely to see.

Agitators

It is common practice for many still manufacturers to at least *offer* a mechanical agitating device as part of the still package. In North America, these are commonly in the form of drive motors mounted onto the shoulder of the still pot. The motor when turned on rotates a steel shaft with blunted blades at the end. These blades stir up the liquid inside the still.

In the Scotland you may occasionally come across what's called a "rummager." These are sometimes found on older direct-heated stills. They consist of a motor that turns a set of copper chain mail along the circumference of the pot bottom.

There are two primary benefits to agitators inside the still. The first is that by keeping any possible solids within the liquid in suspension, you can reduce the potential for scorching or "baking-on" of these solids to the walls and heating surfaces of the still. Scorching is more of an issue with direct-fired stills and can produce burnt and acrid notes in the distillate. In indirect fired stills, it is possible for the solids in a fermented wash to bake on to some of the heating surfaces, thus reducing the efficacy of heat transfer to the liquid inside the pot.

Secondly, the mixing action helps to speed up the heating of the still. Similar to stirring a pot while cooking on the stove, it helps to distribute heat to the liquid more quickly. Vendome Copper and Brassworks, states in some of their materials that the agitator can shave 20–25% off the total heat up time which works out to 10–15 minutes (assuming the non-agitated heat up time is 60 minutes). That 10–15 minutes may not mean much if you're only doing a single distillation a day. However, if you are running multiple batches a day, it adds up really fast.

A final secondary benefit is the technique of "throwing." The theory is that by adding in a physical mixing action to the pot liquid being distilled, you can "throw" off volatiles into the head space at a higher rate, thus increasing your vapor's congener load. Think of it like swirling a wine inside the glass to release the aromas more before you drink it… sort of. In my experience, this is a pretty subtle technique with an equally subtle effect.

Agitators are most commonly used during the distillation of fermented wash. However, some distillers will use them during their spirit distillations as well for some of the reasons mentioned above.

A quick word of caution regarding the use of agitators. NEVER run the agitator motor unless the liquid level is well above the agitator blades. This is particularly problematic on many modern pot stills where the agitator motor, rod and blades are positioned at an angle inside the still as opposed to running straight down through the center. If the blades are turning during the filling or emptying operations and the liquid level does not sufficiently cover them, then an offset force is placed on the rod supporting the blades. This can, over time, loosen the rod from the motor housing and even bend it. The net result is a situation where the blades can eventually turn and hit the inside of the still, causing severe damage to your equipment in the process.

Relief Valves

These devices have become somewhat standard fare for the production of stills by most of the major manufacturers. There are two types that you commonly see employed: vacuum relief valves and pressure relief valves. It's not uncommon to see both types on the same still and some manufacturers will actually insist on using both.

Since batch distillation is essentially an open system, some people wonder why you would ever need such devices in the first place. Well, just look back to earlier in the chapter when I recounted the tragedy that befell Silver Trail Distillery. There was a blockage in the column and the still became over pressurized. The valve they had installed was incorrectly rated and as a result the still exploded and one of the distillers died a few days later.

Blockages are rare, but they can happen. Certainly, a blockage inside a packed column is a concern, but the condenser can also be a potential source for disaster.

Vacuum relief valves help prevent the opposite scenario, where a rushed load of negative pressure somehow gets applied to the inside of the still. The cause of this could be something as simple as an operator trying to quickly empty the still without properly venting it.

Regardless, these devices are relatively inexpensive and help to mitigate against the unlikely event of disaster. Sure, the above scenarios might be rare, but relief valves are a cheap insurance policy against potential tragedy.

Thermometers

I learned how to distill on an old 250-gallon pre-Prohibition era pot still. As for bringing things up to modern standards, the distillery owners had largely left the ol' girl alone save for one thing: they added two digital thermometer probes, one for the pot and one in the lyne arm. But here's the thing: the head distiller and I never used them. We quite literally left them turned off. That might seem crazy to some people. I mean, how on earth can you distill without knowing what temperature everything is?

Well, remember that the thermometer is a relatively recent invention, coming about in a somewhat precise form only a few hundred years ago. (A Dutch inventor named Daniel Gabriel Fahrenheit designed the first modern thermometer in 1714.) However, distillation has been going on for MUCH longer than that. So, clearly one does not need to use a thermometer to distill alcohol.

...But boy, do thermometers make things easier! Look, I'm all for simple, pure and rustic when the results really are equal or better to what modernity can provide, but I don't ride a horse and buggy to work, and I will never try to use leeches to cure a cold. In other words, not all technology is bad, and this is definitely a case where it can really help.

Thoughtfully placed thermometers can help you to make informed decisions about and throughout the distillation process. I generally suggest having probes in the pot, the lyne arm and in the spirit pipe at a minimum. If you are using a hybrid column still to produce neutral alcohol, then you absolutely need a few thermometers placed at strategic points. For a neutral spirit hybrid column still, you should have probes in the above-mentioned spots plus probes at the top plate of every column, in the vapor line exiting each column, as well as in the incoming and outgoing cooling lines of every condenser.

Probes can be either digital or analog. I prefer analog for reasons that would only make sense to the most technologically averse among you. However, I readily admit that digital probes are easier to read and can sometimes be more accurate and precise.

Thermometers can let you know when your distillate is about to first come over, give you clues about the alcohol concentration, indicate possible problems with cooling lines, and aid in making decisions on cut points, among many other things. Trust me. Thermometers make life easier.

I was touring a distillery in Oregon a few years ago. The distiller was using a cognac still that was over 140 years old. It was a beautiful piece of kit. He noted the lack of thermometers on the still. He pointed out that the old French distillers used to take a can of nails and hang it by some paraffin wax around the still's lyne arm. When the vapors from the pot began to travel through the lyne arm, the copper would quickly heat up and melt the wax. The can would drop to the ground and make a loud rattle and crash. The distiller would then know when the distillate was about to start coming over.

Clean-in-Place (CIP) System

The old saying goes, "Cleanliness is next to Godliness." I've never taken much of a holy bent to my cleaning protocols, but I will say that having a clean still makes life a lot easier.

If you are unfamiliar with the term "CIP," it is simply a method of cleaning a vessel or piece of equipment through the use of a cleaning loop that can be left to operate on its own. Your still will get dirty and you will need to clean it. You can certainly stand there with a hose and spray a day's supply of hot water obtaining suboptimal results. Or you can invest in a CIP system that will allow you to set up a loop of cleaning liquid that can be pumped through a spray ball strategically placed inside the still, effectively cleaning the vessel while you attend to other things.

Some stills and some liquids seem to be dirtier than others. I've met distillers who say that the occasional water spray is all they ever have to do, while others have told me they have to clean their still almost every day. Stripping runs seem to cause the most amount of buildup, particularly those from grain-based washes. However, don't get complacent about distillations only containing low wines. These distillations can leave a fair amount of heavier oils coating the inside of the still pot and piping. It's good to clean these compounds off every so often.

What happens if you don't clean your still? Well, you can find yourself with a buildup of unwanted soils on the inside of the various still parts. These soils can contribute unwanted flavors to your distillate. More than that, they can inhibit effective heat transfer in the pot subsequently slowing down your distillations. A CIP system can save you a lot of time and labor in the long run. We'll take a look at some specific CIP protocols in a later chapter.

Vapor/Gin/Botanical Basket

The so called "gin basket" may be referred to by many names such as "vapor basket," "botanical basket," and sometimes even "carterhead" (this isn't quite accurate as a carterhead is a bit different from today's modern designs, but I'm not the name police so...). No matter what you call it, a gin basket is a container usually affixed to the outside of the pot still neck into which you can load a certain amount of gin botanicals. This allows the distiller to pass hot alcohol vapors through the botanical bed and extract their essential oils. As we will discuss later in the book it is most certainly possible to distill gin without a gin basket. Regardless, these are increasingly common little contraptions found in gin distilleries all over the world and may be of interest to the fledgling botanically minded distiller.

Purifiers

Purifiers are odd little devices. They are essentially rudimentary pre-condensers that are situated within the lyne arm. Like any other

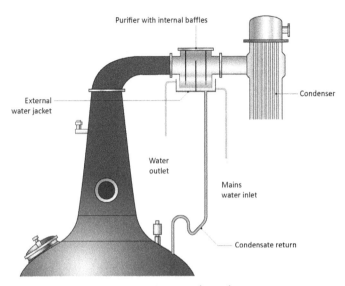

Figure 4-12. Diagram of a purifier
(Used with permission and copyright of the Institute of Brewing & Distilling)

Figure 4-13. Modern pot still with gin basket
(the small stainless-steel canister offset from the still neck is the gin basket)

pre-condenser their purpose is to provide some amount of reflux back into the still. The vapors travel through the length of the lyne arm, are condensed (at least partially) in the purifier and the heavier refluxed components are returned to the pot.

Purifiers are not too common, but they do exist. Perhaps the most famous example is the purifier on the spirit still at Ardbeg on Islay, Scotland. (Figure 4-14)

Specialty Batch Stills

Now that we have a generalized overview of the major components of a pot still, let's take a few moments to look at some more specific still types you may come across in your distillation journey. A still is a tool and nothing more. A given tool can usually be used for all sorts of purposes, but they are typically well suited to only a handful of applications where they might really excel. And so it goes with the following still designs and types. Certainly, you can use them for any type of batch distilled spirit, but they are most often found in specific spirit categories. This section will help to explain how these stills function and why they are used so often to create specific spirits.

Alembic Charentais

The Alembic Charentais is somewhat an iconic still in the spir-

Figure 4-14. 160-year-old alembic Charentais at McMenamins Cornelius Pass Roadhouse Distillery in Hillsboro, Oregon

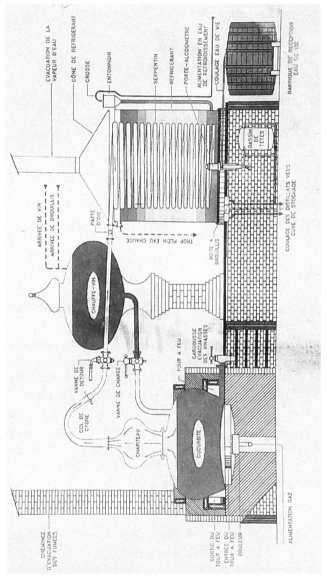

Figure 4-15. Schematic of a modern alembic Charentais

its world. Used primarily throughout France for cognac and certain styles of calvados production, it has become known as the quintessential brandy still.

Ranging in size from petit 400-liter versions to an upper limit of 25 hectoliters, these stills are characterized by their anachronistic operating principles. Most (with the exception of a very few specially manufactured pieces) have a direct-fired pot encased in a brick housing. The flame may be fueled by a gas burner or occasionally wood for some of the older models. Sitting atop the pot is often a squat ogee-type helmet that supports a deeply ascending lyne arm. The lyne arm then extends itself to form a serpentine coil inside a large tub to make up the condenser.

Many examples abound of this simple two-vessel system, but the most recognizable iteration on the alembic Charentais is the three-vessel design. In many distilleries there is a third vessel sitting atop a pedestal in between the condenser tub and the pot. This middle and higher tiered vessel almost looks like a separate pot without a heat source beneath. It is actually a wine preheater.

As the contents of the pot heat up from contact with the direct flame beneath, vapors eventually evolve up and away through the lyne arm. The lyne arm then travels directly through the preheater (there is a bypass pipe to avoid this on most models if the distiller so chooses). As the hot vapors travel at a slightly downward slope along the lyne arm and pass through the preheater, energy is passed from the vapors to the wine or low wines contained in the surrounding vessel. This allows the next batch for distillation to get a jump start on heating so that the next distillation doesn't take too long to begin.

This preheating is incredibly valuable to a number of distillers, because these stills often require long running times to produce quality distillates. It is not uncommon to see distillation times of 12–14 hours for a single distillation.

These stills are not necessarily always so antediluvian in their operation. A few modern firms have begun to add pneumatic valves and semi-automatic operation via touch screen interfaces and other modern flourishes. Some even go so far as to have "recipes" in their operating systems, further limiting any necessary human intervention by automating the process almost entirely. (Figure 4-16)

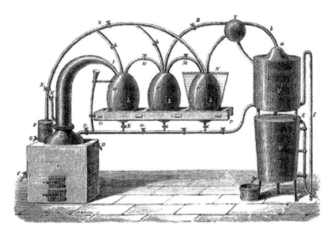

Figure 4-16. Jean Edouard Adam's fractional distillation system

The Retort Still

Depending on your particular spirit of choice, your frame of reference for the retort still likely comes from either the rum industry or the American moonshine tradition. Interestingly, we've actually already seen a retort still earlier in the book...

For all of Edouard's still's operational complexity, it is effectively a retort still. If you run a search for the terms "retort" and "distillation" together, you'll find that retort is generally considered an archaic word for an alchemist's still. However, today we generally take a retort still to mean a batch distillation system with one, two, or more "retorts" connecting the pot to the condenser in a sequence.

The way a retort works is quite clever. The retort is filled with a liquid, usually fermented wash or low wines, though they can sometimes simply contain water. As vapor exits the pot, it is directed into the retort. Often the pipe is submerged, and vapors bubble up through the liquid though sometimes the pipe ends above the liquid line. Regardless, the heated vapors enter the retort chamber condensing a bit and releasing increasing amounts of heat energy into the liquid medium. Eventually the heat causes the vapor pressure of the liquid to reach atmospheric pressure and enriched alcohol laden vapors evolve up and out of the chamber. They may then be directed to another retort or towards the condenser. The resulting distillate is purer and stronger than it would be otherwise, and this permits the distiller to do only a single pass distillation if they choose to.

The sizing of the retort(s) is based on the size of the pot. In general, the working volume size of the first retort is around 13% of the pot capacity. If there is a second retort, it will be approximately 10% working volume of the pot capacity. (Note that we're talking about *working* capacity. This is a bit different than *actual* or *total* capacity. Working capacity is the suggested loading capacity. Total capacity of the retorts is often around 30–40% more than the working capacity which gives the distiller a bit of wiggle room on volume if needed.)

What goes in the retort is just as important as the number of retorts used. If distiller puts water into the retort, then the alcohol concentration will not be increased by much but more water-soluble compounds in the vapors will be better reduced. Distillers may also choose to put low wines, high wines, or feints into the retorts.

Renegade Rum in Grenada uses a three-vessel retort system. The pot contains a wash of about 7% abv. The second vessel (first

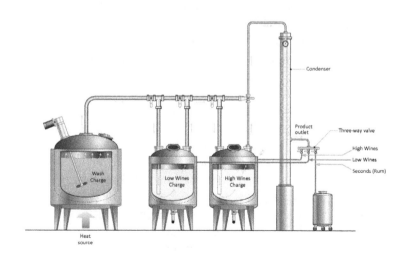

Figure 4-17. Diagram of a double retort still
(Used with permission and copyright of the Institute of Brewing & Distilling)

retort) contains a low wine of around 35% abv and the other retort contains high wines (~70% abv) from the previous distillation. After the vapors leave the pot and go through the two middle retorts, the resulting distillate has an alcohol concentration approaching 80% abv after fractioning (Renegade Rum, 2019).

Quite a few rum distilleries make use of retort stills. In Jamaica most of the distilleries make at least some use of retorts including Hampden Estate, Long Pond, Worthy Park and Clarendon distilleries. Both Mount Gay Rum and Four Square in Barbados use retorts. There are many more examples, which is to say that a lot of quality rum flows through retorts before it hits the bottle.

The use of retorts in moonshine is every bit as fascinating. Of course, moonshiners have not traditionally used the term "retort" instead opting for the more colloquial "thumper keg" nomenclature. Doesn't matter what you call it — it is indeed a retort.

Most moonshiners both historic and modern work on a smaller scale than the massive retort stills found in the rum industry, but the purpose is the same: give some rectification power to some otherwise potentially rough distillate.

One interesting application of the retort still is the "Cousins

Figure 4-18. Reconstructed moonshine still with center "thumper keg";
Photo by Brian Stansbury, 2009 -
This photo is licensed under the Creative Commons Attribution 3.0 Unported license.

Process" for making high ester rums. This is a complicated process, a full description of which is well beyond the scope of this book. However, I'll give you the major bullet points and you can do some digging on your own if your curiosity is piqued.

Herbert Henry Cousins was a brilliant chemist and during the early 1900s he did a lot of work with organic acids and ester formation. This work was able to be transposed onto systems for Jamaican rum production. Through this process distillers had a way to produce extremely high ester rums (purportedly up to 7,000 ppm).

Here is how the Cousins process works. At the end of distillation, the stillage left over in the retorts (Cousins used the archaic term "lees") contains high amounts of organic acids. To this liquid, the distiller would add lime (calcium oxide) which would form calcium salts from the organic acids. Sulfuric acid is then added to form calcium sulfate and precipitate the acids from solution. (This effectively concentrates the acid levels in the medium.) The newly concentrated acid mixture is then added to the high wines retort with rum at about 70% abv. The addition of alcohol plus acids plus heat equals lots of ester formation. The resulting supercharged high ester distillate can then be used to blend into lower ester rums to produce a more palatable level of esters for the drinker.

The "Filipino" Still

A lot has been written over the years about the origins of distillation in Mexico. The discussion has largely been centered on the European distillation practices that were brought over from Spain during the 1500s. And this is absolutely true. Prior to the European incursion into Central America there isn't much evidence to suggest that distillation was practiced in the region prior to that time. However, there is another important component to the story that is becoming increasingly recounted by historians.

During the 1500s the Spanish were not the only foreign visitors to the area of what is now modern-day Mexico. Seafaring visitors from the Philippines reached Mexico's western shores during the same time period. They had their own distillation methods and equipment, and it turns out that quite a bit of mezcal owes a debt of gratitude to those early Filipino voyagers (Starkman, 2018).

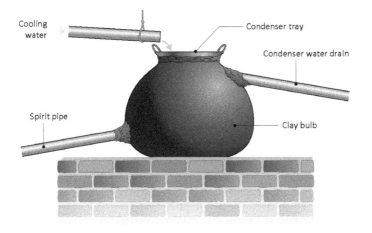

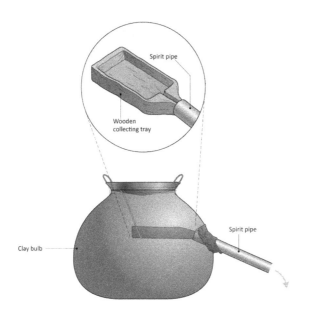

Figure 4-19. (Top) Schematic of a clay "Filipino" type mezcal still;
(Bottom) Collection tray positioning inside the still
(Images courtesy of the Institute of Brewing & Distilling)

It seems that the Filipinos began working their distillation magic in and around the city of Colima in the 1500s producing coconut spirit. Eventually the locals who held the agave plant in extremely high regard, adopted the Filipino distillation technology to distill the primitive beginnings of mezcal (Zizumbo-Villarreal & Colunga-Garcıa Marın, 2008).

The Filipino still is a bit of a departure from many of the other still types we've discussed thus far. It is simultaneously primitive and anachronistic while also being resolutely clever in its design.

These stills are often made of clay as opposed to metals such as copper or stainless steel. This makes them incredibly fragile and subject to heat stress, but also relatively inexpensive to repair or replace.

The still consists of two primary chambers. The bottom chamber is analogous to the pot in other batch stills where the liquid to be distilled is placed. It sits atop a direct fire burner, fueled by gas or wood. The pot opens to a clay bulb chamber above it. Capping the clay bulb is a shallow saucer structure into which cool water is poured and constantly drained off to the side of the still.

As the heat from the flames below warms the contents of our bottom pot, the vapors steadily rise into the bulb above. Eventually they reach the bottom of the saucer which is cooled by the water pouring on top it from overhead. The vapors are then condensed into liquid and drip back down. Much of the condensed liquid will drip back into the pot below, serving as a small amount of reflux inside the still. The rest of the condensed liquid will drip into a small collection tray that leads to a spirit pipe that drains outside of the still. (Figure 4-19).

Due to the simple nature of these stills, rectification is not great, but it isn't as bad as you might suspect. A distiller working with a good fermentation and a deft and attentive hand can produce fairly clean spirits off these stills.

The absence of copper means that the resulting distillate can be a little sulfur laden, but in my experience with mezcals produced this way, that is not much of a concern. The clay does seem to produce an interesting minerality to the distillate that is absent from mezcals produced on more modern type stills.

The Armagnacais Still

I had some internal debate about including the Armagnac still in this book. It is effectively a continuous still and when one is writing a book on batch distillation techniques, such things can seriously muddy the waters. Eventually I settled on its inclusion because it sort of straddles the line between continuous and batch systems. And besides, Armagnac is delicious, so there's that.

The so-called "Armagnac still" is a classic beast of distillation equipment through and through. Its use is not relegated to the Armagnac region. It is commonly employed to distill calvados in Normandy in Northern France. Many of the few itinerant distillers that still roam the French countryside during the winter distillation season haul old armagnacais stills along on their trailers, distilling for the

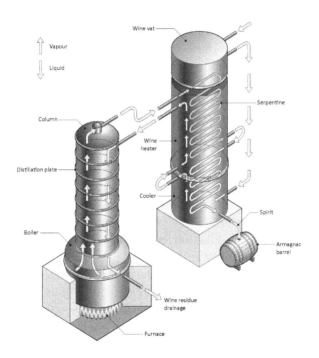

Figure 4-20. Diagram of the Armagnacais still
(Used with permission and copyright of the Institute of Brewing & Distilling)

scheduled small volume cider or wine producer so that they have a smattering of spirits on offer to their thirsty patrons.

The still works simply enough. Wine is fed into a vat atop the condenser column and is used as a counterflow chilling agent to condense the opposite flow of hot alcohol vapors. The wine eventually winds its way to the top of the adjacent column where it falls down a series of rectifying plates. The bottom of the column is heated by a direct-fired furnace, separating the heavy components from the lighter alcohols and congeners.

The number of plates varies by producer. You may see as few as three trays, but by law a maximum of 15 can be used. High volatility congeners are vented to the atmosphere through the top of the still.

Despite these stills being somewhat similar in form and function to the larger continuous columns, they can actually be operated somewhat "semi-continuously" so that start and stop operations are fairly quick and simple. They also don't tend to overly rectify the spirit. In fact, it isn't uncommon to see distillate strengths of 55–60% abv coming of the still. These are fairly high congener distillates that work well for long maturation programs.

The Three Chambered Still

Perhaps an even odder inclusion than the Armagnac still, the three chambered still is an extreme rarity in the world of distilling. In fact, at the time of writing, I can think of only one distillery in the entire world that uses one: Leopold Bros. in Denver, Colorado.

The reason I include it here is not just for its rarity and obscure origins, but its operation is indeed quite interesting.

Leopold Bros is a distillery ever tinkering and researching the unique histories and production techniques of spirits past. Todd Leopold commissioned Vendome Copper and Brassworks to manufacture a three chambered still for the distillery to produce their historically based rye whiskey recipe. Prior to American Prohibition, quite a bit of rye whiskey was produced on these stills. Some estimates suggest that during the late 1800s most of the rye whiskey produced at major distilleries used a chambered still instead of a column still. As we'll see in a moment these stills required a fair amount of hand operation and were subsequently a bit finnicky. Still, companies seem reticent

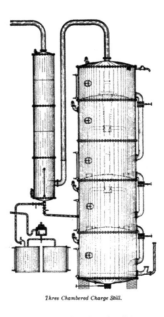

Three Chambered Charge Still.

Figure 4-21. Diagram of a three chambered still (Norton, 1911)

to let them go because the flavor obtained in the distillate was reportedly phenomenal.

From the diagram above, you will notice that our three chambered still is actually a four chamber still. That's only partially true. One of the chambers is merely for the preheating of the still charge and no distillation actually takes place within it.

The three chamber still was (is?) effectively a semi-continuous still. The original designs were partially or completely made from wood but eventually modernity took over and copper became the metal of choice.

The design and operation go like this: steam is pumped up through the still from a pipe below. Fermented wash is allowed to flow downwards and come into contact with the steam at a continuous rate. (Presumably, the wash chamber can be refilled perpetually throughout the distillation for a somewhat continuous mode of operation.) The middle chambers operate like large, simplified distillation trays, allowing for the mixing of vapor and condensed liquid and a certain level of rectification to take place. Each chamber has a valve that can be adjusted to allow a certain amount of wash to flow into the chamber. As the previous chamber is emptied to fill the one beneath, it is refilled with more wash. The top chamber handles the more volatile compounds while the middle and final chambers handle compounds of ever lower volatilities. The vapors exit through the top and then lead to a doubler after which they are condensed into spirit. It's a very labor intensive and hands-on kind of distillation.

Chapter 5

Recommendations for Purchasing a Still

If you are reading this book, which obviously you are because you've just read this sentence, then you certainly fall into one of two camps: you own a still or you don't. If you own a still, then maybe you don't need to read through this section. However, in all likelihood, there will come a time when you will be interested in purchasing a new still. That may be because you are expanding your operations or simply replacing an older still. Regardless, there may be something in this section for you.

If you haven't yet purchased a still but are in the process of thinking about it, I can imagine how you must be feeling. Usually, it's a mixture of exhilaration and trepidation coupled with a certain financial queasiness surrounding what is typically one of the most expensive purchases for your distillery.

Making things worse is the fact that virtually no still is going to be perfect.

In fact, I've never met a distiller who has claimed their still meets the criteria for flawlessness in every facet of production and workflow. That's not to say they don't love their stills. Quite the opposite in fact. Many people have stills that have countless idiosyncrasies and confounding quirks that somehow make working with them more honor than frustration. Of course, I've also met a tragic number of folks that would love nothing more than to melt their current still down for scrap were it not completely necessary for them to continue operating as a distillery.

I've been on both sides of the fence with this one. The old pre-Prohibition era pot still at Corsair Distillery was the first still

I ever worked with. It had leaks, was impossible to clean and had worn out gaskets. I loved every second working on that still. I've also purchased the fanciest of the new-fangled and been at my wits end with the manufacturer over their sale and "workmanship."

So, I don't really believe any still is absolutely perfect, and I'm not sure I would want one to be. Every still is going to have some kind of imperfection or frustration associated with it. The question is whether or not you can learn to live with and even love those peccadillos or if they will drive you off sanity's deep end diving board.

Certainly, if you fall into the other camp where you do not currently own a still, you might have countless questions about where to get started, and even more now that I've frightened you with my imperfect still speech. Afterall, this isn't exactly the same thing as purchasing the wrong pair of headphones and returning to the store for an exchange. Don't worry. Buying a still is just like any other purchase where you are spending an obscene amount of cash on a piece of industrial production equipment: it can be a real f*@#ing headache. Fortunately, I'm here to offer a few words of wisdom and hopefully make the whole process a little bit easier to grit your teeth through.

First, the basics. Establish what you want to make with your still. Whiskey? Rum? Vodka from potatoes? Gin? Be as specific as possible as to your stylistic intent. Most manufacturers will try to convince you that their still can handle most spirit styles with aplomb and all you have to do is turn 'er on. This rarely turns out to be the case. Yes, there are a number of still designs out there that claim to handle multiple spirit styles, but few if any will produce them all perfectly. Some still designs are simply better suited to certain spirit styles than others. This means that if you are wanting to produce a boatload of spirit types simultaneously in your distillery, you will need to purchase multiple stills, or be willing to make some compromises. Most small distilleries with tight margins and less than Rockefeller level bank accounts take the compromise route. This is not to say that they aren't able to make superlative products on their limited production set ups, just that the job may become a bit more difficult to reach the desired level of quality. The reasons for this will become more apparent as you read later chapters in the book.

The question of spirit "perfection" here is a dicey one and it's something that I constantly struggle with. I very much adhere to my oft mentioned credo of "tools not rules" and generally do not believe that there is only ONE golden standard to produce a high caliber spirit. That includes specific production equipment. However, if you want to make a traditional cognac-style brandy with all the stylistic trappings that process entails then using a traditional cognac still is going to make the job much easier for you. If you want to go full Scottie and make single malt bliss, then certain still designs will get you there more easily. If you want to make both of these things on the same still, then your job becomes quite a bit more challenging. Not impossible, mind you, but certainly more difficult.

You also don't want to be sold into purchasing something you don't need. I have a lovely 750-gallon still from Vendome Copper and Brassworks that I produce my single malt whiskies on. The owners of the distillery purchased it before I was a part of the project and they were sold on the idea of having four bubble cap trays and a gin basket…I've never used either the plates or the basket. I love Vendome, but I could've possibly saved my bosses some money by purchasing a simpler design from the same manufacturer.

Next, ask yourself how much are you willing to spend? Inevitably, this is the most painful question for folks. Believe me. You get what you pay for. That being said, be honest with what you are willing to afford, because that will shape the next question you need to ask.

Which company should you work with?

This is a massively critical question that you must be willing to do a lot of research on and give a lot of thought to. There are so many reasons for choosing one manufacturer over another. A far from exhaustive list of such reasons might include:

- Brand recognition
- Price
- Customer service
- Location in proximity to your distillery
- Manufacturer brand value
- Recommendations from friends
- Production lead times
- Proven track record
- Available designs

- It's what other distillers in your category use
- And so much more...

Let's tick our way through a few of these.

Brand Recognition

If you are relatively new to the world of distilling, then you may not know where to start with your still purchase. Many folks simply resort to calling up manufacturers that they've heard of. Maybe you saw the name Vendome a few times on different distillery tours. Maybe you've heard Forsyths uttered among your knowledgeable single malt friends. Or perhaps your obsession with all-things cognac has found a few mentions of Chalvignac Prulho in your searches.

Name recognition is a powerful thing, but it isn't the only thing. There are countless reasons why you might continue to bump into the same manufacturer names time and time again. Often it really is that they are great at what they do. Other times it is simply that they've invested in savvy marketing and have found ways to get into your visual and mental research space. There are more than a few companies I can think of that have in recent years pumped a lot of cash into advertising, but whose products fall well short of something that I would recommend to another distiller. If you keep seeing the same names pop up in your research, certainly call them up and talk turkey (or stills, preferably). However, you should shop around. CARL out of Germany makes excellent stills but doesn't advertise much so you may not come across their name as often as some others. The fact that you aren't being blasted with CARL banners constantly in your Google searches should not be taken as an indication of lack of quality. They are an excellent company and because of their loyal customer base, they generally do not *need* to advertise.

Price

This is the most painful subject for people. Getting that checkbook out sometimes feels like self-exacting a pound of your own flesh. Like many purchases it can be tempting to go with the lowest price, but with distillation equipment you typically get what you pay for. Sometimes the lowest price works in your favor but not as often as you would hope. It's a business gamble that in some situations can be akin to Russian Roulette. If you aren't careful you can wind up with a piece of equipment that is constantly on the fritz, your production slows (or even stops), and your business suffers. I've seen it time and time again. Price should be a factor but not the only one.

But how much should you spend? That's a tough question to answer and I've never been able to give a hard and fast rule about it. Spend what you are comfortable spending on a piece of equipment that is the physical embodiment of you company's livelihood.

Some companies are notoriously more expensive than others. Vendome, CARL, Forsyths and Chalvignac Prulho will all charge more for their stills than many other companies. In part this is because of their overall quality of manufacture, but it's also because they *can* charge a higher amount. These are busy companies, and the simple economics of supply and demand mean they can ask for a premium price on their products. I don't think that any of them are *over*priced, however.

Of course, there are countless companies out there offering deep pocket savings if you'd only give them a chance. Some of these companies are actually offering good value for the money. Others not so much. Buyer beware.

I have a client that purchased a 500-liter still from a new-ish manufacturer in China. They spent approximately $20,000 on the pot, five tray column, gin basket, condenser, and collection tanks. When they were ready to do their first distillations, I went out to the distillery to walk them through everything first-hand for a few days. I was able to get up close and personal with the still and gave it a seriously thorough look over. To my surprise it actually worked fairly well. The stripping distillation went smoothly, and with some typical fine-tuning the column produced a good spirit. However, I noticed a few workmanship issues that I suspect will cause problems down the line. I suggested all the thermometers be changed out for more accurate ones. Some of the gaskets didn't seem to seat properly. The tri-clamps and connections could've been made better and subsequently more

secure. The list goes on. In the end, I think my client
dodged a bit of a bullet on their financial decision. Only
time will tell if the equipment holds true to its promise.

Aside from supply and demand and having a big-name brand, what other factors make these stills more expensive? Quite a few things as it turns out. The copper and metal work are of a higher quality. The welds and brazes are solid and uniform. Valves, fittings, tri-clamps and other accessories come from high caliber manufacturers and are less likely to leak or fail. Piping and connections are angled perfectly. Still geometry has been optimized. And then there's the customer service...

Customer Service

Of all the factors that come into play when choosing a company from which to purchase your still, this is arguably one of the most important. Customer service here is definitely not the same thing as what you may be used to when it comes to so many other consumer products. You aren't laying down a few hundred bucks on a new cell phone, here. Your still could possibly end up costing you more than your house. So, forget about the 1-800 numbers with the automated maze of computer generated "responses." For the kind of money you're forking over, you expect to get a live person on the phone if a question or problem arises. And in many cases, you do, but sadly not always.

I think most manufacturers want to make sure that you are happy with the incredibly expensive distillation device that you purchased from them. They want to help you succeed long after the invoice has been paid. And should something malfunction or break, they are willing to jump on the phone, or sometimes a plane to help you fix it. Other companies seem content to end the transaction as soon as the card has been swiped through the machine. And if something goes wrong, well you'll probably figure it out, right?

Once again, I've experienced both scenarios and guess which one I prefer.

I've worked extensively with Vendome, Specific Mechanical and CARL in my own distilleries. I've tangentially worked with several other reputable companies through friends and clients. I can attest to the excellent customer service I've received in all cases.

When one of my manufacturers sent us our new 2,000-liter dual column pot still for neutral spirit production, they accidentally forgot to send along a couple of important valves. Not surprising; this beast came with what seemed like 10,000 parts to it. I wasn't upset or shocked that a few valves were missing. I emailed the company and my rep responded within 20 minutes with an apology and a guarantee that the valves would be overnighted to me the very next day at no charge. And that's exactly what happened.

When I had questions about the best operational conditions for our new still, I once again got a reply to my query within a few short minutes. The rep patiently went through every step and every answer to my questions to make sure I had a proper and thorough understanding of how to best operate their design.

On the flipside, I've worked with a company that shipped us a small 500-liter still that was promised to produce our neutral spirit at an easy 96% abv with a good flow rate into the collection tank. The still had all the fancy automation a guy could want, and the marketing materials seemed to suggest that all I needed to do was to turn it on and we would be good to go. When the still arrived, I began to put everything together but some of the automated valves didn't make sense to me, so I contacted the company. They asked me why I had removed the valves from the system and disassembled them. When I responded that I had done no such thing and that the valves came to me that way, they claimed that I was lying but that they would help me fix it anyway... how nice of them.

When I got the still fired up and began our first run, I noticed that our "neutral spirit" was coming out at 93% abv and at a much slower rate than their website had claimed. Once again, I contacted the company and once again the response was that I was doing everything wrong. They also claimed that the flow rate I was quoting wasn't real. I pointed out that it was on their website. A few days later I went to their website and they had taken down the promised flow rate numbers. The worst part about this whole experience was that these were some of the *best* interactions I had with that company. In the end we decided to scrap their still (not an easy decision to make considering the amount of money we had put into it) and work with a different company. And we couldn't be happier.

The moral of the story is that customer service *matters*.

Location in proximity to your distillery

This seems like such a simple and quaint idea that you might wonder why I'd even bother with it. Afterall, we live in a world where you can buy limes year-round in Quebec and purchase the latest fashions from anywhere in the world with the click of a button. We are inescapably connected with a disconcerting ease. Why should it matter if the still manufacturer is based across the street or across the ocean?

It is true that manufacturer proximity is not as much of a concern as it once was. However, having the still maker closer to your neck of the woods does have its benefits. Mostly, if you need some onsite maintenance or guidance, this becomes really easy and relatively cheap. If your manufacturer is based on the opposite side of the world and you need some onsite assistance, well I hope you've got a lot of frequent flier miles saved up...

Manufacturer Brand Value

The modern spirits consumer is smart. Virtually everyone these days is carrying around a web-connected supercomputer in their pocket and can obtain information about any and everything they could possibly have a passing interest in, including the liquors they purchase. I've noticed it more and more with the passing years, but consumers that have absolutely no interest in opening a distillery themselves know the names of companies such as Vendome and CARL. They recognize these companies as partial signifiers of spirit quality. Granted most consumers don't mire themselves in such gory details of a distillery, but an increasing number of them do. As such, there may some (slight) value in purchasing a recognized still brand for the (also slight) marketing boost it might confer.

I've also seen distillers purchase a company's stills based in part on the pride it gives them to own something from said manufacturer. Pride can be a silly thing, but in this case it's all about whatever makes you happy. If purchasing a true Chalvignac Prulho alembic gives you some pride (and your pride can afford to write the check from your bank account) then who am I to tell you to stay humble?

Recommendations from Friends

It may seem strange that decisions on still manufacturers could be based on something as casually cavalier as a recommendation from a friend, but it does happen. As a friend you should be able to trust them. If they tell you that still maker A has been wonderful to work with and built a top-grade apparatus, then why wouldn't you at least consider their advice? Reach out to other distillers whom you know and trust. They will likely give you good intel on who you can trust with your equipment manufacture and who you should steer clear of.

Production Lead Times

This can be and often is a huge mitigating factor in who you choose to work with. With the current boom in small distilleries opening their doors, and large distillers rapidly expanding their operations, the still manufacturers out there are getting busier and busier. They are hiring more folks, opening more warehouse space, and dealing with an immense amount of logistics. However, the increased business load for many companies has led to increased production lead times.

If you are hoping to get your distillery open within 12 months, then you should probably have ordered your still six months ago. OK well maybe not, but in some cases that's not too far-off base. In the past few years, I've seen lead times of up to three years! I've also seen smaller companies quote times of only a few months. I would argue that the average lead time for most of the well-known manufacturers is currently (2020) sitting at roughly 10–12 months. And that's for something relatively "stock" in design. If you want a lot of bells, whistles and customization, you can expect to wait much longer than that. However, I have seen some lead times as low as six months from highly reputable companies. So, if time is an issue, you may need to call around and ask about lead times. It could be a major deciding factor on who you work with.

Next Steps

Deciding who you should work with to produce your still can seem a daunting task. To cover all your bases and ensure you're getting the best price for the best equipment, it's not a bad idea to whittle your list of candidates down to two or three and speak with all of them about your needs. You'll get a better feel for how the company and its engineers operate. You're going to be working with these people through phone calls, email and in person for quite some time so it is important that you feel like you can get along and that they understand not just your needs but how you feel they can be best met.

Before you make that final decision on who to work with, ask them for a list of projects they've done before. This is for a couple of reasons.

First, you need to know that they have experience building your type of still. With the current market boom, I've seen quite a few brewery equipment manufacturers get into the realm of distillation equipment. Sometimes these companies offer great results for a fraction of the big-name price. Often though, the finished fabrication is less than stellar. For the amount of money you are about to invest in this equipment you want a company with a proven track record.

Second, you need a list of names that you can potentially contact to see what they think of the company, their experience purchasing their equipment and how well it runs. Really good companies will actually set you up with introductions to some of their other clients who can recommend them. However, I suggest doing your own research and talk to some folks outside of the list the manufacturer will connect you to. You want to make sure that they aren't simply cherry picking from the good reviewers and leaving out all the bad experiences other may have had working with them. If you are really lucky, the manufacturer has installed a few stills within driving distance, and you can go see their equipment in person and talk with the operators to get their true two cents.

After all of this, you should finally be at a point where you can make a decision on who to work with. Now, what are you going to have them build?

Honestly, the order of events and decisions here is less sequential and more in tandem. You probably have an idea of what you want and how much you're willing to spend before you even line up calls with potential still makers. Regardless of when you make the decision, the decision must be made, and you need to have a fairly clear picture of what you need in your distillery.

Reading the various methods and techniques in this book will hopefully give you a good idea of what is possible and what is useful to your particular situation. If you are planning on making traditional single malt whisky, then you probably don't need to purchase the two 20-plate columns with bubble cap trays and a gin basket on the side. But if you're making only vodka straight from grain, then those two columns become incredibly valuable to you.

You don't have to have a perfect image of the still in your mind. If this is your first foray into distilling, then you may not have much of an image at all. The only thing you may know is which products you want to make. That's ok too. Talk with your chosen manufacturer and see what they suggest. A good still maker is not going to try to sell you on things you don't need (though some certainly do), but it's never a bad idea to involve a good production consultant in the process if you are at all unsure.

Deciding on the still design and feature set doesn't have to be hard. It can actually be a lot of fun (if you're like me and you enjoy those kinds of things). What *can be difficult* is deciding on how big of a still you need.

Size Matters

This is where it really pays to have a good understanding of your business and its goals. You should know how many cases of how many products you intend to make over the course of the next five to ten years. How do you predict what the market demand will be in ten years? Well, if I had the answer to that then I'd be a billionaire, (last time I checked, I was still not magically wealthy) so I can't really help you there. Get a good sales and marketing consultant that has experience with spirits to help you put together some figures. From there you can calculate how many proof gallons or liters of alcohol you need to produce in order to reach your sales goals.

Once you know how much you need to produce you can then sus out how big of a still you need. But this question can still get a little bit complicated. How often do you want to run the still? And what kind(s) of spirit(s) are you making?

The type of spirit you produce can have a massive impact on the required still size. For instance, I have a good friend that runs a well-known gin distillery about two hours outside of London. He produces excellent gins using high quality neutral spirit that he purchases from a larger firm. Even though his still is only 500-liters, he produces upwards of 70,000 nine-liter cases per year which is roughly 250,000-liters of absolute alcohol. This is in large part because he doesn't have to make his neutral spirit. Meanwhile my distillery focuses on single malt whisky and produces a small amount of gin and liqueurs. Instead of purchasing neutral spirit from another company we opt to make it ourselves. We have a 2,800-liter still for whisky and a 2,000-liter still for neutral spirit and gin. Running 24/7, I can conservatively crank out around 250,000-liters of alcohol per year roughly equaling my buddy's production. And yet I have almost 10 times the still capacity that my friend has.

Now, note that I mentioned a 24/7 schedule in my estimate above. Currently I've got three employees plus myself running 12-hour days, 7 days per week. We have a lot of room to expand our production. It would require more labor hours, more employees, more maintenance, more, more and more still. It's a lot of work running a distillery and optimizing its production capacity. It also costs a lot of money to make these changes. A large still runs for the same amount of time as a small still making the same product, so size can really impact how efficiently your operations run. A question that you have to ask yourself is "How often do you want to distill?"

This is not an easy thing to answer for a lot of people. What I see happen all too often with new smaller distillers is they get really excited about working in the still house and think that they won't mind running the still for 25 hours per day, 8 days a week. So, why not save some money and get the smaller still? Sure, they'll have to distill more often to reach their production goals, but that just means more time in the still house having fun, right? To them, distillation is a romantic process, one of carefully handcrafting a liquid vision and a far cry from the stale life of former non-distilling jobs past. And some people really do excel with this kind of attitude and can handle the excessive work hours long term, but these folks are definitely in the minority. Most people who adopt this approach end up burning out. They also quickly find that they can't easily distill AND run a business at the same time.

I can't tell you how to manage your time or run your business. I can only offer some suggestions and guidance here. In my opinion you should be able to reach your first-year production goals while operating the still at 10–20% production capacity at most. What I mean is that you are operating the still only one-fifth of the maximum amount of time the still can run in the first year. This gives you room to expand as your sales grow from year to year. If you need to run your still at 100% production capacity to reach your one year's sales goals, then you are going to be in trouble in year two when hopefully your sales go up.

What if you are in a situation where you need to mature your spirit for several years before you can sell a single drop of liquid? Well, then the question is a little harder to answer. Now you are having to predict sales of a product that won't be ready for quite some time. It's hard to calculate those numbers and harder to offer advice on production volumes as a result. In this case, I suggest having a still that can process the contents of one fermenter within a single eight-hour shift. If you can go bigger and faster, then all the better.

Balanced Distillation Design

For many batch spirit types you will perform at least two distillations to reach your quality goal. Some stills and techniques will allow for single passes while other styles and methods require three distillations. However, two distillations is the most common method for a large swath of spirits. This means that you'll be doing a "stripping" run followed by a "spirit" run.

The stripping run is where you distill your fermented wash. If you have 1,000 units of wash, then ideally you have a still that can distill the entire fermenter within a single shift. The wash still generally doesn't have to be a complicated device. For most spirits you really only need a basic still design along with possibly a motorized mixer to reduce the risk of scorching wash solids. The amount of low wines that you get out of the wash distillation is usually 30–40% of the total volume of the initial wash. If you have 1,000 units of wash, then expect something on the order of 350 units of low wines at the end of the distillation.

Because the volume difference between the wash and the low wines is significant, and because spirit distillations require more care in their execution, many distilleries opt to use two stills for their distillation program. One still is a dedicated wash still and the second is used only to distill the low wines.

The wash still in these instances is considerably larger and usually simpler in design. Outside of a mixer, the only other components to the still are often the required safety devices such as vacuum and pressure relief valves. The geometry may even be a little bit different that the spirit still. In Scotland, it is not uncommon to see wash stills with wide descending lyne arms while the corresponding spirit stills have smaller ascending lyne arms (though lyne arm orientation for spirit stills varies considerably between distilleries). The descending lyne arm eliminates a lot of unnecessary reflux from the wash distillation.

This brings us to the discussion on making a balanced distillation system. As I've already mentioned, in most spirit producing traditions, you will typically perform two distillations to reach your final spirit. Distilleries go about this in all kinds of ways.

If you have only one still in your facility that is sized to fit one of your fermenters, then there are a few scenarios to follow. For this example, you would distill two washes, combine them with heads/tails from a previous spirit distillation and then distill everything together. The combined volume of the low wines from the two washes plus the heads/tails should be roughly equal to the total volume of one wash. You could also distill three fermenters separately, collect the low wines and distill them all together. After three distillations you would have enough heads/tails to fill the still with a separate heads/tails run. Or let's say you have two wash stills and one spirit still, all the same size. Distill two fermenters and combine with heads/tails into the spirit still.

In all of the above examples the distillation system is considered balanced. The ratio of wash distillations to spirit distillations is a whole number.

Why is this important, you ask? Let's look at an unbalanced system and the situation should become clear.

Imagine that you have three wash stills of 1,000 units each (gallons or liters). You distill three fermenters and obtain 350 units of low wines each for a total of 1,050 units. Now let's say that you have one spirit still sized at 750 units. One set of wash distillations will not fit inside your spirit still. In fact, it would take nine fermenters to get to a point where you would have enough low wines to come even remotely close to distilling whole even batches. Even then it would take four spirit distillations to make the numbers come out for you.

Aside from the obvious inefficiencies associated with the still-house usage in an unbalanced system, these systems can actually have adverse effects on spirit quality if liquid is not well managed. For instance, let's say that in the above unbalanced system your stills are sized in liters. You also decide to collect all your low wines into 1,000-liter plastic IBC totes which is a fairly common and inexpensive collection vessel for many distilleries (mine included). You could use one tote per wash distillation, but if your system is sized in liters then you would only get 350-liters of low wines per wash, which is not an efficient use of tote space. So, you decide to run the distillate low wines from all three stills into the same 1,000-liter tote. At the end of the distillation, you have 50-100 liters of weak abv low wines that won't fit into the tote. You decide to put that liquid into the next tote. Now tote #2 has 50 or so liters of weak low wines, and because that is also not an efficient use of tank space, you decide to distill your next batch of three washes into that tote. At the end of that run, you now have even less room in the tote that you did during the first set of wash distillations, so you allow the final 100 liters of weak low wines to go into tote #3.

As this process continues of blending weak low wines with the next batch of low wines you eventually wind up with a set of totes with fairly different alcohol and congener compositions. Any subsequent spirit distillations using any combination of these totes will naturally be different from each other. (Keep in mind that we still haven't decided how we approach the redistillation of any heads/tails from previous distillations.) At best this provides a massive amount of batch-to-batch inconsistency that you'll have to contend with.

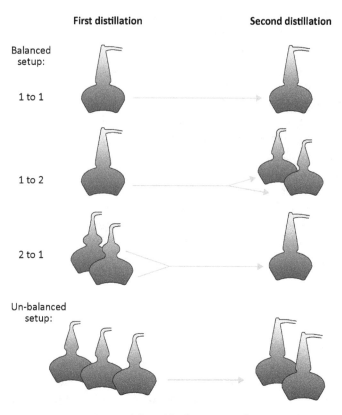

First distillation   Second distillation

Balanced setup:

1 to 1

1 to 2

2 to 1

Un-balanced setup:

Figure 5-1. Common balanced distillation system designs
(Used with permission and copyright of the Institute of Brewing & Distilling)

At worst, your final spirit quality may suffer. Unbalanced systems can be successfully managed, but you need to keep excellent liquid management and storage practices to make the most consistent product possible.

This is not a simple question of finding the right sized storage tanks. You effectively have two routes you can take here. You can combine all the low wines into a single tank and keep your feints (heads/tails) separately stored OR you can combine everything into a single tank. In theory, both situations should result in the same alcohol composition inside the still. But due to production scheduling (especially if you are making several different spirit types on the same still) you can easily find yourself in a situation where you are holding onto the low wines and feints for extended periods of time. Extended storage of these liquids will change their congener profiles and these profiles will differ from each other based on whether or not the feints and low wines are stored together or separately. In many cases the effects will be subtle, but you can produce two different products based on storage differences. See the diagram below for a visual representation of how this can play out.

You may find yourself in a position where you have no choice but to work with an unbalanced distillation system. Or maybe you're simply curious as to how such a system could possibly work. There are some big-name examples out there. Probably the most famous "unbalanced" distillation system is that of single malt whisky, Mortlach (one of my personal favorites, I must admit). The "Beast of Duff-

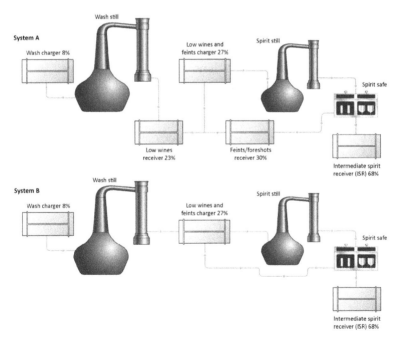

Figure 5-2. Two different liquid collection systems
(Used with permission and copyright of the Institute of Brewing & Distilling)

town" as it is often called, is utterly unique in its elaboration process in that it is distilled 2.81 times. Part marketing copy and part honest calculation, this is the official number that Diageo gives for how one of their secret weapons is distilled. Here is how it works.

Mortlach use six stills, all of which are different sizes and effectively work independently of each other. Three of these stills are considered wash stills and the other three are spirit stills.

- Wash still three is paired with spirit still three. In theory, these would be a balanced pair if they were the only stills in operation at the distillery.
- Wash stills one and two work as a pair. The stronger 80% (volume) of the low wines from these stills then goes into spirit still number 2.
- The remaining 20% weak low wines go into spirit still one (known affectionately as "the Wee Witchie").
- The Wee Witchie is run three times with a hearts cut taken ONLY on the third distillation.
- Hearts cuts are then blended together to reach the desired spirit profile.

It is confusing, confounding and blissfully brilliant on so many levels. It's just one example of how to make an unbalanced system conform to your will to have a consistent end product. Such a route is not the way I would advise most distillers to take, but it can certainly be done and still produce something classic.

In the next chapter we will briefly look at the components of the liquid we are distilling and how they will affect the quality of our finished spirit.

Chapter 6
The Wash

Before we get to actually distilling something, it would probably be beneficial if we have a good understanding of what we are distilling. Sure, you've taken your fermentable substrate and through the addition of yeast managed to produce some alcohol, but are you 100% certain that your wash is going to produce a quality spirit? In this brief chapter let's explore some of the theories and considerations behind some of these pre-distillation conditions and how they affect final spirit quality.

Raw Materials

Every action in the distillery affects everything downstream from it. It's an idea that I continue to bring up in this book, in my own distillery, and in the classes and talks I regularly give. It is an absolutely unescapable dictum like death, taxes and rain after you've just washed your car.

In the grain distillery this means using only high-quality grains that have been purchased from vetted and tested suppliers. This is an area where I see a lot of unnecessary risks being taken by the small distiller looking to produce something from farm to bottle. I certainly understand the appeal, running a farm distillery myself. It is a beautifully romantic notion to offer your customers a whisky that you have produced from grain straight off the local farm, with minimal human intervention in between you and the land. There's also the bonus that often times you can get direct to distillery crops at a good price by simply omitting the middleman grain broker. Everyone wins!

However, unless the grain has been tested for several key parameters you may be welcoming a world of trouble. A representative grain sample can easily be sent off for testing for things such as moisture content, extract and protein. These items can tell you a lot about how a grain will behave in the distillery. Besides, you want to be consistent with your production methods so that your product is also consistent. If you purchase rye from one producer with an extract of 75% and then another producer sells you some of the "same" rye from their farm and the extract is 70%, you are going to produce different whiskies from those two grains. The extract has an effect on the potential starting sugar concentration in the wort and that in turn affects how your yeast behaves and many of the compounds they will produce (ester production often increases with starting gravity for instance).

There are some other items that we should add to the list. Two of the biggies are EC precursors and DON. Let's deal with DON first.

DON stands for deoxynivalenol, but commonly goes by the more insidious name, vomitoxin. Formed as a result of fusarium blight in grains, it is a well-feared issue that occasionally pops up in the brewing industry. It does exactly what its name implies. It will make you vomit if you ingest enough of it. How much you need to consume before vomiting ensues is up for some debate among scientists (it would seem they likely couldn't find enough human test subjects to figure this one out…). One study found that a dose of 16 µg/kg of body weight did not cause one poor test subject to vomit. That dosage equated to 800 ppb of DON in beer and 3 ppm on the original malt. What if the dosage was increased? Well, let's not put someone through the emetic paces to find out (Bergstrom & Schwarz, 2016).

Well, surely we don't have to worry about vomitoxin in distilled spirits, right? Afterall, doesn't the distillation process destroy stuff like that? The answer is a little yes and a little no. It is true that DON levels seem to be somewhat reduced during distillation. Notice that I said "somewhat" as in not completely. It is also true that most beers on the market probably contain some small amounts of DON and we don't see an entire beer drinking populace upchucking their lunch every time they down a bottle of suds. In other words, small amounts of DON are likely not much of an issue. And certainly, when the levels are greatly reduced during distillation, it is probably even less of an issue. However, if you are starting out with a grain that hasn't been tested, you have no idea what level of vomitoxin you may be potentially dealing with. Our customers are our most valued resource, and they are definitely the worth the price of a simple DON test.

The other compound of concern in grain is actually something to be concerned about in virtually all fermentable substrates and that is EC. As you've likely guessed through context alone, EC is not something you want to have in your spirit.

EC stands for ethyl carbamate (also known as urethane) and it is a suspected carcinogen. Suspected means that it hasn't been proven as a carcinogen… yet.

EC rustled quite a few feathers in North America back in the 80s. It was discovered in many spirits, so research and legislation were undertaken to get a handle on the possible health risks posed to the consumer. Concentration limits were set at 125 ppb (voluntary) in the US and 150 ppb (mandatory) in Canada. (In Canada 400 ppb is the limit for stone fruit brandies, the reason for which will become apparent shortly.) The EU regulations are currently left up to the individual member states and are consequently all over the place. Regardless, this is something that every distiller should have a conscious understanding of so that they keep their EC levels under the required maximums.

EC is found in pretty much every fermented beverage. It is formed through the combination of urea and ethanol. Yeast will produce urea through the metabolism of certain amino acids and other precursors. These other precursors include glycosidic nitriles from grains and plants (including barley and sugarcane) and cyanide derived from amygdalin in stone fruit pits (yes, *that* cyanide). To make matters worse, some folks use urea as a nitrogen source in their farming practices and occasionally as a yeast nutrient inside the distillery. All these things combined mean there is a multitude of ways for yeast to produce urea.

Urea on its own is not really harmful. We still need to form the ethyl carbamate. In order for urea and ethanol to combine into EC, you need heat which is something we have in abundance inside our stills. Copper seems to help catalyze the reaction as well.

Most EC formed in the pot never makes into the final distillate. Some studies have shown a 70% reduction in EC after the first distillation and a cumulative 97% reduction after the second distillation (Alcarde, de Souza, & Bortoletto, 2012). However, if you start out with high enough levels of precursors, you can easily produce a spirit that exceeds the permitted EC maximums. One study assessed 84 different Brazilian cachacas and found EC levels as high as 5,589 ppb with an average of 904 ppb (Boscolo, 2001).

Stone fruit brandies are often some of the worst offenders when it comes to EC content. If the fruit pits are too heavily damaged during processing, the amygdalin inside can be enzymatically broken-down during fermentation to produce hydrogen cyanide as an EC precursor. The level of cyanide is too low to be of much health concern for the average person, but as an EC precursor the levels can lead to high rates of formation. Many countries, including my home country of Canada, actually set different (generally higher) EC limits for these types of brandies.

So, what is the best way to keep EC from getting into your spirit? A good defense is the best offense here. Work with your ingredient suppliers to ensure that any known or concerning precursors have been kept to a minimum in the raw material. With stone fruit brandies, it's a good idea to limit damage to the pits as much as possible. Some researchers suggest a 5% limit on the total number of crushed pits accepted in the fermentation (Berglund, 2004).

At our farm distillery, we plant many acres of barley every year. Just like there are different breeds of dogs, there are quite a few varieties of barley and the options for our farm are many. Speaking with a local maltster, he suggested that I stick to only one variety in particular. When I asked him why, he said that every other variety seemed to produce unwanted levels of EC precursors when grown in our area. We've stuck to our single variety ever since.

Raw Materials Processing and Fermentation

Entire books have been written on all the ways you can convert your raw materials into drinkable alcohol. The point of this section is not to recount the contents of these books and articles. You've no doubt done your own research into this area and heard from countless others. By this point you probably have a good idea of the techniques and systems that work best for you and I'm not here to try and get you to change any of it. What follows are simply a few notes on the processing and fermentation of your raw materials to remain cognizant of as you go about your distillation business.

Cereals, Sugarcane and Agave

Process your cereals so that they are able to be completely fermented. Residual sugars might be acceptable for beer brewers for residual sweetness and mouthfeel, but in distilled spirits production they are simply missed opportunities for alcohol formation.

You should distill the fermented cereal wash as soon after fermentation as possible. There is a bit of leeway here, but not much. Many grain distilleries can reach the end of fermentation within 48-72 hours and quite a few of them will begin distillation as soon as possible. However, others will hold off a day or two to ensure that every last bit of sugar has been fermented and to allow the yeast to metabolize some of the young beer character that is typical in cereal fermentations so young.

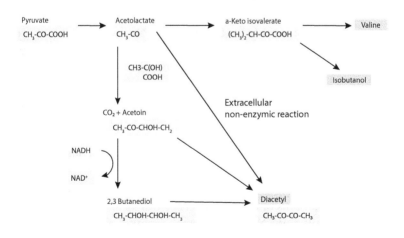

Figure 6-1. Diacetyl formation pathway
(Used with permission and copyright of the Institute of Brewing & Distilling)

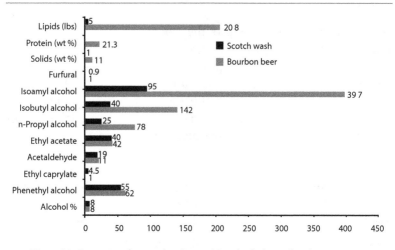

Figure 6-2. Comparison between bourbon and Scotch whisky wash; values in ppm except where noted otherwise (Lioutus, 2002)

Be careful about your timing. Beer has little in the way of microbial protection and can become contaminated rather quickly. Acetic acid bacteria are an especially frustrating nuisance, often forming copious amounts of acetaldehyde and ethyl acetate that can negatively impact the distillate quality. Lactic acid bacteria may produce large amounts of diacetyl if left to their own devices which can also ruin an otherwise well distilled spirit. Be judicious with your timing here. Yeast will often metabolize diacetyl after fermentation to recover important components for cellular function. However, if you wait too long after fermentation, bacterial contamination can make things worse or produce other unwanted compounds.

Of course, not all grain-based washes are created equal. It is an interesting exercise to look at the differences between a Scotch malt whisky wash and a traditional bourbon wash. Even though they both ferment to around the same alcohol concentration, because of the mixed grain recipe of the bourbon wash, the chemical composition is vastly different from the all-malt Scotch wash.

In the above figure you can see several stark differences between the two washes. This of course will cause things to play out differently during distillation. Notably, isoamyl, isobutyl and n-propyl alcohols are all much higher in the bourbon wash. The bourbon wash would be expected to allow higher levels of these compounds to come over into the final distillate. (This is mitigated someone by the use of continuous column distillation, but many bourbon distillers have found isoamyl alcohol to become an issue if they aren't diligent in monitoring their distillates and procedures.)

Another serious difference between the two wash types is that of the lipid contents with the bourbon mash containing significantly higher amounts of lipids than the Scotch wash. Lipids in the form of fatty acids can have a significant impact on new-make spirit character. Some fatty acids such as oleic and linoleic have been shown to increase the perception of nutty and oily characters in the new-make spirit (Boothroyd, Jack, Harrison, & Cook, 2011). For malt whisky producers this is important because you can increase the fatty acid content of your wash by increasing its turbidity. In other words, by not clarifying your wort, you will see an increase in fatty acids. You'll also see an increase in esters as well. Some distillers like to increase these characters while others will shy away from them. You should simply be aware of the effects that these wash parameters can have on your spirit character.

If you are using smoked malt to produce a smoked whisky, be conscious of the fact that the phenolic compounds responsible for smoke aroma in the final distillate can easily dissipate at nearly every step of the production process. Smoked grains should be purchased as close to the smoking date as possible and used quickly. If storage is required, make sure they are stored in a cool area in bags or containers that are not too porous. Too much air penetrating the container can lower the available smoke potential.

Another potential issue with smoked malts is the production of nitrosodimethylamine (NDMA). NDMA is a known carcinogen that can form in grain that has been improperly kilned. This is not going to be much of an issue if you purchase your grain from a well-known supplier. However, with the increase in small malting operations (which I wholly support) and many distillers attempting malt and smoke grain on their own, this can be a serious issue. Nitrous oxides formed during the burning of kiln fuels can interact with hordenine in barley (mostly found in the rootlets) and create NDMA. The solution is to use indirect kilning, but this can be difficult when purchasing directly smoked and kilned grains from small suppliers. Making things worse is that even if the maltster is using indirect kilning, there can be nitrous oxides naturally present in the kiln air if the malting house is located in an industrial area or one with a lot of cars and fuel exhaust.

Fortunately, there are a couple of solutions for the NDMA problem. The most common method is to burn a small amount of elemental sulfur with the fuel. This inhibits nitrous oxide formation. The maltster can also use low flame temperatures on their burners which also seems to help. Regardless, if you are purchasing smoked malt from a small maltster, you should ask about testing for NDMA levels in the malt and anything they are doing to keep these compounds at acceptable levels. NDMA does come over into the distillate and is a health concern for the consumer.

Agave and sugarcane washes have similar concerns in that they are relatively unprotected. It is not uncommon to see agave ferments end at only 4–5% abv (some producers go even lower than that). Rum producers may ferment to higher alcohol levels, but this varies greatly between producer and region.

The length of fermentation can heavily impact congener formation, especially with regards to rum and agave washes. Some mezcal producers will ferment their washes for over a month before they are deemed ready for distillation while many tequila producers finish fermentation after a mere 48 hours. Some rum distillers may practice these lengthy ferments as well, especially in Jamaica where we find the funky, dunder pit produced high ester rums. Light rum producers who are actively trying to keep congener levels low in the distillate will often distill after only 2–3 days of fermentation.

Fruits

Similar concerns exist for fruit washes as for cereals. Be clean and conscious of potential contamination points. I've already mentioned issues associated with stone fruit brandy and ethyl carbamate formation.

Another major concern for fruit washes is the use of sulfur. It is common in many vineyards to spray elemental sulfur onto the grapes and vines to inhibit various fungal diseases. Once inside the winery sulfur dioxide is often added to the juice and/or fruit to further protect against unwanted microbial growth. In a standard winery this is usually a non-issue. In distillation, sulfur can be problem. It easily comes over into the final distillate and can create a stinging burnt match-like character that is easily detectable and unpleasant.

Work with your fruit grower to avoid the use of sulfur as much as possible. Try to harvest the fruit with a lower pH/high acid value. This usually means sacrificing some sugar formation in the fruit, but it provides better protection in the winery from microbes and reduces the need for sulfur dioxide. Since many brandy fermentations can take up to two weeks or more (some Calvados producers will ferment for up to six months), the value of microbial protection should not be underestimated. If left alone and unprotected these fermentations can go south with a surprising quickness.

Something else of consideration for fruit distillers is the addition of yeast lees to the still during the stripping run. (Yes, this is of concern for all wash distillations, but brandy distillers are particularly sensitive to the effects of lees during distillation.) Yeast lees can add a certain spiciness to the final distillate that some distillers love, and others try to actively avoid. You may want to experiment with the amount of yeast lees you allow to be pumped over into the still for distillation to see what distillate character you like best. If you are trying to avoid yeast lees, then try to avoid agitating the fermented wash too much. It is all too easy to stir up yeast lees that have dropped to the bottom of the fermenter and move them back into suspension.

Microbial Considerations

The amounts of aromas and flavors contributed to the distillate by resident yeast and bacteria should not be underestimated. Unfortunately, far too many distillers that I know don't put much thought into their yeast or sanitary practices.

Different strains of yeast will produce different amounts of congeners within the same wash. Some yeasts are better ester producers. Some produce more phenolics. Some produce notes of clove, bubblegum and banana while others produce spicy characters. Still other strains produce little in the way of congeners and are good at letting the raw materials speak for themselves. Which strain(s) you choose is really about the type of character you want to obtain from

Table 1 Factors affecting ester and high alcohol formation by yeast (Table Courtesy of the Institute of Brewing & Distilling)

Fermentation Condition	Effect on Higher Alcohol Product	Effect on Ester Production
Increased temperature	Increase (less available - NH2)	Increase (less recycled CoA)
Decreased temperature	Decrease (more available - NH2)	Decrease (more recycled CoA)
Increased oxygen	Increase (more yeast growth)	Decrease (active acyl alcohol transferase)
Decreased oxygen	Decrease (less yeast growth)	Increase (inhibited acyl alcohol transferase)
Deficiency in amino nitrogen	Increase (less available - NH2)	Usually decrease if less growth (less recycled CoA)
Redox effects		
(a) Deficiency in NAD +	Increase (to generate NAD)	Neutral or increase, if less growth
(b) Sufficiency in NAD+	Neutral or decrease	Neutral or decrease, if more growth
Genetic properties of yeast	Increase or decrease, according to properties of the yeast strain	

your spirit. Let experimentation be your guide.

Strain differences aside, there are various processing and fermentation factors that will influence the congeners formed by yeast. Table 1 illustrates how just a few factors such as oxygen availability, fermentation temperature and amino acid content will affect ester and higher alcohol formation.

The other side to the microbial coin is the issue of spoilage organisms. I've already hinted at some of the potential problems with regards to ethyl acetate production by acetobacter and diacetyl by lactic acid bacteria. Lactic acid bacteria can also produce acrolein which gives a highly pungent horseradish character in the spirit. (Fortunately, acrolein is easily oxidized and reduced in concentration during post distillation resting and maturation.)

One of the more frustrating microbial contaminants is that of various *Clostridium spp.* Clostridium is a genus of bacteria that holds the infamous distinction of housing the same bacteria species responsible for tetanus and botulism. However, the species I'm discussing here are not nearly so insidious. What these species *can* do is produce high amounts of butyric acid. Butyric acid smells like old cheese and baby vomit and it readily comes over during distillation. And once it is in the spirit, there is no getting rid of it. Distillers should be wary of potential Clostridium contaminations by maintaining good distillery hygiene practices and monitoring fermentations for signs of any potential problems.

Early in my career I was tasked with transferring a tote of spirit to ready it for destruction. We were destroying it because the spirit was produced from a heavily contaminated mash and was absolutely riddled with butyric acid. It was one of the worst smelling spirits I have ever come into contact with. During the transfer I accidentally spilled a few small drops of the spirit onto my left hand. The smell of baby vomit stayed with me for three days after that despite washing my hands with scented soap at every available opportunity.

Lest you think that all bacteria are bad for fermentation, remember that most washes have some form of resident bacterial colonies in them. Often this is in the form of lactic acid bacteria that come into the distillery on the raw materials, be it grain, grapes, or cane. And some lactic acid bacteria actually produce positive flavors in the new make distillate. It has been shown that strains of *Lactobacillus brevis* increase "sweet flavors" in new make Scotch whisky distillate. The theory is that some lactic acid bacteria can hydroxylate unsaturated fatty acids such as palmitoleic and oleic acid. The hydroxylated acids are then converted by yeast into sweet/fruity flavored gamma lactones (Wilson, Jack, Takise, & Priest, 2008).

This chapter has hopefully served as a helpful reminder for the issues that can arise from our raw materials and fermentations. How we handle our materials and the subsequent fermentations can have a massive impact on the final quality of our distillate. Now that the groundwork has been laid, we can finally venture into the stillhouse and turn on the still. In the next chapter we will discuss basic pot distillation operations.

Chapter 7

Pot Still Operation and Double Distillation Techniques

For the reader that has experience operating a pot still, parts of this this chapter may not be of much benefit to you. Feel free to skip it. It's your right as a reader. However, you never know. Perhaps I've slipped in some tid bits of knowledge or technique that you are unaware of. All I'm saying is the choice is yours. I'm that kind of writer... the nice, choose your own educational adventure kind. For everyone without such decisional quandaries, feel free to press on.

The assumption is that you have access to a basic working pot still. With this we can begin to discuss the fundamentals behind its operation. Your base fermentable doesn't matter here because we're talking in generalities. You could produce whisky, rum, brandy and more with the guidelines I'm about to set forth. So, without further ado, let's begin.

Basic Pot Still Operation

There are several factors that affect how a pot still operates and the quality of the resulting distillate. We've discussed some of these things earlier in the book when we covered the various components of a basic still. But there are other factors that may or may not be as immediately obvious.

- The number of distillation cycles
- The geometry of the still
- The amount of heating/cooling i.e., distillation speed
- The amount of liquid "charged" into the pot
- The addition of plates/columns

This is by no means an exhaustive list. It does give us a lot to think about, however. Let's start with something simple and build off of it from there.

Picture a basic pot still: a somewhat rounded pot surrounded by a steam jacket. The pot is about 7.5-ft (2.3 m) from the base of the copper to the base of the neck. Let's say the pot holds 1,000 gallons (3875 liters). No strange geometries or gadgetry are at play. The pot is connected to a neck situated above that is the same vertical height as the pot, giving the still a total height of 15-ft (4.6 m). The lyne arm extends away from the neck at a perfect 90° angle for a straight horizontal run to the shell and tube condenser it is attached to. (We could describe some more specific components like the addition of an ogee or the diameters of various pipings but this basic description should more than suffice for our current purposes.)

There you go. Our still is in place. We've got ample steam for heating and plenty of cold water for condensing. The still has been filled to the proper level with our fermented wash and we are all set to go.

The sequence of events for basic still operation is:

1. Turn the heat on
2. Turn the condenser on
3. Collect distillate
4. Turn off heat and condenser once all distillate is collected

It really is that simple. Of course, you're not reading this book to discover the obvious. You want more detail. Fair enough. Let's take a closer look.

We start by opening the steam valve to our jacket to allow steam to come in. It will push through the jacket and steadily heat up the contents of our still. If we have a motorized agitator, this process is even more efficient. But how much heat do you need?

There are competing beliefs here. Some distillers feel that the heat level should be constant and consistent throughout the distillation; meaning whatever amount of heat and subsequent distillate flow rate you want to have is what you should dial your still into from the very beginning and that you should simply leave it there. Others believe that you can safely crank up the heat to maximum until distillation begins and then slow things down to the desired level. Which of these is the "right" way?

If you know me, then you know I don't believe in any one "right" way to do something in distilling. For the folks that believe in maintaining a steady heat throughout the process, they will find that their distillations are a bit easier to control once the spirit starts flowing. However, it will take a lot longer to heat things up. On the flipside, the people that crank their still at the beginning and dial it back once the liquor flows, will find that the distillation can initially be a little unwieldy, but it takes less time to heat up.

Me? I opt for a fast heat up. I have a busy production facility and I'll take any time savings I can get that won't sacrifice the quality of my distillate.

It helps to keep an eye on your still and any thermometers you have installed. You want to know when the initial distillate is about to come over so that you can turn the condenser on. I have a water-cooled condenser that runs through a glycol cooled loop, so my condenser is pretty much always on and it's not a problem for me. But for folks who are using a water supply without a loop, there's little sense in running the condenser until you need it. Otherwise, you would just be needlessly running water down the drain.

If you've been diligent in taking readings on your fermented wash of the initial sugar concentration and the final sugar concentration, you should be able to get a good estimate of the total alcohol it contains. From this you will be able to get an idea of the approximate boiling point of your wash. (Figure 7-1).

In figure 7-1 we can get a decent idea of what the boiling point of our wash might end up being. The diagram shows an 8% abv wash initially boils at about 94°C (201.2°F). A 10% abv wash would boil at closer to 93°C (199.4°F), while a 5% abv wash would boil around 95°C (203.0°F). Honestly, you don't need to know the *exact* temperature your wash will boil. (Though it is a good idea to take notes so that you ensure your distillations are behaving in a consistent manner from batch to batch.) You just need to understand the *approximate* temperature so that you are prepared to turn on your condenser and dial your heat back, if necessary.

Finally, we need to discuss the amount of heat applied during distillation. The more heat you push into the pot then the faster your distillation will go and for those of us with busy lives that sounds

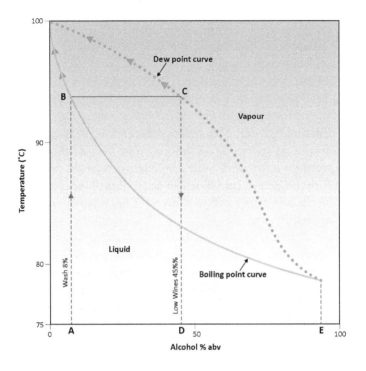

Figure 7-1. Vaporization and Condensation diagram
(Used with permission and copyright of the Institute of Brewing & Distilling)

awesome doesn't it? Except that heat has a significant impact on spirit character. And it doesn't matter if you are using indirect heat or direct fire to run your still. Running it hot and fast versus low and slow will produce vastly different distillates.

In some ways this is more a quantitative issue than a qualitative one. That is to say that the choice of how to run your still, somewhat depends on what kind of characters you want to coax out of the wash into the final spirit. Hot and fast or low and slow. One is not necessarily better than the other. They are simply different. Though many distillers opt for what is essentially a happy medium.

One study found significant character differences in new make malt spirit for every 20°C increase in distillation surface temperature.

As the temperature went up, sensory analysis showed increases in cereal and sulfur notes (Jack, et al., 2005).

The amount of cooling you need is greatly influenced by the amount of heat you are applying. If you've got your pot heating at full bore, then you're going to need more cooling power to compensate. If you are heating gently then cooling power can be dialed back.

> *The analogy that I was given when I was learning to distill was that you can think of your heat as the gas pedal on a car while your condenser acts as the brake. Turn the heat up and things go faster. Punch the cooling higher and things will go slower. It's not a perfect analogy but it helps.*

We don't want our distillate to come out too hot. Hot alcohol spirit can lead to evaporative losses and excess alcohol vapor in the air, neither of which is a good thing. Ideally you should shoot for distillate temperature of around 20°C (68°F). You have a little bit of leeway with this, but it's a good number to shoot for. It might be tempting to go cooler than 20°C but you may just wind up needlessly slowing your distillation down without much benefit to your workflow or spirit quality.

Once the distillate starts flowing you should regularly assess the alcohol concentration. This is most often done using a small container connected to the spirit pipe called a "parrot" which allows you to situate a glass alcohol hydrometer inside and visually monitor the alcohol concentration in real time. You should note however that the faster you run your still, the more the hydrometer will bob up and down, making it difficult to get an accurate reading. I've seen situations where the distillate was flowing so fast that the hydrometer broke inside the parrot…not a great thing to happen. You also need to take a temperature reading when you read from the hydrometer as they are calibrated to specific temperatures.

The other reason to remain vigilant during this distillation is to monitor for signs of foaming and entrainment in the still. As the contents of the still heat up, various residual sugars, proteins and other foam forming compounds can create a massive amount of foam inside the pot. If you aren't careful, it is possible for this foam and some liquid wash to push up through the neck and on into the condenser. This fouls up the neck and condenser piping, lowers the alcohol concentration of your spirit, and changes its chemistry. Not a good situation to be in. You can add silicone-based anti-foam compounds (if they are allowable by regulation in your area), but in my experience these compounds sometimes cause a large amount of sedimentation and buildup on the heating elements of the still. This in turn reduces heat transfer efficiency and can slow down your distillation to unacceptable levels. They are quite effective at foam reduction however, so use them judiciously with caution. I find that by controlling the distillation speed I can better keep foam overflow from happening in the first place.

As the distillation proceeds you will see the alcohol concentration gradually lower as the distillate comes off the still. Eventually, it will get down to around 1% abv or so. Certainly, there is technically still more alcohol that you could distill from the liquid inside the pot, but it is extraordinarily little. It is generally more energetically expensive to continue the distillation at this point than the small amount of potential alcohol would be worth. At this point you can shut the heat off, carefully vent the still, shut down the condenser and dispose of the remaining dealcoholized stillage.

It is really important to vent the still before dumping the stillage. For many smaller stills, this involves simply opening the main still door and allowing the inside still pressure to equalize with the surrounding outside pressure. Some stills may make use of an air valve to accomplish the same task. Regardless, failure to equalize the pressure inside the still prior to dumping can potentially lead to a collapse of some of the still components. Dangerous and extremely costly.

The previous process would serve as a "stripping" or wash distillation. At this point we have simply concentrated our alcohol and collected everything that has come off the still. We have not done any selective fractioning or cuts.

If we started with 1,000 gallons of 8% abv wash, then we should wind up with approximately 350 gallons of 22% abv low wines. The exact volume and alcohol concentration are going to vary between different systems.

Low wines are not the best smelling distillates. Nor do they taste all that pleasant. Besides, the alcohol level is too low for most spirit styles. In order to get something palatable to our loyal customers we need to do some redistillation.

You should take notes and keep records of the distillation process. Here are just a few things worth keeping tabs on and writing down for future reference and repeatability.

- Date and time of the start of distillation
- Still operator name(s)
- Inputs into the still including tank name(s), alcohol concentration, spirit type and any other relevant information
- Heat and condenser settings when turning the still on
- Time and alcohol concentration when first distillate emerges
- Time and alcohol concentration of any fractions taken
- Time and settings of any adjustments made to heating and cooling conditions
- Time and alcohol concentration at time of distillation end
- Weight, volume, alcohol concentration and temperature of each distillate vessel

The Second Distillation

The second distillation is where we will coax our lovely spirit out of its drab low wine shell. Assume we have collected enough low wines to fill up our 1,000 gallon still again. The starting abv should be around 22–23%.

If we look at our vaporization and condensation diagram again (figure 7-1), we can roughly pinpoint our expected initial boiling point. At this alcohol concentration we should see an initial boiling point in the pot of around 86–87°C. We've got more alcohol in the system, so the boiling point is lower than the previous distillation.

So, the still has been charged, all doors and valves are shut and we're good to go. Turn the heat on.

Eventually we will see the first signs of distillate coming over in the spirit pipe and exiting the still. With our condenser turned on, we can dial in our heat. Generally, your heat settings for the second distillation are lower than for the first distillation (assuming you are using the same still for both distillations).

The first distillate coming off the still is your heads fraction. Review the chapter on cuts and fraction management to get a better understanding of how to approach making a good cut here. You will want to direct the flow of liquid into a vessel that is designated for heads collection. This is the smallest fraction by volume so this vessel can be a lot smaller than the vessels for the other fractions.

Once you are confident that the heads fraction is "done" then you can change the flow of liquid into a different vessel and begin collecting your hearts. The hearts collection vessel should be something chemically inert such as stainless steel or glass.

The hearts fraction will last for anywhere from 2–4 hours but can be more than twice that for some distillation techniques. The exact timing is going to depend on distillation speed, technique and equipment among other things.

You will eventually reach a point where you are ready to cut from the hearts to tails. Once again, you will redirect the flow of liquid to a different vessel, this time the tails receiver. At this point, you can speed up the distillation to finish it faster or keep it flowing at the same rate. What speed you choose to run the tails will affect their overall quality and subsequently how you process them in the future. Higher speeds allow for heavier compounds to wind up in the tails fractions (and allow you to finish the distillation run faster). Slower speeds produce a cleaner tails fraction that many distillers prefer, but it will obviously draw out the day a bit more.

At the end of the second distillation, you should have approximately 150–200 gallons of spirit (hearts) at ~70% abv. Your tails fraction will total between 35–40% of the initial charge volume with a final alcohol concentration of ~35% abv. You'll also have a small amount of heads (10–30 gallons) at ~70% abv.

Feints Recycling

I'm of the firm belief that every distillery should recycle their feints whenever possible. It just makes good economic sense.

Now, let me start off by saying that not everything is worth recycling. I don't recycle the heads fraction from my neutral spirit distillations, for instance. However, for my whisky distillations, heads and tails are collected in the same vessel and mixed together to be redistilled later. It's up to you as to what cut fractions you think are worth saving from your distillations.

Once you've decided *what* you are willing to recycle, the next question becomes *how* you will recycle. For our double distillation technique there are a few avenues we can take.

First, we could take our feints and recycle them with the next batch of wash. This would be more common in distilleries that produce a weaker wash in an effort to raise the alcohol concentration of the subsequent low wines. I've heard of some small batch American whiskey producers doing this, but it's honestly not that common. Still, if you are producing washes of only 5% alcohol by volume, then this technique might make sense. It will allow you to bump up the recovered alcohol concentration of the collected low wines.

The second thing we could do would be to recycle our feints in with the next batch of low wines for our spirit distillation. This is probably the most common method for feints recycling. Simply take your feints, add them to your next batch of low wines in your spirit still and start distilling.

The question often gets asked, "How many times can you recycle the feints?" The answer to that is going to depend on who you ask, but the general rule is that you can recycle them for as many distillation cycles as you like as long as the quality of your distillate doesn't change. I know distillers that take the feints from each batch and recycle them into the next lot of low wines ad infinitum with no issues or complaints. Others will run a certain number of prescribed cycles before dumping the feints and starting the cycling at zero again. Taste and constantly assess your distillate to make sure you are happy with the quality.

The follow up question that people often want to ask, is if you recycle the feints infinitely, don't the feints compounds just increase in the still with every cycle? Well, the answer is... a complicated and cloudy "no." That doesn't seem to be the case. A few of the larger distillation firms have looked into this using the various research teams and toys at their disposals and while no one seems to be sharing specific data with the plebes such as myself, the general consensus is that recycling feints does not produce a buildup of unwanted congeners in the distillate. It seems that after a few cycles, the feints and low wine distillations reach a kind of chemical equilibrium with regards to which compounds (and their concentrations) are distilled and which are dropped out through the stillage. I hate offering up such a weak explanation but trust me when I say that for most distilleries, the process just seems to work.

People also want to know what ratio of feints to low wines (or wash) should you distill. This varies between distilleries. The ratio is usually somewhere between 1:1 and 1:2. Looking back at our 1,000-gallon example, we said that for every 1,000-gallon distillation of low wines, you would likely wind up with around ~350–400 gallons of feints, maybe more and maybe less. You could recycle these feints with a roughly equal volume of low wines which is fairly common in some whisky making circles. This would likely produce a "heavier" distillate with a higher congener load. You could also take those 350 gallons of feints and distill them with 700 gallons of low wines. Here, the congener loading would be somewhat lighter. Of course, this all depends on your still sizing and how you would like to process your workflow.

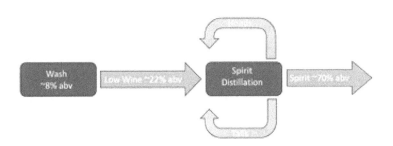

Figure 7-2. Classic Double Distillation Method

Finally, the third option you have is to build up a sizable volume of feints and distill them on their own completely separate from the low wines. The resulting hearts cut from such a distillation can then be added back into the hearts fraction from the low wines distillations.

Another interesting approach to this option is to use the feints to produce a completely different product. In rum circles this is known as a "Queen's Share." The resulting distillate is usually a bit heavier in congeners and can make an excellent candidate for maturation programs.

All three techniques have their advocates and detractors, and you'll have to play a bit to decide which works best for your distillery.

What we've just covered are the basics for doing a double distillation on a simple pot still. And what I've described is effectively the type of distillation that many single malt whisky producers traditionally use. However, there are some style-specific techniques that warrant some discussion, so let's take a few moments to look at some of the most important ones.

The Cognac Distillation

Cognac has strict rules. There are guidelines on the grapes, where they come from, how they are grown and how they are processed. Fermentation has its own set of rules. Distillation has dates, deadlines and dictums. And the maxims behind maturation can sometimes feel byzantine and labyrinthian. In short, it's not an easy spirit to make.

Of course, it's not all rulebooks and stern looking regulators. Many concepts in cognac production remain simply out of tradition. Yes, you have to use a specific style of still, but exactly how you operate it is somewhat left up to you. However, most of the major distillers seem to all follow a similar order of distillation procedures.

Cognac is distilled twice using a traditional Alembic Charentais still. (Figure 7-3).

These stills are composed of two or three vessels, a direct-fired pot, a serpentine (worm tub) condenser and an optional wine preheater that some distillers forgo while others cherish. They are absolutely beautiful in their rustic simplicity. However, don't worry. You don't need to be making calls to French still manufacturers in order to pull off the technique I'm about to discuss. You just need good record keeping and time management skills.

Let's walk through the steps of a traditional cognac distillation and then we will briefly discuss its effects.

The first distillation is done to produce low wines or *brouillis*. This distillation takes three fractions: heads, hearts (which become the brouillis/low wine) and tails. The heads fraction is ridiculously small. By volume of the initial charge, it is usually less than 0.5%. In fact, its primary purpose is to clean out some of the residual fatty acids left in the condenser from the previous run. The hearts are collected until the spirit coming of the still registers around 3–4% abv. The rest of the distillate is considered tails and is collected separately. The brouillis goes onto the second distillation to become cognac while the heads and tails are recycled into the next batch of wine.

The second distillation is done similarly to the first. A heads fraction is taken at roughly 1.5–3% of the initial charge volume. Hearts are collected from around 75% abv down to around 60% abv. A cut is then made to the *first tails, or "secondes."* This first tails cut is allowed to run from 60% abv down to approximately 3% abv. Any distillate that comes afterwards is part of the second tails and is considered junk. (Though you may feel it is worth recycling at some point in your process.) The heads and secondes are recycled back in with the brouillis for the next spirit distillation.

Now, there are a few extra specifics involved as well as a handful of caveats. First, it is suggested that you low wine be no more than 30% abv in strength. The *ideal* low wine strength (with the heads and secondes added back in) is around 28–29% abv for these distillations, at least in cognac. The reasoning is that this is the alcoholic strength that gives the best congener profile in the alembic Charentais.

Also, you should note that on a traditional cognac still, these distillations are *long*. Almost brutally so. The first distillation typically takes around 10–12 hours while the second distillation reaches to around 14 hours in order to achieve the proper flavor and aroma balance in the distillate. It might seem crazy that a direct fired still would take so long to produce a distillate, but further inspection of the still should yield the answer. If you look at the geometry of a classic Alembic Charentais still, you'll notice that there really aren't too many areas where much internal reflux will occur. The boiler pot is quite squat with an equally dumpy looking ogee. The lyne arm and neck it extends from are relatively narrow producing a higher vapor flow. They are also steeply descending towards the condenser. In

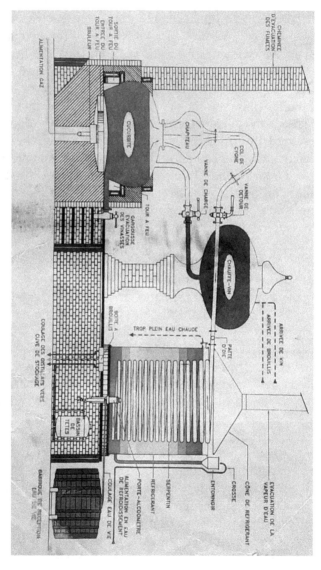

Figure 7-3. Diagram of an Alembic Charentais still

other words, to get a properly clean distillate, these stills need to be operated in a fairly slow manner. For a 25 hL still the typical advised distillate outflow rate is between 0.75–1.0 liters per minute.

Inevitably people ask why cognac distillers do things this way. Why bother with the hassle of cutting the first distillation into fractions? Ask this question of 10 different cognac distillers and you may find that you get 10 different answers. For my part, I believe the technique is simply a way of shuffling congeners around and producing a slightly heavier spirit.

There is some really interesting data on this done by some researchers in Brazil on techniques for cachaca distillation.

The tables of data (page 188) come from distillations of a fermented sugar cane base. The researchers wanted to see how distillation techniques affect the chemical composition of the distillate, in their case, cachaca. A myopic discussion of the numbers is beyond our scope here, but you can certainly see some differences between the distillates resulting from the two methodologies. The cognac distillation saw an 11% increase in overall congeners compared to the whisky distillation technique. That is not an insignificant difference by any means. Much of that increase comes from an increase in higher alcohols and volatile acidity.

The study also looked at another double distillation method which is called the 10-80-10 method.

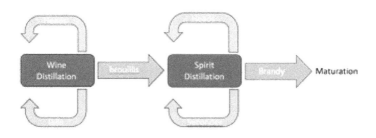

Figure 7-4. Cognac Distillation

	First Distillation			Second Distillation			
	Head	Brouillis	Tail	Head	Heart1 (Spirit)	Heart 2	Tail
Alcoholic concentration[1]	81.10	41.39	1.85	84.15	80.32	31.86	3.25
Copper[2]	0.18	0.10	0.15	0.14	0.06	0.38	0.15
Volatile acidity[3]	11.41	29.42	642.16	7.41	11.09	55.93	639.69
Furfural[3]	0.00	0.00	0.00	0.00	0.00	0.00	0.00
Aldehydes[3]	101.17	19.25	0.00	88.01	9.42	0.00	0.00
Esters[3]	179.11	19.23	0.00	71.38	8.68	0.00	0.00
Methanol[3]	67.99	12.57	0.00	29.41	9.40	7.47	0.00
High alcohols[3]	987.19	497.91	12.33	460.67	448.51	81.95	0.00
Congeners[3]	1278.88	565.81	654.49	627.47	477.7	137.88	639.69

[1]in %v/v 20°C, [2]in ppm; [3]mg.100 mL[-1] anhydrous alcohol

Table 2. Chemical analysis of fractions taken during a traditional cognac-style distillation (Alcarde, Araujo de Souza, & Eduardo de Souza Belluco, Chemical profile of sugarcane spirits produced by double distillation methodologies in rectifying still, 2011)

	Low Wines	Second Distillation		
		Head	Heart (Spirit)	Tail
Alcoholic concentration[1]	39.84	84.19	78.55	35.09
Copper[2]	0.09	0.13	0.08	0.13
Volatile acidity[3]	39.82	7.06	7.56	42.32
Furfural[3]	0.10	0.00	0.00	0.00
Aldehydes[3]	21.11	76.25	9.60	0.00
Esters[3]	20.84	75.24	10.39	0.00
Methanol[3]	14.60	92.32	9.45	6.06
High alcohols[3]	548.19	455.87	401.90	180.79
Congeners[3]	630.06	614.42	429.45	223.11

[1]in %v/v 20°C, [2] in ppm, [3]mg.100mL-1 anhydrous alcohol

Table 3. Chemical analysis of fractions taken during a traditional single malt whisky distillation (Alcarde, Araujo de Souza, & Eduardo de Souza Belluco, Chemical profile of sugarcane spirits produced by double distillation methodologies in rectifying still, 2011)

The 10–80–10 Technique

Brazilian cachaca is one of the biggest selling spirit categories in the entire world. Most of the liquid produced is consumed entirely in Brazil, but exports to other markets such as the United States have proven to be big business for some cachaca producers.

Cachaca is a spirit produced from fresh sugar cane juice. But don't call it rum. The Brazilians feel that cachaca is its own thing. Much of the stuff is produced on a large industrial scale using massive continuous columns. However, quite a few small to medium sized distillers perform a double distillation in traditional pot stills. Of these batch pot still users some have been known to use the 10-80-10 method for fractioning.

The first distillation is similar to our whisky distillation method in that it serves as little more than a simple stripping run. The fermented wash is distilled and everything that comes off the spirit pipe is collected and readied for a second distillation.

The second distillation is where the 10–80–10 numbers come into play. You see these numbers are volume percentages for the fractions. In this method, the first 10% of the expected distillate is collected as heads, the next 80% is collected as hearts and the final 10% is collected as tails. It's a simple program that allows for distillers to work without any testing equipment, even a basic alcohol hydrometer.

Obviously, there are some issues here. The first is that in order to pull this kind of distillation off, you need to have a fairly good idea of your final distillation volume. Otherwise, you'll be flying blind when it comes to deciding where the various percentages stop and start. Of course, this isn't that difficult to overcome, and you should be able to quickly figure out how much distillate you should expect to come out of the still from a given charge volume.

The real trouble is in the chemistry and associated sensorial characters of the final spirit. Note that the heads fraction is a whopping 10%! Even for conservative distillers that's quite a lot of liquid. Though, if you are concerned that your fermentation and/or distillery hygiene practices were not tip top, then perhaps a 10% heads fraction isn't so unreasonable after all. The big issue for me is the low tails percentage. Essentially this technique allows for a LOT of tails compounds to find their way into the hearts fraction. This makes for an incredibly congener heavy distillate and not necessarily in a good way. Let's look at some data from the aforementioned study (Table 4, page 191).

It shouldn't take long to notice some stark contrasts between the results obtained from the 10–80–10 method and the whisky and cognac techniques. First the hearts fraction has a lower ethanol level than the other two, and not by a small degree. We see a drop of approximately 9% abv when compared to the whisky-type distillation. (Remember, the study used the exact same fermented wash for each distillation so starting alcohol concentration is a variable that has been controlled for.)

Next, we see the level of volatile acidity more than double. You'll also note that the concentration of higher alcohols has increased by over 50% from the whisky technique levels.

These results do not paint a pretty picture. This technique produces a very full-flavored spirit, usually to a feinty fault. Indeed, within that same study the researchers ran a sensory preference panel and the 10–80–10 method distillate finished well behind its cognac and whisky technique distilled siblings.

Now that we've discussed some of the basic double distillation techniques, let's take a deeper dive into some of the parameters that affect how the distillation process plays out in real life.

The number of distillation cycles

In the previous explanation of basic distillation operations, we assumed that we were doing a double distillation to reach our quality goals. This is common in all sorts of spirit categories from whisky, cognac, tequila and rum. Of course, each of these spirits has quite a bit of internal variation in this regard and you'll certainly see things such as singly distilled mezcal or triple distilled whisky.

How many cycles you choose to do will have an enormous impact the qualities of your final spirit. Generally, the more distillation cycles you commit to, the lighter the final spirit character you will have. This is perhaps why the double distillation cycle is so popular. It provides a happy medium for flavor intensity and refinement.

It is quite a bit more complicated than this, however. There are other factors that can and will mitigate the effects of multiple distillation cycles. It is possible to produce a fairly light spirit in a single

	First Distillation	Second Distillation		
		Head	Heart (Spirit)	Tail
Alcoholic concentration[1]	39.16	83.60	69.57	6.55
Copper[2]	0.07	0.12	0.11	0.10
Volatile acidity[3]	31.33	7.23	25.45	323.63
Furfural[3]	0.16	0.04	0.31	0.91
Aldehydes[3]	23.71	57.33	14.02	0.00
Esters[3]	21.37	53.93	13.98	0.00
Methanol[3]	14.24	64.62	9.22	5.83
High alcohols[3]	551.64	608.85	606.79	17.47
Congeners[3]	628.21	727.38	660.55	342.01

[1]in %v/v 20 °C; [2]in ppm; [3]mg.100 mL^{-1} anhydrous alcohol

Table 4. Chemical analysis of fractions taken from 10–80–10 distillation technique (Alcarde, Araujo de Souza, & Eduardo de Souza Belluco, Chemical profile of sugarcane spirits produced by double distillation methodologies in rectifying still, 2011)

distillation. You can also end up with a congener rich spirit after several distillation cycles (though this scenario is less common).

The geometry of the still

How your still is designed and shaped will affect how your distillation plays out. It is not uncommon to hear stories both real and apocryphal about distillers retiring or replacing an old still and having the still manufacturer build an exact replica down to the smallest of seemingly insignificant dents and blemishes in the copper so that their spirit isn't affected by a "new" shape. I've never been completely convinced that minor dings and dents in a still will change spirit character in any significant way. However, there are certainly ways that the still shape and geometry will impact the spirit.

Think of distillation like a running track in an Olympic stadium. The ethanol, esters, fusel oils and all the other congeners start out on the starting line and begin their sprints towards the condenser's finish line. If the track is simply a straight line, then the compounds don't have to try that hard to do their job. The race is relatively fair. Sure, some lighter compounds such as ethyl acetate and acetaldehyde will be more lithe and reach the condenser well before our more opulent low volatility runners, but overall a lot of our compounds will get to the same place relatively close to each other.

Now imagine that we start putting some hurdles at various points in the track. All of a sudden, we've got a physical way to help thin the herd of competitors. In order to get to the finish line, the compounds have to jump over these hurdles which will inevitably slow a few of them down. Everyone will get there but we should see more spacing between the competitors at the finish line. The more hurdles we throw up, the more separation we have in the pack.

While it's not a perfect analogy by any means, this does help describe what happens with certain types of geometrical configurations on your still. Some still geometries throw up more hurdles than others so to speak.

Imagine adding a lot of height to the neck of the still as is the case with Glenmorangie's stills. This creates a physical "hurdle" in the form of wider temperature differentials along the neck and causes some reflux to occur, thus providing better separation of lighter and heavier distillation components. The same scenario plays out if you have a steeply ascending lyne arm going towards the condenser. Once again, you are increasing reflux inside the still from geometric changes and increasing temperature differentials.

Now, compare a still with a tall neck, large ogee at its base and a 45° upward sloping lyne arm with a still that has no ogee, a short neck and a descending lyne arm. It should be pretty clear at this point that the first still with the tall neck will produce a spirit that is lighter in character, all other things being equal.

Distillation speed

Remember an analogy I gave earlier in the book about operating the still: the heat tends to act like the gas pedal in your car while the condenser acts like the brake. In other words, these are things that can determine how quickly the distillation proceeds.

Distillation speed is important not just to you, the distiller, but also to the quality of the distillate. Certainly, you don't want a distillation that is painfully slow. It's not an efficient use of you or your equipment's time. However, if you go too fast then your distillate quality might suffer.

Pushing the distillation too fast and hard can make it difficult for the condenser to keep cooling at a satisfactory level. If the distillate is too hot, you can suffer alcohol losses from evaporation and possibly desirable aroma compounds may be lost as well. Besides, distillate vapor in the air is a safety hazard and not worth risking.

Another issue with running the still too quickly is smearing the fractions. If the heat is too high, the vapor components have a lot of energy to move more easily past any physical geometrical hurdles your still has. Your separation will suffer and both high and low volatility congeners will more easily "smear" into the hearts fraction. This can happen even if your condenser is easily keeping up with the added heat load.

If you'll remember from our discussion on congener profiles in batch distillates from earlier in the book, smearing is something that happens in pretty much every batch distillation. It's an unavoidable consequence of the physical and chemical cards we've been dealt. Perfect separation of compounds on our beverage distillation systems is nigh impossible. What we are discussing here is a high level of smearing. This is something that some distillers want while other distillers actively avoid it. And it is certainly an issue of degrees. Depending on your still shape, the wash composition and definitely the distillation speed, the amount of fraction smearing that you encounter will vary from that of your fellow distillers. It is up to you to decide what level of smearing is acceptable and gives you the results you are most happy with.

Condenser Temperature

Closely related to distillation speed is the issue of condenser temperature. In many instances, running the condenser at a warmer temperature allows for a faster distillation to occur. A lower condenser temp usually means a slower distillation. But the factor of condenser temperature is even more complicated than this.

If you are using a condenser with copper tubing, be it a shell and tube or a worm tub, there are important interactions between the copper and the spirit that take place (as we discussed in our chapter on cuts and chemistry earlier in the book). Those reactions are usually faster and more effective while the distillate is still in the hot vapor phase. Obviously, this is complicated by the effect of copper surface area available for these reactions such as the difference between worm tubs and shell and tube condensers.

Glen Ord Distillery actually uses slightly warmer water in their condensers to prolong the vapor contact with the copper. This in turn produces a beautiful grassy charactered spirit.

We have to be careful here. Afterall, it might sound like promoting vapor and copper interactions would be a good thing overall. Certainly, you could save on the energy and water usage for cooling. However, remember that a warmer condenser temp may increase your distillation speed depending on how your still is designed. It may also run the risk of producing a distillate that is *too warm* which can lead to alcohol losses and potentially dangerous levels of ethanol vapor in the air.

The charge volume

It might seem odd that something as mundane as the amount of liquid you put inside the pot would affect how your distillation proceeds, but indeed it does. Obviously, lesser amounts of liquid to distill will reduce the active distillation time. However, the effects go a bit farther than that.

If you have a 1,000 gallon still and distill 1,000 gallons one day and then only distill 500 gallons the next day, the two distillations will likely behave a little differently from each other. The reason is that with a smaller charge you are increasing the headspace inside the pot. By increasing the available headspace, you are also increasing the potential reflux inside the pot.

Many stills have a pot geometry that is a little wider in the top half of the pot than in the bottom half. When you distill a volume less than the working capacity, the vapors will quickly come into contact with more of the walled surfaces of the pot. Unless the still is heavily insulated (which is rare), these walls build up a slight temperature differential between the liquid and the cooler surface air layer just outside of the still. This temperature differential will cause some of the vapors to reflux back into the liquid below.

You should also note that the local climate of whatever room your still is in can subsequently alter the amount of reflux. If the room is really hot like one Tennessee distillery I used to work in many years ago, you are going to have less reflux in the pot because the metal has less ability to form a significant temperature differential. Likewise, if your stillhouse is quite cool then the reflux ability can actually increase.

The addition of plates/columns

Obviously, the addition of extra distillation elements such as plates, columns and purifiers will have a significant impact on your distillation and the resulting spirit qualities. The nice thing about most of these elements is that they are usually by-passable either through the use of toggles for individual plates and/or additional changeover valves or diverter panels for entire columns.

For many years now I've seen a specific type of still design that has become somewhat ubiquitous in much of the industry. (In fact, one of my stills is this very design.) It consists of a basic pot situated beneath a neck containing 4-5 bubble cap trays capped by a pre-condenser. The neck extends to a perfectly horizontal lyne arm that terminates in a shell and tube condenser. I affectionately call it "the craft distiller special."

These stills are fairly versatile in what they can produce. If you are like me, you will never activate the trays and simply treat the still like a simple pot still. However, a large portion of distillers who purchase this design do end up using the trays. With four to five bubble cap trays engaged it is possible to reach alcohol concentrations of around 90% abv. Engage only one or two trays and that number will go down but will still be higher than if you weren't using any tray elements at all.

I've seen some distillers engage the trays for the first portion of the distillation to concentrate the heads and then deactivate the trays as soon as the heads collection is done. This gives a clean and concentrated heads cut but still allows some heavier congeners to emerge into the hearts fraction.

Distillery Yield

When I visit online forums of the various distilling websites, a common question that comes up from new distillers pertains the amount of yield they can expect from their new distillery. I'm not sure I've ever seen someone reply to one of these posts that has answered the question satisfactorily. This is not from lack of trying. It's just that it isn't an easy question to answer. I'll do my best here to clear the mental fog a bit.

In order to run a distillery successfully and stay financially solvent, you need to know how much alcohol you are producing from your starting materials. This not only helps you understand you margins, but to the working distiller it also gives you some important data points for your production efficiencies. And if these numbers change in one direction or the other, you can more effectively and efficiently make production decisions based on your yield numbers.

In order to properly calculate and understand the efficiency of

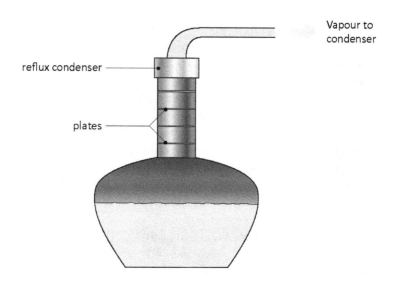

Figure 7-5. Basic pot still with four in-neck trays (Used with permission and copyright of the Institute of Brewing & Distilling)

your distillation process, you need to have a good understanding of how much alcohol you are starting with inside the still. This begins with taking sugar readings at the beginning and end of fermentation.

Depending on your training and, to an extent, your chosen spirit tradition, you may measure sugars using specific gravity, degrees Plato, degrees Brix or possibly Balling (if you are in South Africa). The following calculations use specific gravity. If you use one of the other units for sugar content, refer to the appendix in the back of the book for a conversion to get the correct specific gravity number.

In order to calculate your wash's final abv you need to know the starting gravity and the final gravity. Then you can input these values into one of the following two equations to calculate your alcohol concentration.

There are two commonly used calculations for abv totals. One is rather simple and holds up well for alcohol concentrations of 6% abv and below. The other is a bit more involved, but arguably more accurate for higher abv's. If you are unsure of which you should use, start with the simpler one and if it gives you a value significantly higher than 6% by volume then switch to the second one. For many distilleries, particularly those in the brandy, rum and whisky worlds, the more complicated equation is the better bet. However, note that no equation is going to be perfect. Concrete numbers rarely describe physical phenomena perfectly. Errors from taking gravity readings (which can be common) will lead to inaccurate calculation results. The only way to know the exact abv of your wash is to have it tested, usually through benchtop distillations or gas chromatography. Neither of these things are done that often in small distilleries so we won't cover them here.

The first equation to calculate the abv of your fermented wash is:

$$\text{Eq 1.} \qquad abv = (OG - FG) \times 131.25$$

For example, if your original gravity (OG) was 1.045 and your final gravity (FG) was 1.002 then the equation would look like this:

$$abv = (1.045\text{-}1.002) \times 131.25 = 5.64\% \; v/v$$

The second equation is a bit more involved, but not unreasonably so.

$$\text{Eq 2.} \qquad abv = \left(76.08 \times \frac{(O.G. - F.G.)}{(1.775 - O.G.)} \right) \times \frac{(F.G.)}{0.794}$$

Let's take this equation for a spin, shall we? We have a starting gravity of 1.065 and a final gravity of 1.002.

$$abv = 76.08 \text{ x } \frac{1.065 - 1.002}{1.775 - 1.06} \text{ x } \frac{1.002}{0.794} \quad abv = 8.52\% \text{ v/v}$$

Now, just for argument's sake let's plug those last wash readings into Equation 1.

$$abv = (1.065 - 1.002) \text{ x } 131.25 = 8.27\% \text{ v/v}$$

You'll notice that the Equation 2 gives us a slightly higher abv than equation 1 (0.25% abv higher). This seems small but in your production space it can have a significant impact. Use whichever equation you think is more accurate for your particular situation. For the remainder of this section, we will be sticking with Equation 2.

> *I fully realize that with the ease and convenience of the Internet and smart devices, you can app or web browse yourself into an acceptable answer to your abv question. Most people do this, myself included. However, I think it's important to understand where these online and phone-based calculators get their numbers. Besides, knowing these calculations might make you more interesting at parties. Just sayin'.*

Once you have your abv, then you can easily calculate how much alcohol you have in your wash. All you need to know is the exact volume of wash in your fermenter. I do this by using an inexpensive inline flow meter that tracks the volume of the unfermented wash as it is being pumped into the fermenter. Other people use volumetric markings on a side mounted sight glass or somewhere inside the tank. Whatever your method, just be sure that you are comfortable with its accuracy and precision.

If you have 1,000 units of wash at 8% abv, then simply multiply the volume of wash by the percent alcohol (in decimal form) and you will arrive at the total amount of alcohol in your system.

Remember: this gives you an answer in terms of *absolute* alcohol which is fine for pretty much everywhere except the United States where units of Proof Gallons are the norm. Since one proof gallon is simply one gallon of spirit at 50% abv, the conversion is quick and simple.

So, now you know how much alcohol you can theoretically distill. (Assuming it was possible to distill 100% of the alcohol, which it's not but that's beside the point here.) In the above example, if you have 1,000 liters of 8% abv wash then you would theoretically be able to get 80 liters of absolute alcohol out of the distillation assuming perfect recovery.

So, you put your wash into the still and fire everything up. You collect everything that comes off the still until the spirit exiting the spirit pipe reads 1% abv. You then cut the still off.

Make sure the contents of your low wine are well mixed up to avoid slight concentration stratifications in the tank. (Alcohol and water do mix easily but not as easily as people often assume. Some physical mixing prior to taking an abv reading will help ensure better accuracy of your readings.) You check the obtained volume and alcohol concentrations. In this example we'll say you got 350 liters of low wines at 22% abv. Same as before you can calculate how much absolute alcohol you distilled.

350 liters x 0.22
=77 liters of absolute alcohol (LAA)

Now we can calculate what the loss was.

$$\% \ loss = \frac{Start \ LAA - Distilled \ LAA}{Start \ LAA} \ x \ 100$$

For our example that looks like:

$$\% \ loss = \frac{80 - 3}{80} \ x \ 100 = 3.75\% \ loss$$

So, our total loss for this distillation was just shy of 4%, not terrible, but far from fantastic. There's definitely some room for improvement. And if we do a second distillation, we will likely see another loss so that our 3.75% loss will almost certainly go higher.

Ideally, you keep your distillation losses to less than 2%. In a small distillery, 2% loss would be fine, but larger firms with more controls in place should be able to get closer to 1% losses in many instances.

Now, there are quite a few things we can do with these numbers.

The losses will enable us to see if there is a potential problem with our production systems and may help us to identify the specific causes.

Our yield will also tell us how much it costs to make a certain amount of spirit from a given amount of base material. In the single malt whisky world, we see recommendations all the time on specific strains of barley. Most of these strains come with a PSY value which stands for Potential Spirit Yield. For many modern varieties of barley, the PSY is somewhere around 420 LAA per metric ton. Knowing that this number is the maximum amount of spirit, you can use the cost of the barley and the amount of spirit you produce from it to gain a better insight into your production practices and costs.

Inefficiencies in alcohol recovery can be costly to a distillery. Table 5 was published by the Institute of Brewing & Distilling as part of their learning materials for their distillery students. It gives a fairly accurate accounting of what these efficiencies can cost a single malt whisky distillery in the UK if they aren't properly handled and prevented.

There are all kinds of ways to lose spirit in the production process and there are just as many ways to mitigate those losses.

- Leaks in the still

  ▸ Motorized mixers and agitators are often not perfectly sealed from vapor loss in the pot.

  ▸ Loose fittings (A good maintenance and check schedule should be in place to look for loose fittings and replace worn clamps and gaskets, relubricate DNC fittings and so forth.)

  ▸ Worn copper can eventually cause leaks. Condenser water should occasionally be checked for small amounts of alcohol concentration which would be indicative of a condenser leak.

- Condenser not cool enough
  ▸ High condenser temperatures may lead to high distillate temperatures. If the distillate temp is too hot, then increased evaporative alcohol losses can occur.

- Cutting the distillation off too early
  ▸ Take regular readings and continue collecting until it

Capacity (MLa)	Loss of Efficiency (%)	Equivalent Litres Alcohol	Equivalent Malt (400 La/t)	Cost of Malt £(300.00/t)
5	1	50,000	125 t	£ 37,500
5	5	250,000	625 t	£ 187,500
10	1	100,000	250 T	£ 75,000
10	5	500,000	1,250	£ 375,000
15	1	150,000	375 t	£ 112,000
15	5	750,000	1,875 t	£ 562,500

Table 5. Costs of various alcohol loss points in a distillery
(Table Courtesy of the Institute of Brewing & Distilling)

is no longer feasible or reasonable to do so.

- Cuts/fraction management
  - ► Some distillations allow for easy recycling of heads/tails fractions. In these instances, the alcohol losses are kept to a minimum because of the constant recycling of alcohol.

  - ► Other spirits such as neutral spirit and some gins, don't recycle some or all of the feints and instead send them off for destruction or recycling by a different distillery. In these cases, the alcohol in the heads/tails fractions may be partially or totally "lost" from our distillery inventory.

- Filtration media
  - ► Many kinds of filters and filtration media will retain some liquid from the filtration after the process is done. This means there will be a slight loss in recovered alcohol that we must account for in our production.

- Spillages
  - ► Some processes are more prone to spillages than others such as barreling and bottling operations. Even so, there can be spillage from the distillation operations. While you should always keep these losses to a minimum, be aware that they do occur and must be accounted for.

Probably one of the most effective ways to maximize production efficiencies and minimize losses during distillation is to recycle otherwise discarded fractions whenever possible. Feints recycling can easily bring alcohol losses down to below our 2% per distillation criteria.

Stillage and Effluent Disposal

I think it's safe to say that at least on some level, most people care about the environment in one way or another. Perhaps you're a green crusader who chains themselves to every tree tearing bulldozer they see. Or maybe you just don't like the possibility of paying hefty environmental fines for aspects of your life and business somehow being out of spec. Most people fall somewhere in between the two extremes. And like it or not, most places these days have some degree of environmental regulation at play when it comes to distilleries. If this is the business you want to be in, you have to learn how to play by the rules. Hopefully, you *want* to stay in line with the various laws and regulations. And if you don't, well, let's just say I've never seen anyone get away with such schemes for long.

You should discuss your distillery operations with your local regulatory authorities to make sure that you are toeing the environmental line responsibly. Also, speak with a few different engineers regarding best practices to reduce your environmental impact. The technology is getting better and less expensive all the time. So, do Mother Earth a solid. Go green.

In January of 2021, Filibuster Distillery in Virginia and its owner were brought up on criminal charges of 115 counts of breaking local environmental regulations. How did this happen? Between 2018 and 2020, the distillery allegedly dumped over 40,000 gallons of distillery effluent into a local stream. The distillery waste had high levels of copper and zinc, an environmental hazard (Lake, 2021).

This was big industry news. At least it was to me. Think about the potential fall out here. Not only have the distillery and its owners potentially done serious harm to their local environment, the optics on their brand and business are probably forever tarnished. A lot of folks these days don't look to fondly upon businesses willingly and knowingly hurting the local flora and fauna. Not to mention all the legal costs that the company is going to have to pony up. This is really a shame because with proper foresight and investment, this situation could have easily been prevented.

After distillation of a wash, you have what we call stillage or "pot ale." Stillage generally refers to washes that have large amounts of solids in them such as bourbon on-grain distillations. Pot ale is most often used in the single malt industry and other categories where wash solids are largely absent. Regardless the terminology, the end result is a dealcoholized liquid with proteins, lipids and yeast residues. It is very hot and may have some level of metal content such as copper. It has to be disposed of… properly.

After the distillation of the low wines, we are left with what many people confusingly refer to as "spent lees." "Lees" would typically refer to yeast dropped out of from fermentation, but confusingly that's not what "spent lees" is referencing. It is simply the term for the dealcoholized liquid left in the still after the low wines have been distilled into spirit. Fractious nomenclatural issues aside, spent lees is a dilute liquid composed of organic acids and higher alcohols. It must also be handled in the proper way.

	Pot Ale	Spent Lees
COD (mg/L)	50,000–75,000	1,500–4,000
BOD (mg/L)	25,000–35,000	500–2,000
SO_4^{2-} (mg/L)	100–450	<40
PO_4^{3-} (mg/L)	150–600	<0.5
Copper (mg/L)	2–12	8-50
Solids (%wt/wt)	4–7	0.02–0.175
Total N (mg/L)	2,000–4,000	100–150

Table 6. Typical composition of pot ale and spent lees (Bennett, 2015)

The table above details typical compositions for pot ale and spent lees in a malt whisky distillery. These values will vary somewhat between different distilleries and the different spirits being produced. However, these figures give us a nice grounding point to work with.

Most municipal water companies will place some kind of limits on the quantity and quality of your distillery effluent. It varies between municipality, but you may come across rules regarding the following effluent parameters:

- Total Solids
- pH
- Volume per day
- Volume per dump/Instantaneous flow
- Chemical Oxygen Demand (COD)
- Biological Oxygen Demand (BOD)
- Temperature
- Metal content
- Chemical content (controlling for things such as methanol)

Failing to meet these specifications can result in heavy fines or even temporary shutdowns.

In order to meet any proposed specifications, you will likely need to treat your effluent in some way or another. And there are generally three levels of treatment.

Primary treatments are practiced by virtually all distilleries, big and small. These effluent treatments involve taking care of the core basic parameters such as effluent temperature, pH and solids loading.

Effluent Temperature

In small distilleries temperature can be handled quite simply in most cases. A lot of sewer systems can't or don't want to handle large amounts of near-boiling liquid, so an effort to cool things down is usually in order. I've seen this manifested in dumping the stillage into tanks or IBC totes and letting it sit over night to cool down. In some cases when there isn't a concern on volume for the municipal system, I've seen distillers simply run cold water down the drain along with the stillage to instantly cool the liquid down to acceptable levels.

Solids Reduction

If you are producing spirits distilled from washes with high solids contents such as American whiskies like bourbon or rye, then you'll likely need to strain out much of the solids prior to liquid disposal. Stillage from these spirits often contains around 7–8% solid material

(Hickey & Motylewski, 2006). All those grain solids are usually way too much for water treatment plants to handle.

There are a couple of ways to reduce the solids content of stillage. Many of the most common methods are simply industrial strainers where the solids heavy stillage enters a container and a screen inside strains out the solids which can be collected separately and dried. The strained water exits through a different pipe and can then go down the drain or onto more treatment stations.

Other options for high solids stillage, especially with grain-based liquids is to turn it into a co-product such as feed for livestock. I've seen distillers simply take the stillage straight from the still, put it into a tote and let the farmer take it away to deal with and treat as they see fit. This is OK, but not great. Smaller distilleries can occasionally get away with this type of program because of the smaller volumes. But even they will often have a hard time finding a farmer who wants to deal with that much liquid. Trust me: most farmers want to feed solid food to their animals, not watered-down slop. Larger firms know this and generally build entire operations around the production of distiller's dried grains (DDG).

DDG production can be done a multitude of ways. It was common at one point to use large centrifuges to settle out the solids and separate much of the water. This reduces the water content of the solids to below 10%. Other technologies involve running the stillage through a screw press, producing a wet cake of stillage solids which can then be sent to a dry house for further water removal.

Of course, we can't talk about stillage without mentioning the sour mash process. The technique of using a volume of stillage and adding it to the next mash (at a rate of 15–40%) is well-known throughout the whiskey and rum communities. It has a few standout benefits such as adding nutrients to the next fermentation, reducing mash/wash pH to inhibit bacterial contamination and batch flavor consistency. The very practice does reduce water usage and effluent discharge, though in many spirit categories such as malt whisky and brandy, the technique is less useful due to the lower levels of solids in the stillage and hence fewer nutrients. (Malt mashes are typically nutrient rich and adding nutrients can actually adversely increase things such as higher alcohol production.)

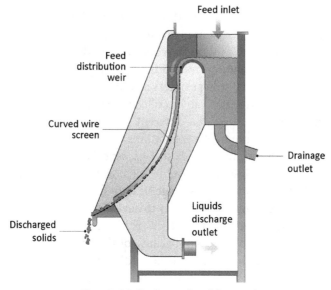

Figure 7-6. Inclined screen for solids removal
(Used with permission and copyright of the Institute of Brewing & Distilling)

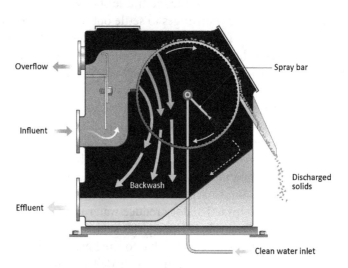

Figure 7-7. Basic rotary drum screen for solids removal
(Used with permission and copyright of the Institute of Brewing & Distilling)

Regardless of the method, if you have high solids in your stillage, then you need to consider the most responsible and cost-effective way of removing them prior to disposing of the water. There are many companies out there that specialize in this kind of thing, and they usually offer a slew of solutions that will work for your distillery and your local regulators.

pH Adjustment

The pH of stillage is often around 4.0–4.5 for whisky distilleries and sometimes even lower for other more acidic spirits such as brandy. Talk with your local water authority as to whether the pH of your stillage needs to be adjusted.

For many smaller distillers, this is rarely an issue. However, for larger plants an intermediary pH adjustment tank may be necessary. The pH of the stillage can be raised through the addition of any number of suitable food-grade bases such as caustic soda. However, cleaning effluent that has used caustic as the detergent has the opposite problem in that the pH may be too high. In this case the effluent will need to be treated with an acid. In large plants that have the capability, carbon dioxide from fermentations can be bubbled into the high pH wastewater which will neutralize the caustic and bring the pH down to suitable levels.

Further Treatments

There are quite a few options for distilleries to further treat their distillery waste. In recent decades many distilleries have implemented anaerobic digestion systems which utilize bacteria to breakdown the effluent into biogas and smaller amounts of "sludge." The sludge can be relatively easy to dispose of and the biogas can be piped back into the distillery and used as an energy source such as a fuel for your boiler.

Beyond that there are multiple types of water recycling and collection systems to reduce overall water usage. The science and engineering behind all these different treatment options is really impressive and as your distillery grows it may be worth your time and money to speak with one of the many companies that provide these systems to see what will work best for you in your area.

Cleaning the still

For all our talk about basic distillation operations and alcohol recovery, we really shouldn't leave this chapter without quickly discussing the cleaning of your still. There are two primary reasons for maintaining a clean still:

- Organoleptic quality of the distillate
- Heat efficiency of the still

The organoleptic (sensory) quality of your distillate can be heavily impacted by the cleanliness of your still. First, if you have large amounts of solids and/or oils caked on to the various pipings and pot of the still, then you are lessoning the available surface area for copper contact. As such, your spirit may have increased sulfur contents.

Some of the caked-on compounds can leach into the liquid you are distilling and come over during distillation. These compounds may have been changed and negatively impacted by being subjected to so much heat over time that their existence in your distillate may contribute some flaws. Where this can be a huge problem is with small distillers who use their stills to make a multitude of spirits such as gin and whisky. The oils from the botanicals in gin can coat the surfaces inside the still and then pass into the liquid of a different spirit, giving botanical notes where they may not be desired.

Another reason for keeping the still clean is the heat efficiency. Any surface that is supposed to radiate heat to the liquid in the pot cannot be effective at its job if it is covered by layers of built-up oils, sugars, lipids and proteins from previous distillations. I've already mentioned the trouble that can occur in some stills with the use of anti-foam compounds causing precipitation of various solids that can coat heating elements and drop the heat efficiency. If your heat efficiency goes down, you will see increased distillation times and changes in the amount of internal reflux that naturally occurs in your still.

So, how should you clean your still and how often?

Multiple theories, procedures and opinions on the subject abound. Here are my thoughts, but certainly talk with other distillers to get their opinions and processes as well.

First off, the frequency. In my distillery, we do a full clean on the whisky still after every two wash distillations and one spirit distillation. That's where we do a complete CIP cycle on the inside of the pot with a 1–2% w/w citric acid solution (dependent on the amount of soiling). After every single distillation however, we simply spray out the still with warm water and remove as much soiling as possible.

These are not hard and fast numbers in our distillery. If the still is running well and looks clean, we don't bother. But generally, we're cleaning the still 3–4 times per week on average.

Our procedure is simple.

- Mix together a 1–2% citric acid solution into hot water (70-80°C). This works out to 10–20 g (1/3 – 2/3 oz) per liter of water. For heavier soiling we err on the higher end of the range.
- Circulate the citric acid solution through a rotating spray ball in the center of the pot for 30 minutes.
- Rinse with warm water and spray out any excess loose soils.

Be careful with the amount of citric acid you use. You don't need much. Too much can potentially damage the copper over time.

Some people like to use a small amount of caustic solution prior to acid washing to remove organic soils. I don't generally do this, but if you feel so inclined, just be sure that the caustic compound you are using doesn't damage copper. If you aren't sure, ask your supplier. If they don't know or you can't otherwise find an answer, move on to a different compound that you do know is safe. Some caustics can cause serious damage to copper inside of the still.

Troubleshooting

There will be times when things just don't seem to go right. Try hard as you might, not every distillation is going to be perfect. That is just the way of things. However, by taking proper notes and referring back to them when needed, you can be better prepared to solve issues and problems should they arise. The following items are by no means exhaustive, but they are some of the more common issues that occasionally pop-up during distillation. I'll do my best to offer some troubleshooting advice to get you through a few of these issues.

Distillation too slow/too fast

As I've mentioned previously, distillation speed can have a huge impact on the quality of your spirit. The exact speed you need (which I usually base on the distillate flow rate) is going to be largely based on the type of equipment you are using, the techniques you are employing, and your desired spirit character.

Eventually, you will have a good understanding of what your distillate flow rate should be. And if there is a deviation from that flow rate when all normal procedures have been followed, you need to understand what to do.

In the case of a slow distillation speed, there are typically three common culprits.

1. Heat is too low.
2. Condenser is too cold.
3. Heating elements are dirty.

First, check to see what your heat settings are. Assuming you've followed your normal procedures, and everything looks as it should, you may need to check your heat supply source. Perhaps your steam boiler has had a pressure drop (which then requires its own set of troubleshooting). Maybe the propane tank that supplies your direct-fired pot is empty, or you forgot to pay the natural gas bill. (Hey, it happens.) If everything looks normal, then move onto the cooling side of things.

Check your condenser temperature. If you have a lyne arm that is angled upwards towards the condenser then a cooler than normal condenser temperature may slow your distillation down. Dial back the cooling. Check the incoming coolant temperature to see if it is cooler than normal. If so, then try to figure out why that is. Condensers that use ground water or municipal water supplies will have to contend with cooler temperatures during colder months of the year as the water supply temperature naturally drops.

Finally, if everything in your cooling and heating looks ok then the issue is likely that you have a dirty still. When the heating elements or jackets develop a layer of built-up proteins, lipids, sugars, or other fouling, they will not radiate heat to the liquid inside the still as efficiently. The best thing you can do is to clean your still frequently and don't allow the heating elements to get fouled in the first place. Avoid the use of too much silicone-based anti-foam compounds inside copper stills as they seem to promote fouled build-up on heating surfaces. Don't turn off the heat to the still unless the distillation is done as in some stills this also seems to cause substances to settle and foul the heat surfaces. If you do have to turn off the heat for some reason before the run is over, make sure you have an agitator running to keep everything in suspension as much as possible.

However, if you find yourself in this situation where you are already in the process of distilling, your only recourse is to simply ride it out and clean the still thoroughly after the fact. In extreme situations you can stop the distillation, pump out the liquid and clean the still, but that's hard to do in many operations.

There are occasions where your distillation may be going faster than normal. Granted this is rarer a problem than the distillation going too slow, and in some cases, it may not even be deemed a problem. However, too fast of a distillation speed can cause quality issues so it is best to investigate if something seems amiss.

As with the distillation being too slow, you'll want to check your heat and cooling. Look to see if your heat settings are where they should be. If they look fine, then check to see if something has changed with your heat source. Is your boiler working at a higher pressure than normal? Is your propane burner somehow burning hotter than it should? These are things you'll want to figure out.

If the heat is fine, then check your condenser. It is possible that the condenser is not cooling properly. Turn up the flow to the condenser to see if that helps. Look at the incoming coolant temperature to see if there is a variation from the normal temperature. During hotter months of the year in many areas the ground water gets warmer. This may affect the cooling power of your condenser. If that's the case, then the best solution is to simply dial back your heat to compensate.

Distillate too hot/too cold

The ideal temperature of your distillate coming off the still whether it be low wines or actual spirit is around 20°C (68°F). A few degrees in either direction is not dire, but ideally you keep things tightly centered around 20°C.

If your distillate is too hot, then check your condenser. Make sure the settings are correct and that you have the correct coolant temperature and flow rate. Adjust if necessary. You may need to dial back the heat a bit on the still if your condenser for whatever reason can't easily be adjusted.

If the distillate is coming out too cold… well, that may not seem like much of a problem to some folks. What's the harm, right? The issue is really of efficiency. If the distillate is too cold, then you are likely using more water and order power to cool your condenser than is necessary. That can get expensive fast. Dial it back a bit. However, there is potentially a quality issue, here as well. With the condenser working overdrive, you may be condensing the vapors too quickly and not getting the right amount of vapor interaction with the copper which can produce more sulfur notes in the spirit.

In this situation I would not necessarily push the heat harder to compensate. By increasing the heat you'll change some of the internal chemical and physical dynamics inside the still such as lowering reflux and pushing more sulfur compounds through. Best to leave the heat alone in this instance and deal with the cooling only.

Higher/Lower yield than expected

The importance of understanding your expected yield is huge in the distillery. You need to know what you're going to get out of every process you implement and if your yield somehow deviates away from the expected value, you can then take appropriate steps to investigate. The amount of tolerance for deviation is something you have to decide for yourself. For me, I tend to look hard at the numbers if the deviation is anything above 1–2% in liters of absolute alcohol.

Yield can vary one of two ways. It can be higher than expected or it can be lower than expected. Let's tackle the issue of higher yields first.

It might seem like a higher-than-expected yield would be cause for celebration and not, you know, *a problem*. And that's possibly true in some instances, but you have to immediately ask yourself three questions when this happens: Is the distillate of the same quality? Why did it happen? Can I repeat it?

Sometimes a larger yield may be due to something unfortunate such as an employee forgetting to cut to tails at the right time. In this case, the quality of the spirit would almost certainly suffer, and you would want to take steps to remediate and prevent such situations in the future.

However, perhaps you've struck gold and really hit the quality vs quantity jackpot. Maybe you really did get a higher yield and the spirit quality is still high. Why did it happen? It could be an issue of running the still at a slower rate and getting better separation, thus increasing the amount of good alcohol you get at the end. Of course, this would certainly mean the character of the spirit has changed in some way and you would need to accurately assess whether it really is for the better and how the customer will perceive it.

Maybe the yield of your fermentations is higher. You will only know this if you've kept thorough notes of all your procedures.

Finally, can you repeat the yield? Well, if you can't repeat it, then there is little reason to get excited about any supposed break throughs. Regardless, a sudden increase in yield should always be treated with a little bit of caution and the quality should always be assessed against your expected standard distillate to ensure nothing has changed.

The more common problem is that of a lower yield. Once again, similar questions need to be asked. What is the effect on quality? Why did it happen? And finally, how can you prevent this from happening in the future?

There are all kinds of reasons for a drop in yield.

When this situation occurs, I try to think procedurally backwards. I start with the distillation itself. Were there any parameters that were out of normal spec during the process such as heating and cooling? For instance, not enough cooling in the condenser can cause evaporative alcohol losses. Obviously, this is where taking good notes can come in handy.

If the distillation was fine, the next line of investigation for me is the fermentation. What was the finishing and starting gravity of the wash? Was the fermentation temperature acceptable? Were there any signs of microbial contamination that might cost me some alcohol? Was the gravity and/or pH drop over the fermentation a normal curve or did it deviate from the standard?

If the fermentation looked ok, then I move back to processing and the raw materials themselves. I'll check to see if there was anything different about the material lot that I was using. Were the materials processed in the correct way using standard procedures and methods?

Truthfully, it's rare that I have to go this far back for anything. In fact, if you have been taking good notes and readings throughout your processes, you should be able to predict ahead of time if there is going to be a distillation yield issue by simply paying attention to variations in raw materials and processing. Admittedly, that level of distillation soothsaying requires a certain level of experience but as you progress with you distilling education, you will begin to see the patterns of these processes and get better at making the big judgement calls.

Cloudy or colored distillate

There are a few instances where you will come across a cloudy looking spirit. Many types of low wines, for instance, are naturally a bit cloudy looking due to their high oil or fatty acid contents and lower alcohol concentrations. In many instances it is nothing to worry about.

Of course, if your product spirit is cloudy then you might have cause for concern. The most common distillation that I see cloudy spirit in is with gin (or other botanical spirits). The essential oils in the botanicals can throw a slight translucent haze, particularly those that come over in the still near the end of the distillation. If your gin spirit appears cloudy then you likely need to adjust your cut point and fraction from hearts to tails earlier. You may be able to filter the spirit to correct the haze, but this will invariably change the spirit character. You're better off starting over in many instances.

Sometimes you may come across a distillate with a slight tint of color. This is most often either a yellow or green to bluish green color.

Blue green is usually associated with copper sulphate salts being rinsed into the distillate from condenser piping. They generally come over early in the distillation in the heads fraction and are usually not a concern by the time the hearts fraction rolls around.

You may also encounter a slight yellow or green hue in the heads of some spirits. I've seen this with rum and whisky and have heard about it occurring with other spirits. There are a few possibilities. It could be from the still not being thoroughly cleaned. It could also be from a small amount of foam over in the still from the wash. In either instance if the problem persists into the hearts of the spirit then you may need to redistill.

Feinty/Heady aromas in distillate

Feinty or heady aromas in the distillate would obviously come from fractioning or smearing issues. Look through your distillation notes to see if the cuts were made at the appropriate points. If they were then it is possible there was too much heat being applied or not enough cooling. This could cause a congener smearing effect in the distillate with various fractions bleeding into each other.

If everything about the distillation looks right, then something has changed in your processes prior to distillation. This could be from a higher alcohol fermentation or out of whack fermentation temperatures. Maybe there were issues with your yeast strain(s). Perhaps something changed you're your raw materials. High levels of nitrogen in your raw materials can cause an increase in higher alcohol production, for instance. This would in turn lead to greater concentrations of things such as iso-amyl alcohol contributing to the character of your spirit.

Alcohol concentration too high/too low

When my guys come to me with a tank reading for our whisky tails that says something like 65% abv, I tell them to go mix up the tank and take the reading again. This is because I KNOW what it SHOULD be (which is ~39% abv).

At some point you will get a distillate reading that is either too high or too low from the norm. And sometimes it really is that simple. The tank just needs to be properly mixed and a new reading taken. As the distillate pours forth into the tank, the steadily decreasing alcohol concentration of the spirit doesn't usually mix perfectly in the receiving vessel. It's a good idea to mix up the liquid through agitation or manual stirring to ensure that the alcohol concentration is even throughout the entire tank. Otherwise, you risk sampling a "pocket" of alcohol that reads a different concentration than the average of the entire tank.

Now, what if you've mixed everything up to kingdom come and taken the reading a hundred times and the abv is still out of spec? Well, then you need to do some more investigative work.

Chances are a fraction was taken improperly giving your spirit cut an out of spec reading. If that turns out to not be the case, then I would look at how the heating and cooling settings were made on the still. Running the still too slowly could increase reflux and may have the end result of increasing the alcohol concentration in the final distillate in some instances.

For cases of having an alcohol concentration that is too low, you might find that you didn't get enough reflux. In the case of wash distillations that produce low wines, a low alcohol concentration is usually indicative of a lower-than-normal alcohol percentage in the wash, perhaps from a lower starting gravity or an incomplete fermentation.

Particulates in the distillate

You might occasionally run the still and find that the final spirit has small flecks of particulate matter in it. This is usually one of two things: copper from the still being worn and washed into the distillate or solid wash material riding the vapors through the condenser. Of these two my experience is that the latter is more common, especially in grain-based distilleries.

If you have a large amount of foaming in your still, solid material from the foam can collect on the walls of plates and piping. The rising vapors can take some of these particulates and carry them on through the condenser. While not pretty, they are largely harmless and assuming they are not excessive, they are usually not worth worrying too much about. Clean your still thoroughly and you should see them go away.

If your still is as clean as can be and yet you are still seeing particulates in the spirit, then you may have small amounts of copper coming over. This can actually be the result of *too much cleaning*. Usually this occurs when you are using too strong of an acid solution to clean the copper. Check your cleaning formulation to make sure you are using the proper amount of citric acid and dial it back if necessary. The acid can eat away at the copper over time and while it is rare, this cleaned and worn copper can come over as visible flecks into the distillate.

You'll notice that in this troubleshooting section, I have spoken more in generalities and problem-solving directions rather than give you specifics. This is not me being lazy or purposefully vague. It is my way of trying to show you how I think through these occasional issues. However, if there is a pervasive theme throughout this section, it's that taking good notes throughout your production process is the only way to know where to look if you have a problem.

In the next chapter we are going to begin discussing specific techniques for batch distillation with plates and hybrid stills. The first thing we are going to discuss is arguably one of the more difficult distillation types to effectively manage: the production of neutral spirit.

Chapter 8

Batch Distillation Techniques Using Hybrid Stills for Vodka and Other Spirits

Neutral spirit and vodka are by definition "neutral." They should have no discernible taste or smell other than alcohol. Of course, the modern distillation landscape has offered up a lot of interpretations for what "neutral" actually means. Nowadays it is not uncommon to see "neutral" spirits with a little bit of, dare I say, character to them. These spirits are offering refreshing hints of aroma, flavor and mouthfeel to what has for decades been an industry of criminal banality.

The amount of "character" you allow in your neutral spirit is a choice that only you can make as a distiller. To a large extent this has a lot to do with where you are operating your distillery. If you are in the EU, then you have the following regulations to answer to:

Ethyl alcohol of agricultural origin*

Ethyl alcohol of agricultural origin possesses the following properties:

(a) organoleptic characteristics: no detectable taste other than that of the raw material;

(b) minimum alcoholic strength by volume: 96.0 %;

(c) maximum level of residues:

(i) total acidity, expressed in grams of acetic acid per hectolitre of 100 % vol. alcohol: 1.5

(ii) esters expressed in grams of ethyl acetate per hectolitre of 100 % vol. alcohol: 1.3

(iii) *aldehydes expressed in grams of acetaldehyde per hectolitre of 100 % vol. alcohol: 0.5*

(iv) *higher alcohols expressed in grams of methyl2 propanol1 per hectolitre of 100 % vol. alcohol: 0.5*

(v) *methanol expressed in grams per hectolitre of 100 % vol. alcohol: 30*

(vi) *dry extract expressed in grams per hectolitre of 100 % vol. alcohol: 1.5*

(vii) *volatile bases containing nitrogen expressed in grams of nitrogen per hectolitre of 100 % vol. alcohol: 0.1*

(viii) *furfural: not detectable*

*Ethyl alcohol of agricultural origin is the EU's clumsy name for neutral spirit.

In the EU, vodka is defined thus:

(a) *Vodka is a spirit drink produced from ethyl alcohol of agricultural origin obtained following fermentation with yeast from either:*

(i) *potatoes and/or cereals, or*

(ii) *other agricultural raw materials, distilled and/or rectified so that the organoleptic characteristics of the raw materials used, and by-products formed in fermentation are selectively reduced.*

This process may be followed by redistillation and/or treatment with appropriate processing aids, including treatment with activated charcoal, to give it special organoleptic characteristics.

Maximum levels of residue for ethyl alcohol of agricultural origin shall meet those laid down in Annex I, except that the methanol content shall not exceed 10 grams per hectolitre of 100 % vol. alcohol.

(b) *The minimum alcoholic strength by volume of vodka shall be 37.5 %.*

(c) The only flavourings which may be added are natural flavouring compounds present in distillate obtained from the fermented raw materials. In addition, the product may be given special organoleptic characteristics, other than a predominant flavour.

(d) The description, presentation or labelling of vodka not produced exclusively from the raw material(s) listed in paragraph (a)(i) shall bear the indication 'produced from ...', supplemented by the name of the raw material(s) used to produce the ethyl alcohol of agricultural origin. Labelling shall be in accordance with Article 13(2) of Directive 2000/13/EC.

If you live in the United States, then neutral spirit is defined by the Tax and Trade Bureau as:

Spirits distilled from any material at or above 95% alcohol by volume (190 proof), and if bottled, bottled at not less than 40% alcohol by volume (80 proof)

With the definition of vodka addended to it as:

Neutral spirits distilled or treated after distillation with charcoal or other materials so as to be without distinctive character, aroma, taste or color

Regardless of where you operate your distillery, you should have a thorough understanding of what regulations you must adhere to in order to hit your spirit style targets. The EU definitions for neutral spirit are stricter in many ways than the ones in the United States. And while there is a lot of room to experiment and interpret some of the rules, the mere fact that the minimum alcohol concentration for neutral spirit in the EU is 96% while it's only 95% in the U.S. should give you pause.

A 1% abv difference may not seem like much but in the world of distilling neutral spirit, it's huge. That one percent increase in the EU typically sees a massive reduction in character and congeners compared to the US definition.

Now, it is true that most neutral spirit in the world is produced on large industrial continuous column stills with a zillion plates, fusel oil decanters, multitudes of columns and more. This is the most efficient and cost-effective method of producing neutral spirit. It argua-bly produces a *better* neutral spirit as well assuming your definition of neutral coincides with that of the big brand manufacturers. With these systems you have more options for the near complete remov-al of most congeners. And the sheer economy of the massive scale means you won't pay an arm and a leg per liter.

Most neutral spirit used by distillers both large and small is purchased from distilleries like this. The purchasing distillery gets a truly neutral character spirit that they can then use to make gin, bitters, liqueurs and more. And all they had to do was pick up the phone and place an order. No physical labor required.

However, these days there are growing numbers of distillers who are opting to take the arduous road less traveled and produce their own neutral spirit/vodka from scratch. Many of them are doing it on hybrid pot stills in a batch process. These distillers want total control over their spirit's flavor and process and the only way to truly do that is to do everything themselves.

I have spent several years making neutral spirit for vodka, gin and liqueurs in my distilleries. I've always produced it from grain that I've mashed, fermented and distilled on my own. It's a lot more work and certainly more expensive, but for me the effort is totally worth it. Other distillers agree with me. My friend Kirsty Black who heads up Arbikie Distillery in Scotland makes an incredible potato vodka straight from the spud. Could she make her life easier and purchase bulk alcohol from a larger supplier? Certainly. Would she be as happy with the results? I seriously doubt it.

Yes, it is cheaper to simply purchase neutral alcohol from the large continuous distilleries operating throughout the EU and North America. There is absolutely nothing wrong with doing that. You get a great product and eliminate a lot of hassle and pain from your production process. However, if you are like me and a growing list of DIY oriented distillers looking to take total control of your produc-tion processes and flavors then come join us in the world of neutral spirit production. It's not easy, but I promise that it is rewarding.

This chapter will outline some of the equipment, techniques and methods for producing neutral spirit from fermented wash in your distillery.

Goals, Expectations and Equipment

Neutral spirit, despite its ubiquity, is actually a fairly difficult spirit to produce. Even more so if you want to produce it *well*. It helps to set up some realistic goals and expectations.

Remember: we are using a hybrid pot still with these distillations. This is not a book about continuous distillation processes and equipment. As such we have a relatively limited equipment set available to us. There is no fusel oil decanter, and you aren't likely going to have more than 40 plates in your column(s). (You certainly can get more columns and plates, but this is something that costs quite a bit of money and you will need to discuss it with your chosen manufacturer.) In other words, you are simply not going to be able to produce something as clean and neutral as Smirnoff Vodka on a pot still. But if you are interested in making your own neutral spirit then chances are your goal isn't to make something as neutral as Smirnoff. You probably want something with a little bit of character in it.

So, we know that our neutral spirit might be stretching the definition of "neutral" a bit, and we're good with that. What about the alcohol concentration? Remember that in the EU we need to start with 96% abv and in the U.S. we can do 95% abv. This one percent is actually a tricky increase for a still. If you need to produce 96% abv neutral spirit, then I would argue that you need at least 40 plates. You can go down to as few as 20 if you only need to produce 95% alcohol. The number of plates is going to be dictated in part by the efficiency of their rectification elements. Bubble cap trays are more efficient than many other tray elements, but they cost more. You could probably get to 95% abv using sieve trays which are less expensive, but you're going to need a lot more of them so the price may actually be more than you expect.

You also need to consider the footprint of your hybrid still. It is energetically and spatially more efficient to use a single tall column. This design is also easier to control during the distillation process. But a single column can be prohibitively tall, and your distillery may not have the ceiling height to accommodate it. Far more common is to break up your total tray needs into several separate columns standing next to each other. This takes up a larger distillery footprint but at least you won't have to cut open the roof to make it work. Once again, work with your manufacturer to decide on the best options for your distillery.

For this chapter I am going to make a few assumptions.

First, I'm assuming you want to produce something fairly neutral at 95.5% abv. Obviously, this would not be considered neutral spirit in the EU. However, it will make a spirit quite suitable for gin production and liqueurs.

Second, I'll assume that you have a dual column hybrid pot still. This is a fairly common kit design for many distilleries venturing into neutral spirit production. The size, type and number of plates are really not that important for the purpose of discussing the techniques in this chapter. These techniques can be easily adapted for one or three columns (or more if you have such a system).

Basic Hybrid Still Operations

You have a few choices to make when distilling neutral spirit. First, you need to decide if you are going to distill to 95.5% abv directly from your fermented wash or if you will do an intermediate stripping run before the neutral spirit distillation.

I know a few folks that go with the first route. They argue that distilling neutral spirit from wash means fewer distillation cycles and therefore less time. Honestly, I've never been completely convinced by this argument. Certainly, by distilling the wash straight up to 95% plus you are limiting cycles, but in order to reach such a high abv from a comparatively low alcohol concentration you have to distill at a slower pace to ensure the right amount of rectification occurs (and also to limit the risk of foam over into the column). In contrast, by doing a series of relatively fast stripping distillations of the wash, collecting the subsequent low wines and distilling them together for one large batch of spirit, you may end up spending the same amount of time and the distillations will be easier to control.

This is the method that I use for my neutral spirit production and it is what I suggest most people to use when starting out with these distillations. Once you have some experience working with the equipment and the techniques you can more easily attempt to cut out the stripping distillation and see which route you prefer.

For most twin column systems, the initial low wine strength in the pot should be between 20–30%. The fewer plates you have, the higher in that range you should shoot for. It will make reaching your target alcohol concentration a lot easier. On my 20-plate system I often start with low wines at roughly 23% abv and we have little issue hitting our target of 95% abv. However, if I was shooting for 95.5% abv or more, then I would try to use a stronger low wine (or add more plates to my system, but that costs a lot of money).

So, we've got our low wine of ~20–30% abv inside the pot of our two column still. Turn the heat on to the still. You can run a motorized agitator if you have one during the heat up phase to speed things along. Just remember to turn it off (or reduce the speed to low) when the distillation is about to begin. Make sure that all your plates are active (if they are able to be toggled "on" and "off"). Also, check to ensure that any pot return piping valves from the individual columns are open. We want to make sure the reflux from the columns can properly drain back into the pot.

While things are heating up, we should take a quick look at the components of the still to better understand how these distillations operate. First, for these distillations, it is absolutely crucial that you have multiple thermometer probes installed throughout the system. At a minimum you should have probes in the following parts of the still:

- Pot
- Lyne arm
- Column #1 top plate
- Column #1 vapor
- Column #2 top plate
- Column #2 vapor
- Spirit pipe

Other areas that may prove beneficial to have a temperature probe would include the dephlegmator in and out piping as well as the primary condenser.

The other thing you should look at is the coolant streams running into the dephlegmator. You should have individual valves for both pre-condensers and your main condenser to control the amount of

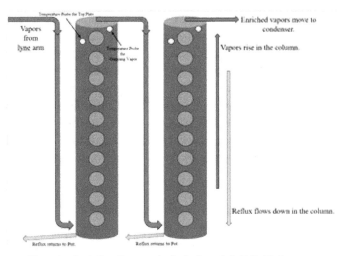

Figure 8-1. Basic flow diagram of a dual column hybrid distillation system
(Note: pre-condensers have been removed for ease of understanding)

cooling going to each column. Ideally, you also have a small flow meter installed on the inlet piping of each cooling line. This is so that you have a real time number from which to gauge you cooling abilities. For a myriad of reasons, coolant flow rates can change during the distillation and you need to make sure that your cooling ability stays as constant as possible throughout the duration of the run.

This is perhaps the most important point surrounding the use of a column for batch distillation. Like their continuous patent still cousins, these systems work best under solid-state conditions. This means that variations in the cooling and heating should be kept to a minimum. The reasons for this will become more apparent as we move forward in this chapter. For now, we can say that obviously changes to cooling and heating will likely have to be made throughout the distillation on most systems. However, you should try to make these changes as slowly and as delicately as possible so as to not upset the internal balance of the columns.

We need a base temperature to use as a reference for when and where to make certain decisions. Since we're doing a neutral spirit distillation the easiest temperature to use would be the boiling point of pure ethanol (78.4°C/173.1°F). Of course, we know that we aren't distilling *pure* ethanol, but if we do our job right, we will get fairly close.

With that in mind, we will know that our distillation is about to start when the pot temperature reaches 78.4°C. At this point we want to dial the heat back down. How far the heat needs to be turned down really depends on the system and some experimentation will usually be in order.

> It is totally normal for these neutral spirit distillations to require several runs to get your settings dialed in. There are usually so many variables and valves to play with that it is rare the first distillation ever goes exactly how you want it to. These distillations beg for constant tweaking, but once you do find the proper settings, you can generally count on good consistency and repeatability with the subsequent distillations.

Once your heat is turned down, go ahead and turn on the coolant lines to the pre-condensers and the primary condenser. Now, why would you want to turn on the primary condenser if we still haven't had anything go through our columns yet? It's because unless your condenser is operated on a cooling system completely separate from the pre-condensers, any change in condenser flow will affect their flow as well. So, if you wait to turn on the main condenser until after the columns have equilibrated, you are going to reduce their cooling which will quickly upset the balance of your system.

If this is the first distillation on the system, turn up the cooling all the way to each condenser in the system. We will dial them in as the distillation proceeds.

Once the pot reaches the boiling point of ethanol, it won't be long for initial vapors to begin flowing through the lyne arm. Shortly after that you will begin to see small amounts of liquid pooling into the base of column one. (Each column should have a base chamber below the bottom plate. This is where vapor from the lyne arm will enter the column. The base chamber has a pipe that drains back into the pot. As vapors from the lyne arm are pushed into the base chamber, they are initially cooled by ambient air temperature and the natural temperature differential from the cool metal of the column. Hence why you should be able to see liquid forming in this section at the beginning of the distillation.)

A few moments later you will notice that the temperature of the top column plate will begin to rise. If you look inside the port glass on the top plate you will see droplets of liquid coming down onto the plate from the column "ceiling." This is the result of the pre-condenser in column one doing its job. It acts as a cooling barrier to keep the hot vapors from moving forward into the second column. That's a good thing because before vapors begin moving heavily into column two, we want to make sure that we are getting good levels of reflux in column one.

After a minute or two you should see the liquid level on the top plate of column rise above the weir. The plate will look active with lots of liquid movement and flow. Liquid can now flow down through the downcomer pipe onto the plate below. After a brief minute, this plate will also fill and become active. The process of filling and draining onto the plate beneath will continue until we reach the bottom plate. At this point all plates should have an active layer of liquid sloshing around and draining back down lower in the column. The liquid draining back down is reflux and the sloshing is the result of the constant stream of hot vapors pushing up from beneath. This allows for vapor and liquid to properly mix, exchange heat and produce more reflux.

Once all the plates have been properly "stacked" you can begin to slowly reduce the cooling on column one. Think of this as slowly opening a water dam. You want the vapors rising up to ever so gently begin to push over into column two. Similar to column one, when this happens you will begin to see some liquid trickle into the base chamber of column two.

From here, the program is the same as before. After a few moments we will hopefully see the temperature probe on the top plate of column two rise indicating the vapors have reached the upper portion of the column. As before, the plates should stack themselves going from top to bottom.

Once all plates on both columns are loaded, set a timer. You need to wait for both columns to completely stabilize after reaching full reflux. How long should you wait? There is some debate here and factors such as starting abv in the still, heating levels and coolant availability all play a role. However, I find that thirty minutes does the job nicely.

After you've allowed the columns to equilibrate, you can begin to slowly dial back the cooling on column two. Do this slowly over the course of several minutes. Eventually you'll notice that the vapor temperature in column two begins to rise meaning the most volatile vapors are beginning to move towards the condenser. In fact, these first vapors should have a temperature somewhat lower than 78.4°C, more likely around 65°C. (Unsurprisingly since methanol has a boiling point of 64.7°C and it forms a not insignificant portion of the first distillate fraction.)

It helps to pay attention to several of your thermometers at this point. The most important ones to follow are the probes on the column top plates and the vapor probes at the top of the column. **The temperature of the vapor probes should be lower than the temperature on the top plate.** Depending on the system (and the accuracy of your thermometers) the difference may be slight. The vapors should be cooler than the plate beneath them because you are trying to evolve the most volatile (lower boiling point) compounds and move them to the next point in the distillation system. In the case of the final plate on my second column when I distill neutral spirit, I will typically see a plate temperature of 78.7°C and a temp of 78.5°C on the outgoing vapor. That small difference is huge in terms of spirit quality. If the vapors register as hotter than the plate temperature, then you have some smearing from higher boiling point compounds getting into your precious distillate. You'll need to increase the cooling on your pre-condenser(s) to get everything back in check.

This being a neutral spirit distillation you will note that the outcoming spirit has a high alcohol concentration. It will start low and rapidly get higher as more ethanol begins to come over from column two. Once the spirit smells clean and you are above 95% abv you should feel comfortable cutting over to hearts. The heads in these distillations are usually so riddled with methanol and ketones that they aren't worth keeping. I personally choose to dispose of them.

The hearts are allowed to continue unabated until the alcohol concentration dips below 95% abv. You can then cut to tails. The tails can be collected until 60-30% abv. The actual cut point is often decided based on the sensory qualities of the outcoming spirit. You'll find the tails for these distillations to be quite pungent so use your best judgement. Without the aid of things such as a fusel oil decanter there is not a great way to recover every last drop of pure alcohol in these distillations. However, much of the tails can be redistilled so the overall alcohol loss is somewhat minimized in the end.

You should also notice around the point of when you cut to tails that the temperature in the pot is incredibly high. On most systems it will be close to (if not right at or even above) 100°C. This is because virtually all the alcohol has evolved off from the pot and is now in the column(s). I actually use the pot temperature as one of several indicators for when my tails cut may be getting near.

From start to finish, these distillations often take 8–12 hours. That's quite a bit longer than a typical pot still run, but the added time is usually necessary. You need to be able to get ample separation of ethanol and congeners in order to reach the desired alcohol concentration.

Distillation Management and Troubleshooting

If there was ever a distillation that I would call "hands on" it would definitely be the two-column neutral spirit batch distillation. For most systems, you will find that you can't really leave the distillation space. The still must always be watched for signs of potential problems. Once you've done this distillation enough times, you'll be able to point out general trends and indicators that announce an impending issue. Learning to recognize these things early on will allow you to make meaningful changes to the distillation parameters to ensure that a problem never has the chance to start. It takes a lot of practice and experience to be able to make these kinds of judgement calls. Nothing I write can fully prepare you to run a neutral spirit distillation absolutely perfectly on the first go. However, in this section I can offer some words of advice and give you a few tools to help you start off on the right foot with this kind of spirit production.

First, always pay attention to the liquid levels on your plates. If your still has explosion proof lights that will shine on the plates, then all the better. At the very least keep a small flashlight nearby to shine on the plates through the port glasses. This comes in handy at the beginning of the distillation when you might want to observe the top plates to ensure they are loading properly. However, for the rest of the distillation run, the plates you will spend the most amount of time observing are the bottom two or three plates of each column. There are a few reasons for this.

The bottom plates of a column are the first point of contact for the vapors. They are also the hottest plates in the column. This means that if something changes in your distillation system, the effects will be seen on these plates first (typically in order of lowest plate moving upwards).

Let's say that you have too much cooling going through your column's condenser. What this can translate to is the bottom plate will eventually become completely flooded and entrained. If the situation is not corrected, then the entire plate will fill with liquid and eventually the plate above it will also flood. This can continue all the way up the column if you aren't paying attention.

The opposite situation can also easily occur where the plate completely dries out. If you have too much heat and not enough cooling in a column then the bottom plates will not form enough of a liquid layer on the plate elements. Eventually the plate will run dry which means you won't get much in the way of vapor or liquid mixing.

The net result of both scenarios is that your distillate quality will suffer. For neutral spirit, the most obvious (and arguably damaging) qualitative change is a drop in distillate alcohol concentration. You'll also likely see a bleeding effect of unwanted low volatility congeners coming over into the distillate.

Problem	Likely Cause(s)	Solution(s)
Bottom plate(s) dry	Too much heat Insufficient cooling Vapors not diverted to column	Slowly dial back heat Add more cooling load to condenser Check valves and piping to ensure that vapors are running into the column
Bottom plate(s) flooded	Too much cooling Not enough heat	Lessen cooling load If too many plates are flooded, turn off heat, allow column to drain and "reset"
Distillation too fast	Too much heat Insufficient cooling	Dial back heat Turn up cooling
Distillation too slow	Too much cooling Not enough heat	Usually, to speed up these distillations it's a good idea to increase the heat AND the cooling at the same time in small increments so as to not upset the balance inside the column(s).
Entire column is flooded	Operator error: not paying attention to how the plates are stacking.	A column reset is in order. Turn off heat and allow column(s) to completely drain before starting over. Pay closer attention to the column.
Distillate alcohol concentration is dropping or is too low	Distillation speed too fast Vapor temperature higher than plate temperature Not all plates in reflux	Slow distillation speed using method(s) from above Raise cooling to keep vapor temperature lower than top plate temperature Adjust cooling/heating to ensure all plates are in reflux
Distillate stops flowing through spirit pipe	Cooling load has increased Not enough heat Column is flooded	Check cooling flow rates; reduce if necessary Check to ensure proper heat is being supplied; adjust as necessary Check to see if plates/entire column is flooded; possible for top plate to flood check and reset column if necessary or reduce cooling

Table 7. Troubleshooting Hybrid Pot/Column Distillations

In Table 7 I offer some pointers on how to troubleshoot some of the most common issues surrounding these types of distillations. These tips can be applied to any hybrid still design whether it be a single column with four plates or an enormous multi-column setup with more than forty plates.

As you read through the table it should become clear that much of what you're doing to manage these distillations is playing with heating and cooling rates. This shouldn't be surprising at this point in the book. As you've likely realized by now, distillation is largely about controlling these two variables and no matter how complicated the distillation system may be, you will still be altering heating and cooling to affect the final outcome. Yes, things get a bit more complicated with hybrid systems, but after a bit of practice and some attention to detail, these distillations are not that difficult.

One thing to note is that in many situations, if you change one variable you need to also change the other in the same direction in order to maintain the same vapor and distillate flow rates and the same equilibrium in the column(s). In other words, if you turn up the cooling you will likely also need to turn up the heat to compensate for the change. Turn the heat down, then you should probably dial back the cooling a bit. This can sound a little counterintuitive to some people so let me explain.

Let's say the distillation is running a bit slow for your liking and you want to speed things up a bit. It should seem obvious that you could do one of two things. 1. Turn up the heat. OR 2. Dial back the cooling.

Let's say you decide to turn up the heat and nothing else. Now, you've got more hot vapors pushing up through the column which will upset the internal reflux balance. The vapors are pushing through harder and not mixing as effectively with the refluxed liquid. Instead, more vapor is simply pushing through the liquid layer relatively untouched and unscathed. You may even see some of the lower plates dry out completely. Regardless, you will likely see your alcohol concentration begin to drop. If you opt for option two, the same scenario will generally play out. So, what are you to do if you want to speed things up a bit?

You need to turn up the heat AND the cooling at the same time.

You do this slowly, making small adjustments to every few minutes. Eventually, you will notice that the speed does in fact increase but you have managed to keep your plates and reflux in balance.

The concept of making small changes slowly over time during these distillations cannot be stressed enough. Patience is the order of the day, especially with neutral spirit distillations where you are constantly trying to maintain a precarious balance of high alcohol concentration (within very tight tolerances from deviation) with an acceptable level of distillation speed. When an adjustment is needed, make a small tweak to one or both variables, wait 5–10 minutes to see if a change occurs then reassess before making another small adjustment. It takes time and is tedious, but it is the best way to maintain a high level of quality and consistency with these distillations. Note: on many systems, changes to heating take longer to register a noticeable effect on the distillation system than a change to cooling. Be Patient and Do Not Rush.

Of course, not every adjustment requires a movement of both variables in tandem. After the plates have all entered reflux and equilibrated, you will only lessen the cooling load (in small increments) to allow the vapors to come over into the condenser. You are already in total reflux and your vapor speed is largely set at this point so making a change to the heat is usually not necessary. Likewise, many adjustments made when trying to correct a problem such as an overly flooded or dried out plate usually only require the movement of one variable. However, every system is different, and you may find that yours requires slightly different approaches to these issues. Pay attention. Take notes. And eventually, you'll understand the methods that work best for your system.

A Few Words on Distillation Speed

Using hybrid pot/column systems requires a delicate balance to be maintained. Go too fast and your spirit quality will certainly suffer.

Go too slow and your plant efficiency will take a dive. Especially in the case of neutral spirit production, these distillations can take a painfully long time. In my own distillery, my guys know that a single batch of neutral spirit on our dual column system will take around 12–14 hours from heat up to clean out. That's pretty rough when most of your production is centered around whisky distillations that take only half the time.

It can be tempting to try and speed things up as much as possible, but I think that you'll find on most systems there is an upper limit to how fast you can go with hybrid systems. Certainly, by applying more heat and more cooling you should *in theory* be able to manage a fast and powerful distillation while keeping your quality and alcohol concentration within acceptable limits. In general, that idea would work for a simple pot still with no plates. (Up to a point. There is always an upper limit to speed on any still no matter how much cooling you have to "compensate.")

The problem we have with columned systems is one of sizing. The columns are designed to effectively hold and maintain a certain amount of liquid and vapor to ensure that they are properly mixed, refluxed and evolved. Therefore, there is by default an upper limit to the amount of vapor flow and subsequent distillate flow before your spirit quality will start to suffer. If you are unsure of what that upper limit might be, then speak with your still manufacturer. They should have an idea of how fast and hard you can push the equipment before quality suffers.

Feints Recycling for Neutral Spirit

The final issue we will consider in this chapter is what to do with the feints from a neutral spirit distillation. The cut point for neutral spirit often occurs when the distillate dips below the target alcohol concentration. So, if you were shooting for a 95% abv spirit or higher, then you would cut to tails the moment the outcoming spirit dips below 95% (assuming there are no abnormal issues with the distillation that might otherwise cause the drop). After the cut you will wind up with a not insignificant amount of tails/feints. Depending on exactly where and when you cut off the distillation, these feints may be quite heavy in fusel oils or (relatively) lighter in low boiling point congeners. What do you do with them?

Short of disposing of them, there are two things that immediately come to mind. I've used both of these techniques in my distilleries to good effect and so it's up to you to decide which works best for your situation.

The first thing you can do with the feints is to simply recycle them with the next batch of low wines that you are distilling into neutral spirit. This is a nice way of recovering more alcohol for your neutral spirit repository. However, because you are adding more feints into the still with your low wines, just be sure that your distillation technique is consistent and clean. Don't let the distillation get away from you or you may find some of the heavier congeners from the feints more easily smear into the distillate.

The other thing you can do is make a different product out of them. At my whisky distillery, we make neutral spirit for our gin. The base fermentation, grain, yeast and everything else are all the same whether we are making whisky or neutral spirit. This only real difference is the distillation. For every 2,000-liter neutral spirit distillation we usually have around 200-liters of feints at about 70% abv. After five distillations we will take our 1,000-liters of feints, add an equal amount of water to dilute them to approximately 35% abv and redistill them using a single 10-plate column. (Our standard neutral spirit distillation uses two 10-plate columns.) This gives us a light whisky of about 94% abv. We then dilute this down to 70% abv and place it in ex-bourbon casks for a few years.

Either method works well, and both are a great way of maximizing recovery of ethanol. Just pay close to any distillation with a recycling of feints. You don't want to upset the delicate flavor balance with an over-abundance of heavier feinty compounds creeping into your distillate.

Extractive Distillation

Occasionally, you may come across the term "extractive distillation." This is a technique used in large neutral spirit rectifiers to further purify their spirit, diving deeper into the realm of flavor neutrality.

The concept is simple enough to understand. It is based on the idea that many congeners will show different volatilities at different alcohol concentrations.

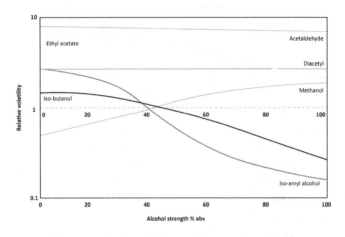

Figure 8-2. Relative volatilities of different congeners in relation to varying alcohol concentrations (Used with permission and copyright of the Institute of Brewing & Distilling)

We've seen the above plot before in our chapter on cuts and chemistry. In the plot you can see that a few important congeners such as iso-amyl alcohol and iso-butanol are less volatile than ethanol when the alcohol concentration is above 40% abv. However, their volatility rapidly rises above ethanol when the alcohol concentration dips below 40% abv. We can use this to our advantage.

Large neutral spirit plants will sometimes utilize these volatility differences to more effectively remove congeners such as iso-amyl alcohol. A high ethanol feed concentration of around 94% abv enters onto a feed plate higher up in the second half of the column. Live steam is pushed up to meet the spirit from the bottom while water comes in from the top. Eventually the alcohol concentration is diluted to around 15% abv near the bottom of the column. At this point, congeners with volatilities closer to ethanol can more easily rise to the top of the column and be stripped away from the alcohol. The further purified alcohol stream can then go onto another distillation column to have high volatility congeners such as methanol and diacetyl removed while simultaneously increasing its strength to above 95% abv.

Batch distillers can actually do something similar with their own spirits. By reducing your high abv spirit down to below 20% abv and redistilling very slowly, you can affect a greater removal of some of the more bothersome congeners such as iso-amyl alcohol. If you are trying to produce a very neutral spirit on a batch system, then this is a technique worth considering. I've actually known some distillers to do this with bulk neutral alcohol that they have purchased from larger distilleries, effectively cleaning up these bulk distillates to make something a bit more delicate and nuanced for their vodka or gin production.

"Breaking the Azeotrope"

There are countless numbers of folks on countless numbers of distillation forums, both pro and "amateur" that claim to have a method for "breaking the azeotrope" and distilling beyond 97% abv. I find most of these claims a bit dubious. But if you read these discussions long enough you will likely come across the term "salt effect distillation." Unlike many of the other effectively bogus techniques based on old timey apocrypha, this one actually holds a little water. Will you be able to distill 100% pure lab grade ethanol using this technique? Absolutely not. Does it have some interesting potential for your own spirit production practices? Quite possibly.

Salt, and by this I am speaking of non-iodized sodium chloride, when added to a low wine, will change the volatility of some substances. Without getting into the ugly chemistry of it all, NaCl aids in separating congeners from ethanol.

One study looked at the addition of various salt concentrations and their effects on pear brandy production. The researchers found a dramatic decrease in higher alcohol concentration in the final spirit using 2% and 5% w/w salt concentrations when compared with their conventional non-salted double distillation. They also saw a decrease in total esters in many of the fractions using salt during distillation. However, the salt additions seemed to promote an increase in methanol and acetaldehyde concentrations in some of the fractions so there was a bit of trade off (Memic, Mujcinovic, Smajic-Murtic, & Spaho, 2017). The study also showed that overall distillation time for the salted treatments was lower than that of the conventional distillation.

It was an interesting study, but I would make the case that this technique isn't too interesting for non-neutral spirits. It seems like it messes with the chemistry too much and possibly poses a risk to maintaining the proper spirit character. However, it could be useful in producing neutral spirit and further separating out congeners such as iso-amyl alcohol in a batch process. With the addition of efficient plated columns, you should have little issue separating the high volatility methanol and acetaldehyde while at the same time, you would be able to better drop out some of the higher alcohols that can negatively impact your spirit quality.

If this all sounds too good to be true, it's because in a way it is. There's always a "but," right? Yes, it does seem that salt additions of 2–5% w/w can improve alcohol recovery in neutral spirit distillations, BUT there are some caveats here. First, is the issue of corrosion to equipment that can occur when chloride ions are allowed to run rampant inside your still. This is especially important when your pot is composed of stainless steel as steel and chloride don't get along too well over time.

There's also the added cost of the salt. If you are distilling 1,000 gallons (~3,800 liters) of low wines into neutral spirit, then the total weight of that liquid is north of 8,000 lbs. (~3,600 kg). That means for a 2% w/w salt addition you would need around 160 lbs. (~73 kg) of salt! The cost of that salt adds up really fast.

Finally, there is the issue of spirit quality. The truth is that small amounts of some of these congeners can actually *improve* your neutral spirit flavor in subtle and nuanced ways. Removing them brings you closer to something more neutral which is a bit boring in my opinion. Besides, if that's what you are shooting for then I might suggest just purchasing neutral spirit from a larger supplier that has already done the job for you. It will cost you less and the bigger distillery will likely be able to do it better than even you could with the salt addition. As for myself, I don't use this technique. However, I think it's important that you know your options.

Using Plates for Other Spirit Types

Hybrid stills are used for many other spirit types beyond neutral spirit and vodka. Hundreds of craft distilleries across North America and Europe have gotten their starts by purchasing hybrid stills. These stills can offer the distiller an immense amount of flexibility, providing a way to easily produce heavier or lighter styles of spirits based on the whims of the producer. I've lost track of how many distilleries I've walked into that use a large pot still with four or five bubble cap trays situated in the neck directly above the pot. It is the same design that I use for my whisky (though I have never used the trays) and it works beautifully. If I wanted to, I could use my still to produce a lighter whisky, rum, or brandy simply by enabling the trays to be in active positions.

Most styles of whisky are not well suited to the use of plates in my opinion. They remove a little too much character for my taste and don't produce the best type of spirit suitable for maturation. However, in both the rum and brandy categories there are ample examples of spirits that will benefit from enabled plates. Typically, these products are designed to be released unaged and may include spirits such as light rums or various eau de vie.

When trying to make these spirits, you really need to have a good understanding of the category you're interested in. This should be the case for everything you produce, but it becomes all the more imperative for spirits you release unaged. These spirits are completely naked and exposed. There is no cask or external modifier to hide distillation defects or fermentation issues. You have to be precise and clean in your operation. It's the same reason why in my homebrewing days I always felt that producing a quality pilsner was far more challenging than making a double IPA or a fattened imperial stout. The flaws in a poorly made pilsner are immediately apparent while other beer styles can be somewhat more forgiving.

When approaching these kinds of distillations where only a few plates may be necessary, some experimentation will likely be in order. Every still and every producer's wash will be a little different and you'll have to take some time to figure out what works best to reach the profile you're after.

If you have a column where all the plates can be enabled or disabled independently of each other, then you have a lot of flexibility at your fingertips. It might be tempting for the consummate tinkerer to go in an do all sorts of odd configurations of active and disabled trays just to see what happens, but I'd argue that it would likely bear little fruit. Instead, a better use of time would be to start by enabling the top tray(s) while leaving the lower ones disabled and see what distillate results you get. Continue to experiment by working your way down the column trays in sequence enabling or disabling them in subsequent runs until you get the desired result.

Once you've decided on your tray settings, you can really dial things in to best suit the type of distillation you are trying to achieve. Running a hybrid system with only a few plates is not really that different from operating one with 40 plates. All the theory, operational parameters and troubleshooting suggestions mentioned earlier will apply here as well.

Chapter 9

Triple and Single Distillation Techniques

Up to this point we have really only dealt with double distillation methods. It's an elegant and classic system that produces absolutely fantastic spirit as long as we've been scrupulous in all the other areas of our production. But these are not the only techniques for batch distillation out there. A whole world of spirits from all categories are produced using methods beyond that of our double distillation system. In this chapter we will take a look at a few of these techniques including triple and single distillation systems. Let's start with triple distillation techniques.

Triple Distillation

The concept of triple distillation is inherently wrapped up in the world of Irish whiskey. At least in the eyes of distillers outside of Ireland. The commonly held belief is that *all* Irish whiskey is produced using triple distillation techniques. True, at one point quite a bit of the drams sunk off the bar in Irish pubs next to burnished black pints of stout were indeed produced using triple distillation. Many still are, in fact. However, with the rise and resurgence of the Irish distilling industry in the 21st century, one could argue that triple distillation is fast becoming the exception rather than the rule.

In general triple distillation produces a lighter styled spirit than most double distillation methods. This fact is what has given Irish whiskey the sometimes-dubious reputation of being "light" and deli-cate. Of course, the effect and efficacy of a tool depends on how it's used, and triple distillation is no different. You can certainly use triple distillation and all its various permutations to produce a heavier and fuller spirit.

The history of the technique is muddier than a Jamaican distillery muck pit and no one is quite sure exactly how or where triple distillation started. The general consensus seems to be that yes, it did begin in Ireland and probably sometime during the 19th century. One of the most interesting theories regarding the initial use of triple distillation methods involves, as these things often do, the excise tax man.

In 1785, the Irish government put a tax on malted barley, which was a serious buzzkill of a move on their part. Irish distillers, ever clever and forever frugal, figured that they could avoid paying much of the tax if they substituted unmalted barley in for a portion of the malted barley in their whiskey production. In fact, this was the beginnings of what would become known as "Pure Pot Still" Irish whiskey, a fairly unique style of spirit.

The use of unmalted barley was a nice workaround. Unfortunately, distillers quickly found out that their alcohol yields suffered as a result. So, they began to run a third distillation to better extract more alcohol from the process. Over time, many iterations of the process popped up and what we're left with now is a veritable cornucopia of triple distillation techniques used not just in Ireland but in Scotland, Australia and even in U.S. bourbon production.

The Basic Triple Distillation

The process of triple distillation can be almost comically simple. Note that I say it *can* be simple, not that it *is* simple. In theory, you could take our basic double distillation technique and simply add another distillation to the mix.

- Distill a fermented wash in the first distillation and collect the low wines.
- Redistill the low wines to a high wine without separating fractions.
- Distill the high wine to a final spirit making separations between fractions where and when appropriate.
- Recycle the feints back into the next batch of high wines.

This technique certainly works and has a few advocates, though it really isn't that common. The reason is that it serves little necessary purpose. The only real beneficial outcome of this technique is that it raises the alcohol concentration in the final spirit. Now, this might be useful to you if you are starting out with little alcohol to begin with. For instance, if you were starting out with a wash that was only 3–4% abv, then this might be a way to boost the alcohol a bit in the final spirit. However, if you have access to a hybrid column still, then the same effect can be had by enabling one or two plates.

The Woodford Reserve Method

Bourbon might seem an odd place to find triple distillation techniques, but it does happen. The most prominent example is Woodford Reserve. Woodford uses a slightly more advanced version of our basic triple distillation technique to produce a fraction of their bourbon that is then blended in with distillate from a continuous column. Their version of the method is simple but elegant.

1. Wash and tails from the previous low wines distillation (see next point) are distilled in the beer still and low wines are collected at ~20% abv.
2. Low wines are distilled in the intermediate still along with feints (both heads and tails) from the previous high wines distillation (see next point) to reach a high wine of ~55% abv. Tails are fractioned and recycled with the next wash distillation.
3. High wines are distilled in the spirit to reach a spirit with 78% abv. Heads and tails are recycled with the next batch of low wines in the intermediate still.

This technique does a few different things. First, is that similar to our basic method it allows for the use of low alcohol washes. Second, it cleverly recycles the tails and "pushes" the heavier distillation components back towards the wash distillation, thus giving a greater efficacy of removal through the spent stillage. The net result is a lighter spirit.

A word of caution for would be American whiskey distillers thinking about using this process. For most American whiskey styles, the maximum allowable average alcohol concentration of the finished distillate is 80% abv. Many triple distillation methods including Woodford's will easily go above 80% abv if you aren't careful. If you are interested in playing with this technique or any of the others discussed in this chapter, you might need to dilute your low wines and/or high wines with filtered water. This dilution has the interest-

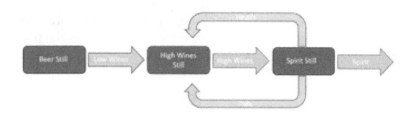

Figure 9-1. Simple Triple Distillation Process Flow

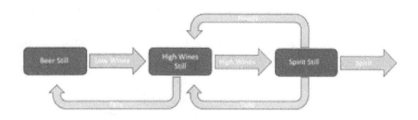

Figure 9-2. Process flow of the Woodford Reserve Triple Distillation Method

ing effect of volatilizing some compounds and dropping others out of solution making their removal during distillation that much easier. This could be a good or bad thing depending on your goals.

The Midleton Process

The Midleton Distillery (it's more of a distillery complex) is located in Midleton Ireland. Owned by multinational drinks conglomerate, Pernod Ricard, it produces several important brands of Irish whiskey including Jameson, Powers, Redbreast and the "Spot" line of whiskies (Green, Red, Blue and Yellow). The distillery has three 75,000-liter pot stills coupled with three continuous column stills and can produce around 64 million liters of absolute alcohol per year. So, yeah. Not a small distillery.

Midleton is large, modern and incredibly clever. The variety of whiskies they produce require a variety of techniques. Here, we will home in on the triple distillation technique they use to make a portion of Jameson. (Jameson is a blend of pot and column distillates).

Jameson is produced using a slightly more complicated process than that of Woodford's.

1. Wash is distilled to a low wine in the beer still. No fractions are made.
2. Low wines are combined with weak feints and heads from previous low wines distillation AND weak feints from previous spirit still distillation. Hearts (Midleton uses the term "strong feints") are collected and sent to the spirit still.
3. Hearts from the intermediate "feints" still are combined with heads and strong feints from previous spirit distillation. Heads, hearts, strong feints and weak feints are all fractioned separately and recycled accordingly.

If it seems complicated, I can assure you that it really isn't too bad. The fractions are made the same way as they are in other distillation methods. The one wrench thrown into our system here is the concept of strong versus weak feints. Strong feints are in a way analogous to cognac's secondes. The hearts are cut around ~60% abv and the strong feints fraction begins. When the alcohol level reaches between 30–20% abv and cut is made to weak feints and the distillation is allowed to run to conclusion.

Here again, we see a method where an immense amount of recycling techniques come into play. The alcohol concentration will certainly be boosted in the end, but the heavier tails components are mostly dropped out during the intermediary distillation. If you are interested in producing an Irish Single Pot Still type of whiskey, then this is a technique worth considering.

The Benrinnes Process

Irish distillers get most of the attention when it comes to triple distillation. Interestingly, there are arguably just as many Scotch whisky producers that also use some kind of triple distillation at some point in their process. One of these is Benrinnes.

Benrinnes is not the most well-known of Scotch distilleries. You'll not likely ever hear it uttered in the same breath as Glenfiddich, The Macallan, or Bowmore. And that's a real shame because they produce some damn fine whisky.

Benrinnes currently distills using a traditional double distillation process. However, prior to 2007 they were using an interesting iteration on the triple distillation technique. Let's give it a quick look, shall we?

1. Wash is distilled in the beer still. Heads and hearts are sent to the spirit still (the third still in the series). Tails/feints are sent to the low wines still (intermediate still).

2. Feints from the beer still are combined with weak feints from the spirit still and feints/tails from the previous low wines distillation. Heads and hearts are sent to the spirit still. Feints/tails are recycled into the next low wines still distillation.

3. Heads and hearts from the beer still AND the low wines still are combined with heads and strong feints from the previous spirit still distillation. Hearts are collected and moved forward to storage. Heads and strong feints are recycled into the next spirit still distillation. Weak feints are sent back to the low wines still to be recycled.

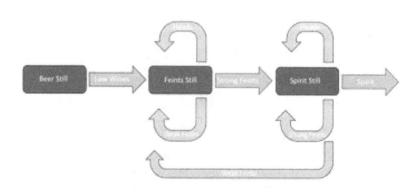

Figure 9-3. Midleton Triple Distillation Process

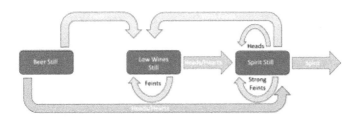

Figure 9-4. Benrinnes Triple Distillation Process Flow

This is arguably one of the more complicated triple distillation methods out there. It does, however, perform an excellent job of recycling and extracting good alcohol from "junk."

The Curious Case of Mortlach

I love Mortlach. I firmly believe it is one of the crown jewels in Diageo's vast whisky empire. However, until recently it just wasn't getting the attention it deserved. "The Beast of Dufftown" as it is known, was flying under too many people's radar. Thankfully, that's all starting to change. Diageo has invested more time, money and energy into the brand, and it is gaining more deserved recognition all the time.

This is a distiller's distillery that makes a distiller's whisky to be sure. There is just so much about the distillery for the interested practitioner of the alchemical beverage arts to geek out about. Perhaps the most famously nerdtastic thing about Mortlach whisky is that it is distilled 2.81 times. Yep. You read that correctly. If you're confused, rest assured you should be. And I promise you it's about to get worse (but in a good way).

Remember from several chapters back our discussion on balanced still operations. If you need a refresher, a balanced distillation system is when the ratio of wash distillations to spirit distillations equals a whole number. So, a distillery that does two wash distillations for every spirit distillation is considered balanced. However, a distillery that does one wash distillation for every two spirit distillations is considered unbalanced. And guess what? Mortlach is about as unbalanced as they come.

Mortlach uses six stills. They have two 7,000-liter wash stills and one 16,000-liter wash still. They have three spirit stills with 8,000-liter (affectionately known as "The Wee Witchie"), 9,000-liter and 10,000-liter capacities. You can tell that we're already off to a strange start when two of the wash stills are smaller than any of the spirit stills. However, this is part of the beauty of Mortlach's system. Let's carefully track our way through their process.

1. Wash still #3 (16,000-liters) is paired perfectly with spirit still #3. Wash is distilled in the wash still to produce low wines. The low wines are then distilled in the spirit still to produce heads, hearts and tails. The hearts are sent to a storage tank while the heads and tails are recycled into the next spirit still distillation.

2. Wash still #2 is partially paired with spirit still #2. The first 80% of the low wines produced from the wash distillation are sent to spirit still #2. The remaining 20% (the weaker portion of the low wines) are sent to The Wee Witchie. The stronger first 80% of the low wines are combined with the strong first 80% of low wines produced from wash still #1 and distilled. Hearts are sent to a storage tank while the heads and tails are recycled with the next batch of strong low wines in spirit still #2.

3. Wash still #1 produces a low wine, the first 80% of which is sent to spirit still #2 (as per point 2 above). The last weaker 20% of the low wines are combined with the weak low wines from wash still #2 in The Wee Witchie.

4. The Wee Witchie is distilled twice in two "blank runs" where no cuts are taken. These are simply concentration runs to bring up the alcohol concentration and to drop out heavier unwanted congeners.

5. The third run of The Wee Witchie produces a heart fraction as well as heads and tails which are recycled back into the next Witchie distillations. Hearts are sent to a storage vessel.

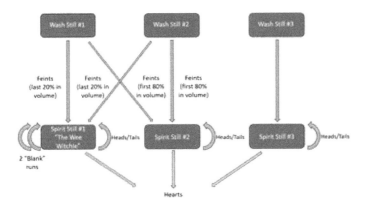

Figure 9-5. Mortlach 2.81 Distillation Process Flow

It is beautifully convoluted in its execution. I would never recommend a distillery attempt anything like this. It is just too bizarre and complicated for most teams to attempt. However, it does produce some magical whisky. Now, go buy a bottle of Mortlach and enjoy the fruits of their anarchic labors.

Single Distillations

Moving away from the dizzying world of triple distillations, we can find sanctuary in the concept of single distillation. However, the supposed simplicity of these distillations belies the difficulty in their execution.

There are quite a few spirits in the world that are producing using a single distillation. The techniques exist in rum, brandy, whisky and agave. And I'm not talking about the use of a column still to distill a wash to finished spirit in one go. I'm not even referencing the use of a hybrid still for these distillations. Spirits such as shōchū and Peruvian pisco are often distilled on the most rudimentary of pot stills.

These types of distillations are notoriously time consuming and finicky to properly pull off. They must be done at an awfully slow distillation rate to inhibit congeners from overly smearing into different fractions. Another caveat with these distillations is that the raw materials, processing and fermentation steps all must be carried out in a careful and detailed manner. You need a high-quality wash going into the still because it will be more difficult to remove off characters during fractioning with a single distillation.

Peruvian pisco and Japanese shōchū are perhaps the most prominent practitioners of single distillation. Fractions are carefully taken during slow and low heat distillations (in the case of shōchū the distillations are sometimes carried out under vacuum making for incredibly low heat distillations).

Peruvian pisco is an odd example in that as per governmental regulations, the distiller is not allowed to add water to the pisco at any step in the process. This includes when the spirit is being prepared for bottling. That means that the pisco must be distilled to bottle strength. To do this, the distiller must be ever vigilant, carefully mixing and checking the distillate's alcohol concentration and then stopping the hearts fraction at the precise point when the desired bottle strength has been reached.

Single distillations are arguably a bit easier to pull off when the initial alcohol concentration of the wash is high. I would suggest a bare minimum of 10% abv. Japanese shōchū generally starts with a wash between 14–20% abv. This will make reaching an acceptable alcohol level much easier.

Because these distillations are often so slow and difficult, many distillers avoid them. However, some folks prefer these techniques arguing that a single distillation gives a fuller flavored spirit. Others counter that in many cases the resulting spirit is a bit rough around the edges and that a double distillation would provide a more nuanced spirit.

Chapter 10

Batch Distillation Techniques for Gin

When I got into the distilling industry, I honestly didn't care much for gin. The breathy sensation of drinking the extract of a pinecone just didn't suit me. My gin education started in earnest the moment I started working for a company that made gin. Suddenly I was forced to drink the stuff on a regular basis. And one day everything just started to click for me. I *got* it. The juniper. The coriander. How they layered with the base spirit and the supporting cast of botanicals lending their unique attributes. It was revelatory and I became a convert.

I've been fortunate to learn gin production from several award-winning gin producers. I've picked up tips and tricks from small boutique producers all the way up to folks from Diageo and Bombay Sapphire. And what I've learned from all these people is… gin is complicated. Much more complicated than the majority of distillers give it credit for. There are so many techniques and considerations to be factored into a successful gin and that's before you even get to the concept of the actual botanical recipe itself.

Gin is a botanical spirit with juniper as its heart. The base alcohol is usually some kind of neutral spirit and can be made from all sorts of agricultural bases. Yes, there are a few styles of gin such as Dutch jenever that are made from non-neutral spirit, but these are more the exception than the rule. Regardless, the base spirit quality needs to work well with your botanicals in order to produce a cohesive final gin. I've seen base spirits for gin made from corn, apples, grapes, molasses, barley, wheat and so much more. The world of base spirits can be dizzying, almost as much so as the world of gin botanicals. This is especially true if you've opted to produce your own neutral spirit. However, above all else, everything needs to play nicely together in the glass just like any other spirit. That is all that matters.

I am assuming that you are interested in making a distilled gin and not an infused or compound gin. Those gins are perfectly acceptable and quite a few of them are excellent, but their manufacture is beyond the scope of this book, so I won't be talking about them. I'm also not going to be discussing botanical choices or recipe building in this chapter. There are ample sources for that information elsewhere. What I want to focus on in this chapter are concepts that affect the physical act of distilling gin and the overall quality. So, I am operating under the assumption that you have chosen your botanicals and their approximate recipe percentages. From there, you should be able to make sense of the techniques and concepts in this chapter and easily apply them to work with your still and botanical recipe. And while this chapter speaks to the gin distiller at large, the points discussed can also be applied to other botanical spirits such as absinthe.

First, we need to look at the basics of gin distillation. Then we can look a bit closer at the individual conceptual trees that make up our gin distillation forest. If this chapter feels a bit like a quilted patchwork of ideas, that's because it is. Gin can be a strange beast and there are several seemingly disparate decisions you have to make during the production process, any one of which can have a significant impact on the final character of your gin.

The Basic Gin Distillation

They say there's more than one way to skin a cat. And despite the gruesome (and in most cases illegal) analogous subject matter, that saying holds true for gin production. However, for the majority of distillers making gin, there is an overarching template of techniques that we can discuss to help make sense of the other concepts in this chapter.

There are generally two primary methods to producing gin. You can:

- Distill the botanicals after a maceration inside the pot.
- Use a vapor basket to extract the essential oils of your botanicals into your alcohol.

The two techniques are not mutually exclusive. You can use both during the same distillation as I'll discuss later. For now, we just want to give a general outline of events that occur when using each technique.

- Measure out all botanicals for your recipe and mix them together.
- Measure out the proper amount of base spirit for the recipe.
- Place botanicals and base spirit inside the still and macerate. (Note: the maceration step is omitted if using a vapor basket for your botanicals.)
- Begin heating the still and turn on the condenser when necessary.
- Begin collecting distillate. The first 0.5–1% is fractioned as heads.
- Collect hearts until spirit coming off the still reaches 60–30% abv then cut to tails.
- Collect tails.

It really is that simple. However, the astute observer will notice that there are quite a few areas where you can play a bit. Things like total botanical load, charge strength and much more will affect the qualitative outcome.

You'll also note that the skeleton of gin distillation, the core principles, are not really that different from the basic batch distillation practices we've already discussed in the book. You can heat up the still rather quickly, dialing the heat back to a gentle simmer when the distillate begins to flow.

There are even fractions that must be accounted for. Even though you may be starting with a neutral spirit, where (hopefully) most of the low boiling point congeners have been removed from precise fractioning, you still need to remove the first small volumes of distillate away from the hearts. This is because just like any other spirit, the first distillate to come over during distillation serves the partial purpose of rinsing the condenser piping of residual compounds clinging on from the previous distillation. The first amount of gin distillate is often slightly bitter as a result, so we separate it.

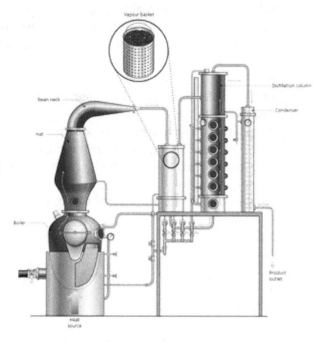

Figure 10-1. Gin distillation still
(Used with permission and copyright of the Institute of Brewing & Distilling)

Similarly, we also need to cut the hearts away from the tails fraction. Botanical oils have different preferences for alcohol and water so as the distillation proceeds and the alcohol concentration in the distillate steadily goes down, you will find that different aromas evolve in the outcoming spirit. Eventually, we reach a point where many of the oils are more water soluble than alcohol soluble and they can easily throw a cloudy haze in the spirit. (They also tend to have a negative impact on flavor.) We will discuss more about cut points in a bit. For now, let's begin to work our way through a list of important factors and considerations that can affect the quality of our gin.

Botanical Load

The running joke is that gin is nothing more than juniper flavored vodka. Yeesh. The gin distiller knows better. The trick is to convince everyone else that your gin rises high above such condescension. You want to make something that leaves the consumer with a heightened impression on what the gin category really is and what it can be. In other words, you want them to feel more strongly about it than, "Meh. Tastes like 'gin.'"

How do you go about reaching for that lofty goal? You are shooting for the juniper-inflected stars. You know which botanicals you want to use. You know what their proportions are going to be. You're all set, right? But there is another question that you must ask yourself. What is the total amount of botanicals you are going to use in your recipe? What is the *botanical load* in the still?

This is an important question to tackle because the answer has an immense impact on the final quality of your gin, notably in the overall flavor and aromatic intensities. Fortunately, there is some general guidance to be offered here.

> *The total amount of botanicals used in making gin typically ranges from 10–30 grams per liter of 50% alcohol charged inside the still.*

As we will soon see this range works well for most, but not all, gin distilling conditions. A botanical load of 10 grams per liter is a fairly light and delicate gin while something as high as 30 grams per liter can be quite intense. An amount of 15–25 grams per liter seems to work well for many gin styles. There are a few other factors that will affect the botanical intensity so you will want to do a number of test batches to see what combination of techniques and botanical loading works best to get your desired profile.

To Crush or Not to Crush

The next thing to consider in your gin distillation is whether or not you want to crush your botanicals. As always, there are pros and cons to both.

- **Crushing botanicals**
  ▷ Pros: exposes more surface area to the base spirit or vapor for better extraction of essential oils; creates a more intense character in the gin with less botanicals, potentially allowing

the distiller to use a lower botanical load

▷ Cons: Requires crushing equipment such as a dedicated roller mill, commercial grade food processer, etc....; Can be time consuming; risk of imparting heat to the botanicals during the crushing process which can contribute "cooked" characters to the gin

• **Using whole botanicals**

▷ Pros: No extra work or equipment required; produces a lighter styled gin which may be desirable

▷ Cons: Need to use higher botanical load to reach a desired character intensity

There is no right or wrong answer, here. I know distillers who crush everything in their botanical inventory. I also know folks who forgo the process entirely. Both make great gin. The choice is up to you. Play with each technique to compare the character differences and see which one you prefer.

Infusion Bags or Loose Botanicals

If you opt to macerate your botanicals in the still, you have two choices. You can blend all the botanicals together and put them in a bag or series of bags which are then placed inside the still with the base spirit. This is akin to steeping tea leaves in a tea bag. You could also simply throw your botanicals loose into the still. This might sound like a silly debate for some, but it holds some serious implications for our gin.

Using a muslin, nylon, or cheesecloth steeping bag makes your job easy. The botanicals are all in one place. Macerate, distill and pull the bags out after everything is done. No mess to clean up and everyone is happy. However, some people feel, and not without reason, that steeping the botanicals lessens the extraction of essential oils into the base spirit. There is also a (albeit low) risk of clumping of botanicals in the middle of the steeping bag. This reduces their available contact time with the base spirit, thus lowering their extractive contributions.

Me? I use the steeping bags. It makes my life easier. The loose botanical method is great if you have a wide discharge pipe on the bottom of the still. Unfortunately for most distillers, their stills probably don't have a wide enough diameter discharge pipe to avoid getting clogged by a sudden influx of botanicals all rushing to get dumped down the drain at the same time. The pipe inevitably gets clogged and it takes forever to drain out and clean your still. Plus, you invariably get a mess of botanicals running all over your production floor. Never mind the potential problems of dumping that much solid botanical material down your pipe drains...

Maceration Time

It's important to consider how long you want to macerate your botanicals in your base spirit prior to distillation. The goal of maceration is to extract essential oils into the base spirit allowing them to pass into the heated vapor more easily and into the final gin during distillation. Longer maceration times mean more essential oils are extracted. It also means that your still (or adjacent dedicated maceration tank) is tied up for longer periods of time.

Industry maceration times vary from 6–24 hours. Twelve hours is common for many distilleries and allows for a good extraction time coupled with ease of production workflow. Simply charge the still with your base spirit and botanicals the evening before you plan to distill. Come in the next morning and fire everything up and you're good to go.

Beefeater famously macerates for 24 hours. I've heard of a handful of gin distillers macerating for 48–72 hours but this is rare. Other botanical spirits such as absinthe will sometimes see maceration times of two to three days, but even with these spirits a single day or less of maceration is more common.

Maceration Alcohol Concentration

So, we understand some of the factors at play with the botanicals during maceration, but what about the base spirit? Perhaps most importantly, what alcohol concentration should the botanicals be macerated in? Once again, we have a lot of options here.

The alcohol concentration you choose for maceration heavily impacts not just the *rate* of essential oil extraction but also the *type* of essential oils that get extracted. As I've already mentioned, different oils show different levels of hydrophobicity (solubility in water). Macerating with 96% abv neutral spirit will favor essential oils that are more soluble in alcohol with little in the way of hydrophilic compounds being readily extracted. High alcohol concentrations also seem to speed up extraction, so in theory you can lessen your maceration time if you are using 95% abv base spirit as opposed to 50% abv diluted spirit. However, you are favoring the essential oils that have high alcohol solubilities and ignoring others that come out better with a little water in the mix.

I personally find a balanced approach to be best. Most distillers I know macerate their botanicals somewhere around the 50–60% abv mark. It strikes a good extraction speed and flavor balance. However, you should certainly experiment with different alcohol concentrations to see what gives you the best profile. Note that maceration alcohol concentration does not have to be the same as the distillation alcohol concentration. Speaking of which…

Distillation Alcohol Concentration

Most distillers when macerating their botanicals opt to choose a base spirit alcohol concentration and simply begin distilling when the time is right. However, if you are macerating your botanicals at 96% abv, then you most definitely will need to dilute down to an acceptable distillation charge strength.

The initial alcohol strength in the still just before distillation affects the oils that come over into the distillate as well as the final alcohol of the spirit. I've heard some people recommend a charge strength of 30% abv as this seems to promote a lot of aromatics coming over in the still. However, if you are using a simple pot still, you'll find that your final distillate strength will be lower as a result. In many cases this may not be a problem, but if you are trying to make, say, a London-Dry Gin then the EU rules stipulate that the spirit strength be at least 70% abv. In some stills, starting at 30% abv may not quite get you there.

Others prefer starting higher at 60–70% abv. This can also work, but you may find that the aromatics are a bit more delicate and lighter in some instances. Once again, this isn't a problem if that's the style you're shooting for. It's just something you should be aware of.

Most distillers shoot for an initial charge strength of around 50% abv with some going as high as 60% abv. For dry style gins, these starting concentrations seem to give a great balance of character and strength to the final spirit. I know I keep saying this but experiment, experiment and experiment some more. It's all part of the fun of making gin.

If you choose to use a maceration concentration that is different than your charge concentration and need to dilute the base spirit, you can simply use non-chlorinated filtered water for the task. I've even known some producers to use filtered water from their hot liquor tanks to do the dilution just before distillation which quickly raises the temperature of the macerated spirit inside the still and lessens the distillation heat up time.

Multi shot vs. Single shot Distillations

A large amount of a gin's intensity is based on its overall botanical loading and the distillation technique used to make it. We've already discussed the basic gin distillation, and we've looked at considerations for botanical loading. Now we will somewhat combine these two factors to explain the concepts of multi shot and single shot distillations.

The basic gin distillation method that I have previously described is what we would call a "single shot" gin. The botanicals are added to the still with the base spirit. Things are heated up, vapors flow and get condensed, and eventually the spirit is diluted with water to give us our final gin. This is a simple method that is easily understood. Many distillers use it, especially the smaller craft producers. However, there is arguably a more time efficient way to make gin. Enter the multi shot process.

A multi shot gin is distilled the exact same way as a single shot gin except that a greater amount of botanicals is used thereby creating a sort of gin "concentrate." This concentrated gin is then diluted with an appropriate amount of neutral spirit to get the botanical levels back down to a more consumer friendly level.

Let's say that your recipe uses 20 grams total botanicals per liter of 50% abv neutral spirit. In a multi shot distillation you might use 40 grams per liter. Once distilled you would blend an equal amount of neutral spirit on an absolute alcohol basis to get back down to your original recipe concentration of 20 grams per liter.

This is how most of the major gin producers make their gin. They see the distillation time as one of the main limiting factors to their production efficiency so the use of multi shot distillations make sense. I have just outlined what would be a "2X" concentration, but you could certainly go much higher if you like. Rumor has it that one of the major London-dry gin producers uses a 30X concentration factor with their gins.

The multi shot technique can be a great time and energy saving tool in the gin distillery. However, it does have some drawbacks. First, this is really only much of a time saver if you are purchasing your base spirit from a larger supplier. If you are distilling your own base spirit, then the time savings aren't that great because you will still have to spend time producing the spirit that you blend back with. Second, some people argue that multi shot gins have a harsher profile and alcoholic burn than single shot gins. I will agree that this is indeed sometimes the case though not always.

Overall, I think this is a technique that many gin distillers could really benefit from. It is certainly worth considering as you continue to grow your production.

Botanical Placement

When it comes to botanical placement there are generally two modes of thought: either inside the pot or inside a vapor basket. However, if you're feeling particularly clever there may be other options. Some distillers that use hybrid stills with short columns to produce their gins will actually place some of the botanicals on one or more of the plates. Even if the plates are disabled and not allowed to build much in the way of reflux, the vapors still have to pass through them. You can use these plates as a partial vapor basket.

Some distillers will place core botanicals such as juniper and coriander to steep inside the still and then place other botanicals on the plates for vapor infusion. The most common botanicals used in this technique are citrus peels.

A few years ago, I was tasked with making a mint liqueur for the distillery I worked at, using fresh locally harvested wild mint. I had never made a mint liqueur before, but I had a fairly good idea of the approach I wanted to take. I took the fresh mint and stuffed as much of it on top of the distillation plates in my four-plate hybrid gin still as I could. I then distilled my neutral base spirit through it. In the end I had the most expressive mint aromas in a spirit I had ever experienced. The integrity of the mint was maintained, and I didn't get any stewed or cooked aromas from the heating elements in the still.

Using Plates

It might seem counterintuitive to use distillation plates for producing gin. Afterall, don't these devices *remove* flavor? Well, yes and no. Let me explain.

Don't think of plates as a way to lower flavor but rather a way to raise alcohol. When the alcohol level is raised, you will have more alcohol soluble botanical fractions carried into the final spirit. These aromas are generally a bit more delicate and nuanced than the heavier compounds that are more water soluble and that come over later in the distillation. By enabling reflux on a few plates (it may only be one or two in many distilleries) you can produce a bright and nuanced gin.

I know of one distillery in the UK that distills their gin on a 500-liter German hybrid pot and column still. The hearts fraction stays around a steady 90% abv for most of the run. The end result is a classic London-dry gin, full of fragrant juniper and nuanced floral notes.

Cut Points

I've already mentioned basic cutting criteria for gin. Heads are typically fractioned merely to rinse the condenser piping of any bitter components. As a result, heads are rather quick and low in volume, perhaps only a fraction of a percent of the total still charge.

Hearts are allowed to run until the distillate coming of the still reaches a predetermined point. For many distilleries that point is often around 60% abv. If you are enabling some plates for a small amount of reflux, that number will likely be somewhat higher. However, some distillers choose to allow hearts to run out until the alcohol concentration off the still is as low as 30% or even 20% abv. At around 30% abv the spirit often begins to look fairly cloudy and will become cloudier as the alcohol continues to drop. Still, these distillers feel that allowing small amounts of these compounds to smear into the hearts will create a certain amount of complexity in the final gin. Experiment to see what you think tastes best.

Vacuum Distillation

In the past decade we've seen a slight upward bubbling of a few distillation aùteurs promoting the use of "cold" or vacuum distillation. We most often hear about this technique in the realm of Japanese shōchū production, but in recent years quite a few botanically minded distillers have taken up the low-pressure distillation mantle.

Remember that the boiling point of a liquid is when the vapor pressure equals that of the surrounding atmospheric pressure. In the majority of gin distilleries, the atmospheric pressure inside the still is more or less in the range of the atmospheric pressure outside of the still. Therefore, the boiling point of the liquid inside can be predicted fairly easily. However, in a vacuum distillation system, the pressure of the inside of the still is reduced, sometimes dramatically, so that the boiling point is also reduced. In many systems you will often see boiling points of around 50°C (122°F) and some go even lower than that. Bacardi owned Oxley Gin purportedly distills some of their gin at -5°C (23°F)!

The reason this is important is that when these conditions are set up inside the still, the volatilities of the various congeners in the gin also change. You also get a different set of congeners that come over in the still and you don't have to contend with the potential cooking or "stewing" effects that higher pot temps have on the botanicals.

Of course, just like any tool, the potential benefits of vacuum distillation to the gin world are largely based on how it's used. You can make fantastic gin using this technology, but you can also make utter rubbish if all your other ducks aren't in a proper row. Regardless,

I present this method as mere food for thought for those interested in the botanical arts.

Feints

Finally, what do you do with the heads and tails of a gin run? While there are distillers out there who may recycle the feints into the next run, many more avoid the process. Gin feints often have copious amounts of unwanted heavy congeners that are bitter or otherwise off tasting. Feel free to experiment but many distillers simply dispose of them after distillation. If you must recycle them, then converting them into neutral spirit using an appropriately sized and refluxed column may be your only option.

A Few Words on Grappa

Wait. Grappa? What does a polarizing pomace spirit from Italy have to do with gin? Well, not much really, but it was the only place I could think of putting it in the book that made even the least amount of sense. And perhaps after I explain you will understand how grappa is loosely a "botanical" spirit akin to gin.

This chapter has looked at the myriad of considerations that go into the gin making process. These concepts are easily transferrable to other botanical spirits such as aquavit and absinthe. Likewise, it turns out that some of these concepts can also play a role in grappa production, specifically the use of a vapor basket... sort of.

Grappa is the distilled essence of left-over grape pomace (mostly grape skins, but also often including small amounts of seed and stem material as well). It is well known throughout Italy and has analogues in other wine making countries such as France and Greece. The grape skins after fermentation and pressing have small amounts of alcohol left in them. They also contain immense amounts of various aroma compounds. Well-made grappa can be a truly divine drinking experience showcasing the varietal character of the grape in a way that no other brandy can.

The best grappa is produced from fresh pomace, lightly pressed. Work with your supplying winery on obtaining pomace that has not been exposed to extreme pressures. This can be tricky as some wineries will aim to press the grapes extremely hard to extract as much juice/alcohol as possible. However, this often produces an overly tannic and bitter wine and when the winemaking standards are low, the grape and pomace quality will also be low. It might be best to search out a winery that uses a light press and is known to produce high caliber wines. Talk to them about what you want to do. You never know. They may be willing to simply give you the pomace (many wineries will charge for it, but it never hurts to negotiate a little). They may also be willing to co-brand the resulting spirit which can be a nice marketing bump for both companies.

Distilling grappa can be approached from a few different angles. A common technique is to simply throw the pomace into the still with an equal weight of water and distill it. Considering that the alcohol content of the pomace can be as low as 2% abv (it will vary depending on the pressing regime, grape variety and fermentation conditions), you will likely need to do at least two distillations to reach an acceptable alcohol level in the spirit.

The other batch distillation method used in grappa production uses a kind of vapor basket for the pomace and this is why we're discussing grappa in the gin chapter. (Now let me put down this shoehorn...)

Quite a bit of grappa produced in Italy uses specially made stills that have rather large vapor baskets. The distiller will load the basket with fresh pomace. The pot will be filled with water. As the still begins to heat, water steam will eventually rise and push through the mass of pomace above, picking up alcohol and varietal congeners in the process. These newly enriched vapors are often ran through a plated column to further enrich them to an acceptable alcohol level and profile.

Unless you are interested in producing grappa as one of your primary spirits, you would likely opt to distill using the first method. However, for those that are interested, there are certainly Italian still manufacturers that can fabricate a high-quality grappa still for all your pomace distilling needs.

Conclusion

Well, that's it, folks. For better or worse I've done the best I could to present these ideas and philosophies on distillation to you. It has been an absolute pleasure, and I hope you come away energized, inspired and professionally hungry.

Distillation really doesn't need or deserve to be so heavily shrouded in technical mystery. The art and science of using distillation to make beverage alcohol has been around for at least a thousand years. And here we are with all our technology and science and yet in many ways, distillation hasn't really changed all that much. Our industry is one for the antiquities and perhaps that's why it's so attractive to so many people. It is liberating to practice an art so old and so primal in nature.

I welcome more and more people joining the industry. For me, this means more ideas coming to the fore, more innovation, and hopefully more delicious spirits to try.

As I write this, it's a cold Quebec January in the middle of the COVID-19 pandemic. There's a local lockdown, and while I'm allowed to continue my distillery work (alcohol is deemed "essential" to the Quebecois) I'm not allowed to sit down with my neighbor or friend to share the fruits of my labors. Spirits should be enjoyed with friends and as the world slowly ambles back to some semblance of normalcy I look forward to a time when I can hopefully sit down over a nice dram with you, the reader and talk all things distilled spirits. Until then I wish each and every one of you nothing but success and enjoyment as you continue on in your distilling career. There really is no other industry I would rather be in and I hope you agree. Cheers!

References

Alcarde, A., Araujo de Souza, P., & Eduardo de Souza Belluco, A. (2011). Chemical profile of sugarcane spirits produced by double distillation methodologies in rectifying still. *Food Science and Technology, 31*(2), 355–360.

Alcarde, A., de Souza, L., & Bortoletto, A. (2012). Ethyl carbamate kinetics in double distillation of sugar cane spirit. *Journal of the Institute of Brewing*, 27–31.

Al-Hassan, A. Y. (n.d.). *Alcohol and the Distillation of Wine in Arabic Sources*. Retrieved from www.history-science-technology.com: http://www.history-science-technology.com/notes/notes7.html#_edn1

Bennett, J. W. (2015). Avenues for bioenergy production using malt distillery co-products. *5th World Wide Conference on Distilled Spirits* (pp. 303–312). Nottingham: Context Publishers.

Berglund, K. (2004). *Artisan Distilling: A guide for small distilleries*. Michigan State University.

Bergstrom, G., & Schwarz, P. (2016). DON From Field to Glass. *Great Lakes Hop and Barley Conference.*

Boothroyd, E., Jack, F., Harrison, B., & Cook, D. (2011). The impact of increased wash fatty acid levels on the nutty/cereal aroma volatile composition of new make malt spirit. *World Wide Distilled Spirits Conference*, (pp. 167–173).

Boscolo, M. (2001). Caramelo e carbamato de etila em aguardente de cana. Ocorrência e quantificação. *Ph.D. Thesis*. Brazil: Instituto de Química de São Carlos, Universidade de São Paulo.

Curtis, E. (1907). *The North American Indian*. Johnson Reprint Corporation.

Davis, C. (2014, July 18). *Armagnac: Virtuous by Nature*. Retrieved from Drinks International: https://drinksint.com/news/fullstory.php/aid/4621/Armagnac:_Virtuous_by_Nature_.html

Duff, P. (2009). *France, Wine & Juniper: The True History of Gin*.

Ewbank, A. (2018, March 26). *The Long, Strange History of Medicinal Turpentine*. Retrieved from Atlas Obscura: https://www.atlasobscura.com/articles/is-turpentine-medicine

Ferrari, G., Lablanquie, O., Catagrel, R., Ledauphin, J., Payot, T., Fournier, N., & Guichard, E. (2004). Determination of key odorant compounds in freshly distilled cognac using GC-O, GC-MS, and sensory evaluation. *Journal of Agricultural and Food Chemistry*, 5670–5676.

Forbes, R. J. (1948). *A Short History of the Art of Distillation:*.

Harrison, B., Fagnen, O., Jack, F., & Brosnan, J. (2012). The Impact of Copper in Different Parts of Malt Whisky Pot Stills on New Make Spirit Composition and Aroma. *Journal of the Institute of Brewing and Distilling*, 106–112.

Hastie, S. (1925). The application of chemistry to pot still distillation. *Journal of the Institute of Brewing & Distilling*.

Hickey, R., & Motylewski, M. (2006, October). An alternate approach to distillery waste management. *The Brewer and Distiller*, pp. 23–24.

Hudson, J. A., & Buglass, A. J. (2011). History and Development of Alcoholic Beverages. In A. J. Buglass, *Handbook of Alcoholic Beverages*. John Wiley & Sons, Ltd.

Irish Whiskey Museum. (2019). *It's True, Whiskey Originated In Ireland*. Retrieved from Irish Whiskey Museum: https://www.irishwhiskeymuseum.ie/news/its-true-whiskey-originated-in-ireland/

Jack, F., Brosnan, J., Campbell, K., Fagnen, O., Fotheringham, R., & Goodall, I. (2005). Sensory implications of modifying distillation practice in Scotch malt whisky production. *World Wide Distilled*

Spirits Conference, (pp. 205–211).

Jackman, M. (2020). Sales Engineer. (M. Strickland, Interviewer)

Jefford, A. (2004). *Peat Smoke and Spirit*. Headline Publishing Group.

Kockmann, N. (2014). History of Distillation. In A. Gorak, & E. Sorensen, *Distillation Fundamentals and Principles*. Elsevier.

Lake, S. (2021, January 15). Shenandoah County distillery faces environmental violation charges. *Virginia Business*.

Lioutus, T. (2002). The renaissance of American Bourbons: developments and technical challenges of theproduction of premium Bourbon distillates by batch distillation. *World Wide Distilled Spirits Conference*, (pp. 233–243).

Memic, A., Mujcinovic, A., Smajic-Murtic, M., & Spaho, N. (2017). Effect of Sodium Chloride Addition During Williams Pear Mash Distillation on the Dynamics of Evaporation of the Volatile Compounds. *Works of the Faculty of Agriculture and Food Sciences, University of Sarajevo*, 199–208.

Mikuka, W., & Zielinska, M. (2020). Distillery Stillage: Characteristics, Treatment, and Valorization. *Applied Biochemistry and Biotechnology*, 770–793.

Miller, G. H. (2019). *Whisky Science: A Condensed Distillation*. Springer Nature Switzerland.

Nicol, D. (2014). Batch Distillation. In I. Russell, *Whisky: Technology, Production, and Marketing* (pp. 155–178). Elsevier.

Norton, C. (1911). *Modern Yeasting and Distillation*. Chicago.

Principe, L. M. (2013). *The Secrets of Alchemy*. Chicago: University of Chicago.

Renegade Rum. (2019). *The Adam Still*. Retrieved from Renegade Rum: https://renegaderum.com/element/the-adam-still/

Ricardo Alcarde, A., de Souza, P. A., & de Souza Belluco, A. E. (2011). Chemical profile of sugarcane spirits produced by double distillation methodologies in rectifying still. *Food Science and Technology*, 355–360.

Rummel, R. (n.d.). *Kumis*. Retrieved from Atlas Obscura: https://www.atlasobscura.com/foods/kumis-mare-milk

Spaho, N., Dürr, P., Grba, S., Velagić-Habul, E., & Blesić, M. (2013). Effects of distillation cut on the distribution of higher alcohols and esters in brandy produced from three plum varieties. *Journal of Institute of Brewing and Distilling*, 48–56.

Spedding, G. (2015). Flavors Found in Distilled Spirits: Origins, Descriptors, Controls. *American Craft Spirits Association Conference*. Austin.

Starkman, A. (2018, August 13). Distillation And Mezcal History In Mexico: Indigenous Or Foreign, Agave Or Coconut. *The Mazatlan Post*.

The Life and Times of Aqua Vitae. (n.d.). Retrieved from Difford's Guide: https://www.diffordsguide.com/encyclopedia/407/bws/the-life-and-times-of-aqua-vitae

The Whisky Professor. (2019, September 10). *Why Some Distilleries Use Fire-Heated Stills*. Retrieved from ScotchWhisky.com: https://scotchwhisky.com/magazine/ask-the-professor/27217/why-some-distilleries-use-fire-heated-stills/#:~:text=Out%20of%20interest%2C%20Glenmorangie%20was,%2Dheated%20stills%20%E2%80%93%20in%201887.

Underwood, T., & Underwood, C. (1830). *The Repertory of patent inventions [formerly The Repertory of arts, manufactures and agriculture]. Vol.1-enlarged ser., vol.40, Volume 8.* London.

Whitby, B. (1992). Traditional distillation in the whisky industry. *Ferment Institute of Brewing*, 261–267.

Wilson, N., Jack, F., Takise, I., & Priest, F. (2008). The effects of lactic acid bacteria on the sensory characteristics of new-make Scotch whisky. *World Wide Distilled Spirits Conference*, (pp. 49–52).

Zizumbo-Villarreal, D., & Colunga-García Marín, P. (2008). Early coconut distillation and the origins of mezcal and tequila spirits in west-central Mexico. *Genetic Resources and Crop Evolution*, 493–510.

Appendix A — Resources

Supplier Directory*

*My intention with this supplier directory is to only showcase vendors that I personally trust. That means I've either worked directly with a company or know someone else who has. If I can't personally attest to a vendor's qualifications or ethics, I won't list them. This does not mean that a non-listed company is *bad*, just that I don't know enough about them to put them on the list.

I cannot tell you how much I appreciate you, the reader, for reading this book. And it is because of that appreciation, the last thing I want to do is to potentially steer you into a vendor relationship that causes you problems. Also, I don't receive any compensation from these companies, monetary or otherwise. I'm listing them because I believe they are all superior vendors and hopefully they will be of assistance to you.

Distillation Equipment

Barison Industry
Trento, Italy
+39-0461-1788800
info@barisonindustry.com
barisonindustry.com

Bavarian-Holstein
USA and Germany
1-310-391-1091
info@potstills.com
bavarianbrewerytech.com

CARL Distilleries
USA and Germany
1-212-242-6806
info@carl.info
carl.info

Chalvignac Prulho
Philippe Bannier
Châteaubernard, France
p.bannier@chalvignac.com
http://www.chalvignac-prulho-distillation.fr

Forsyths
Rothes, United Kingdom (Scotland)
44-(0) 1340 831787
enquiries@forsyths.com
forsyths.com

Frilli
Monteriggioni, Italy
39-0577 307011
info@frillisrl.com
frillisrl.com

Kothe Distilling
USA and Germany
1-312-878-7766
info@kothe-distilling.com
kothe-distilling.com

Mueller Pot Stills
Oberkirch-Tiergarten, Germany
+49-7802-93-55-0
info@brennereianlagen.de
brennereianlagen.de

North Stills
Ontario, Canada
1-416-371-9239
contact@northstills.com
northstills.com

Specific Mechanical Systems
British Columbia, Canada
1-250-652-2111
Michael.jackman@specific.net
Specificmechanical.com

Vendome Copper & Brassworks
Kentucky, USA
1-502-587-1930
office@vendomecopper.com
vendomecopper.com

Educational Resources

Heriot Watt University
Edinburgh, United Kingdom (Scotland)
+44 (0)131 449 5111
https://www.hw.ac.uk/study/uk/postgraduate/brewing-distilling.htm

The Institute of Brewing & Distilling (IBD)
Institute of Brewing & Distilling
London, United Kingdom
+44 (0) 207499 8144
www.ibd.org.uk

Lallemand Alcohol School
Milwaukee, WI USA
1-800-583-6484 (US and Canada only)
or +1 414 393-0410
https://www.lallemandbds.com/contact-us/

Moonshine University
Louisville, KY USA
1-502-301-8139
registrar@moonshineuniversity.com
moonshineuniversity.com

Niagara College
Niagara-on-the-Lake, Ontario Canada
1-905-735-2211
myfuturenc@niagaracollege.ca
niagaracollege.ca

Oregon State University
Corvallis, OR USA
1-541-737-6486
holly.templeton@oregonstate.edu
oregonstate.edu

Siebel Institute
Chicago, IL USA
1-312-255-0705
info@siebelinstitute.com
siebelinstitute.com

University of Adelaide
Waite Campus
Glen Osmond, SA Australia
61-8-8313-4455
faculty.sciences@adelaide.edu.au
Adelaide.edu.au

Professional Organizations

American Craft Spirits Association (ACSA)
Louisville, KY USA
1-502-807-4249
membership@americancraftspirits.org
americancraftspirits.org

American Distilling Institute (ADI)
California, USA
1-510-886-7418
admin@distilling.com
distilling.com

Artisan Distillers Canada
British Columbia, Canada
Artisandistillers.ca

The Distilled Spirits Council (DISCUS)
Washington, DC USA
1-202-628-3544
Distilledspirits.org

The Gin Guild
Essex, United Kingdom
+44 (020) 33-97-27-37
Nicholas.cook@theginguild.com
theginguild.com

The Institute of Brewing & Distilling (IBD)
Institute of Brewing & Distilling
London, United Kingdom
+44 (0) 207499 8144
www.ibd.org.uk

Scottish Distillers Association (SDA)
Scotland, United Kingdom
info@distillers.scot
distillers.scot

Appendix B

Plato/Brix/Balling/SG conversions

Degrees Balling/Plato/Brix are effectively the same thing. You would have to go a few decimal places out for the average distiller to see a difference and as such we will treat them as interchangeable here. The column on the left holds the values for Balling/Plato/Brix while the column on the right contains the corresponding converted specific gravity value. I've only included values up to 30°Balling/Plato/Brix because it is rare that a distiller would need numbers above that. However, should you find yourself in such a position, the equation below will be able to convert whichever number you need to specific gravity. (These equations are "simplified" from much more complex versions. Unless you need your sugar concentration values to extend out to five decimal places, these should be accurate enough.)

Some people say you can get away with simply dividing the specific gravity points by 4 to give you degrees Plato. So, if you have a specific gravity of 1.004, then you have "4 gravity points" and that divided by four gives you 1°Plato. Obviously converting the other direction is also simple. Just multiply degrees Plato by four and you have your 'gravity points'.

This is a quick and easy way to convert between the two, but the equation quickly falls apart above 12.5°Plato/1.050 S.G.

°Balling/°Plato/°Brix	Specific Gravity
0.5	1.002
1	1.004
1.5	1.006
2	1.008
2.5	1.010
3	1.012
3.5	1.014
4	1.016
4.5	1.018
5	1.020

5.5	1.022
6	1.024
6.5	1.026
7	1.028
7.5	1.030
8	1.032
8.5	1.034
9	1.036
9.5	1.038
10	1.040
10.5	1.042
11	1.044
11.5	1.046
12	1.048
12.5	1.050
13	1.053
13.5	1.055
14	1.057
14.5	1.059
15	1.061
15.5	1.063
16	1.065
16.5	1.068
17	1.070
17.5	1.072
18	1.074
18.5	1.076
19	1.079
19.5	1.081
20	1.083
20.5	1.085
21	1.087
21.5	1.090
22	1.092
22.5	1.094

23	1.096
23.5	1.099
24	1.101
24.5	1.103
25	1.106
25.5	1.108
26	1.110
26.5	1.113
27	1.115
27.5	1.117
28	1.120
28.5	1.120
29	1.122
29.5	1.124
30	1.127

Appendix C

Distillation Record Sheet Sample

Below is an example of the basic records you should keep during your distillation processes. This is the sheet that we use in my distillery and as you can see it is very simple in design. This is a template that I was able to design in Microsoft Word within ten minutes. Feel free to take the general design and come up with a record sheet that works best for you and your distillery.

Date/Time:

Operator :

Distillation Type:

Distillation : _____#

Inputs (Tan/ABV/LAA/Spirits Type)

Fraction(s) Readings

Fraction	Time	ABV	Temperature

Heat and Condenser Notes

Output(s)

Tank	ABV	Temperature	Weight	Volume	LAA

Notes

Acknowledgements

Over the years, I've been fortunate to work and study with so many people much smarter and more talented than me. Their cumulative impact and influence on my work as a distiller and this book cannot be underestimated.

I'd like to start out by thanking the fine folks at the American Distilling Institute. Bill and Erik Owens have been immeasurably supportive of my endeavors the past few years and I'm profoundly grateful to consider them both good friends. Brad Plummer and Gail Sands have both had to suffer through editing and preparing my work to be published. I apologize to them both if my work has ever provided undo stress or late-night crunches.

Certainly, I owe a huge debt of gratitude to my Institute of Brewing & Distilling family. Jerry Avis, Alan Wolstenholme, Kirsty Black, Mike Partridge, Dan Griffiths, Steve Curtis, and Graeme Walker, you've all been unbelievably influential to me and I've learned so much from all of you. A special thanks goes to Douglas Murray, Jeremy Stephens, and Shernell Layne for helping me sus out a few of the finer distillation details contained herein. And certainly, I owe quite a bit to my good friend and mentor, Steve Wright, who decided to throw professional reputational caution to the wind and write the foreword for this book. I apologize if the industry decides to blacklist you for being associated with this work.

To my incredibly talented team at Cote des Saints, Michel, Yves, Jean, Guy, Francois, Ann, and Denis, thank you all for your support. Very special thanks go to my assistant distillers, Nico, Mathieu, and David. I probably learn more from you than any of you realize. Hopefully, you don't think me too much a poor student.

To Kyle Grant at Vendome Copper & Brassworks and Mike Jackman at Specific Mechanical. Thank you both for answering many a dumb question and always providing support at the drop of a hat.

To my wife Kerri, thanks for keeping me around all these years. I promise that one day I'll make it worth your while.

Index